THE GERMAN REARMAMENT QUESTION

THE GERMAN REARMAMENT QUESTION

AMERICAN DIPLOMACY AND EUROPEAN DEFENSE AFTER WORLD WAR II

Robert McGeehan

UNIVERSITY OF ILLINOIS PRESS
Urbana   Chicago   London

To Hanneke

ACKNOWLEDGMENTS

It is a pleasure to express my gratitude to the persons and institutions upon whose generous assistance this study frequently relied. My special thanks are expressed to William T. R. Fox, who originally sponsored the research and who offered valuable counsel and helpful suggestions throughout the study's development.

I am grateful to the persons who by interviews or correspondence kindly provided much valuable information, and numerous equally valuable opinions and judgments relevant to the German rearmament question, including Robert R. Bowie, John C. Campbell, General Harrison A. Gerhardt, Colonel Michael J. L. Greene, Perry Laukhuff, General George A. Lincoln, His Excellency Jules Moch, Jean Monnet, Ben T. Moore, Jacques J. Reinstein, General Dr. Hans Speidel, Charles M. Spofford, and Shepard Stone.

Numerous persons whose comments or advice were offered at various points in the project's development included Amitai Etzioni, Louis Henkin, Roger Hilsman, Morton A. Kaplan, Laurence W. Martin, Philip E. Mosely, Frank Trommler, and Gerhard Wettig. I am very grateful for their assistance.

The libraries of Columbia University and of the City University of New York were especially helpful, as were the staff members of the library of the Council on Foreign Relations.

Shirley Lerman's indulgence in the preparation of the manuscript is particularly appreciated, as is Bruce McDaniel's valuable assistance in copyediting the manuscript. Finally, I would like to thank my friends and colleagues Catherine M. Kelleher, Wilfrid L. Kohl, and Wesley B. Truitt, whose encouragement and criticisms were as enjoyable as they were indispensable.

Contents

Introduction

THIS book is a study of the American attempt to rearm Germany after World War II. The German rearmament question was among the most important, and frustrating, concerns of American diplomacy during the postwar period. Abruptly raised by Secretary of State Dean Acheson, it was the result of a unilateral U.S. decision in 1950, when neither the French nor the Germans themselves could accept a remilitarized Federal Republic. Its long evolution produced effects quite unconnected with the original concern which prompted its emergence, and resulted in political settlements unanticipated at the time it was first articulated.

The outbreak of the Korean War was the specific stimulus for the decision to strengthen the security of the NATO area by adding German troops. It was widely thought that aggression in the Far East signaled the possibility of a similar Communist move against a militarily feeble Western Europe. Since the other members of the Atlantic Alliance were unable or unwilling to undertake a major rearmament effort, the United States considered the utilization of German military potential indispensable.

Prior to mid-1950, the expectations upon which American policy was based were pessimistic but not grim; the end of the Berlin blockade and some progress toward an Austrian treaty had produced a partial atmosphere of détente and possible disengagement in Europe. Judgments about the trend of Soviet behavior were mixed, but Moscow had given no clear indication that military force would be used to achieve political objectives. American policy planners looked to a period of containment of Soviet power which would not involve the direct use of force.

Overnight, the Korean attack discredited the predictions of those who had argued that Russian ambitions—while great—were to be pursued by means other than armed aggression. Once force had been used in the Far East, there was little doubt in Washington that the same could occur in other areas. Communism, U.S. officials concluded, no longer eschewed war as an instrument of policy.

If Europe was to be defended at all, it was believed, it had to be held from the outset and on the ground. Soviet nuclear capabilities, though limited, were thought ample to preclude definitively the possibility of repeating the World War II–type Normandy landings to liberate the Continent once it had been lost. This was compounded by U.S. atomic weakness; the American nuclear arsenal was then so small that there was no question of the necessity of more ground troops.

Even if the Korean attack was an isolated Communist probe rather than an indication of imminent hostilities elsewhere, allied planners reasoned, the question was still whether NATO could responsibly remain patently unable to defend the Central European front. Because of the gaps between NATO commitments and capabilities, and between the size of the forces of East and West, U.S. policymakers did not doubt the appropriateness of demanding a military contribution from the Federal Republic. The Korean analogy with the situation in Europe allowed American leaders to call for immediate German rearmament, and this at once provoked the French rejection and German demands which effectively deadlocked the question for the next four years.

This study concerns itself in particular with the evolution of the U.S. demand for a German military contribution, from a simple call for more troops into an elaborate scenario for the future political unification of Western Europe. Its concluding thesis is that the German rearmament question, in leading to the

European Defense Community (EDC) project, brought political results far more important than the military frustrations which attended the delay in the Federal Republic's remilitarization. Despite eventual French abortive action on EDC, its long gestation period was vital; it granted sufficient time for the adjustment of attitudes in Washington, Paris, and Bonn which in the end made it possible for Germany to be rearmed and admitted to NATO on mutually acceptable terms. Without the intervening period of the American diplomatic pursuit of German rearmament and European political unification through EDC, the settlements of later years would not have been achieved as rapidly or perhaps as auspiciously.

The political rehabilitation of Germany and its integration into the Western cooperative framework were, in the long run, far more significant than the eventual reappearance of German soldiers. The restoration in the individual Western European states of conditions of stability was more profoundly in the American interest than the supranational political framework envisaged under EDC would have been. American policymakers mistakenly believed that Europe was ready for unity in the 1950's because of the multiple benefits which they imagined unity would bring. The political outcome of the German rearmament question, however, did not depend upon the accuracy of this kind of expectation, and the German problem in the Western context was handled without the merger of America's European allies. United States diplomacy during the years of the German rearmament question produced mixed results; but given the complexity of the issues involved and the confusion inherent in the psychological, political, and military aspects of the rapid restoration of German military power so soon after the war, the results—it is argued—were, over all, consistent with the interests of the United States, NATO, and international political stability.

The narrative covers the setting, particularly the impact of the Korean attack, from which the American decision to seek a German military contribution emerged; the inflation of the diplo-

matic goals of the United States, as France continued to frustrate
the American desire for German rearmament and as the Federal
Republic bargained for sovereignty and equality; and the successive shifts of the U.S. position on the European army solution
to the German problem, from initial hostility to the Pleven Plan
to complete commitment to the EDC project. The book's conclusions reflect on several questions which were considered as the
material was examined.

Under what conditions, for example, will the leader of an alliance undertake a major policy reversal involving the restoration
of the military power of a very recently defeated enemy? If the
defeated state is unwilling to rearm, but uses this as a bargaining
device to regain its independence, what interaction will result? If
the consent of a key ally is indispensable to the new policy, will
the alliance leader respect the rule that a coalition must agree?
Can a mutually palatable organizational device be devised to cir-
cumvent the dilemma of having to choose between several un-
appealing alternatives? If necessity is the major factor which might
motivate sovereign states to unify, especially the necessity associated
with an external military threat, why did Western Europe in the
early 1950's reject political unification when this seemed necessary, rational, and logical? Why did U.S. officials become so
wedded to EDC when there were so few indications that the prospective members of the new entity desired to embrace it or that
it would work even if attempted?

These questions are considered from the perspective of American diplomacy, rather than as parts of a study of either Germany's
position on remilitarization or France's effort to block this. The
German rearmament question lends itself to expansion easily, and
the author has tried to avoid the inclusion of relevant but not
indispensable material. The criterion used has been whether a
particular point seemed helpful for an understanding of the U.S.
effort to achieve agreement on German rearmament.

The concluding remarks offer some perspectives of policy
relevance, including the degree to which American diplomacy
was successful and how its outcome on the German rearmament

question served or damaged U.S. interests. The role of Germany has been one of the most important problems of international affairs in the twentieth century, as a destabilizing element in the European balance, a cause of hot war, an arena of cold war, and a possible catalyst for future conflict. The present position of the Federal Republic is to a great extent due to the effects of the rearmament question and the direct and indirect results of the American endeavor to work it out in a manner compatible with U.S. objectives and the interests of the Atlantic community.

Robert McGeehan
The City College of the
City University of New York

THE GERMAN REARMAMENT QUESTION

CHAPTER I

The Emergence of the Question

PRIOR to the summer of 1950 American officials agreed that European security required a greater defense effort on the part of the North Atlantic Treaty states. On June 2, Secretary of State Dean Acheson referred to the defenses of the area as totally inadequate, and a fortnight later Secretary of Defense Louis Johnson spoke of "the dangerous disparity in strength between the armed east and the disarmed west." There was, however, little sense of urgency felt in connection with the creation of the balanced collective forces agreed upon in May by the North Atlantic Council (NAC).[1] Reporting to Congress on this meeting, Acheson said it was the unanimous view of the twelve foreign ministers that there was no indication of an immediate threat of war.[2] The unexpected outbreak of the Korean conflict in late

[1] Secretary Acheson said in August, 1949, that U.S. and European security "are one and the same thing and are in fact indivisible." Senate Foreign Relations and Armed Services Committees, Hearings, *Mutual Defense Assistance Program, 1950*, 81st Cong., 2nd Sess., 1949, pp. 6, 15, 22. See also Seyom Brown, *The Faces of Power: Constancy and Change in United States Foreign Policy from Truman to Johnson* (New York: Columbia University Press, 1968), Part II. Raymond Dennett and Robert K. Turner, eds., *Documents on American Foreign Relations, 1950*, Vol. XII (Princeton: Princeton University Press, 1951), pp. 206–8.

[2] Dennett and Turner, *Documents, 1950*, p. 210. The assumptions which underlay NATO plans counted on a combination of American atomic deterrence and

June made previously accepted time estimates seem irrelevant
and prompted a reappraisal of Soviet intentions and the requirements for European security. This led, during the summer, to
policy changes which included the decision to press for an immediate military contribution from Western Germany.

EUROPEAN SECURITY PRIOR TO THE KOREAN WAR

Writing early in 1950, John Foster Dulles noted that a defense
on the Rhine would mean the loss of Germany, while holding a
line along the Elbe was problematical due especially to a lack of
troops. He asked questions which in a very few months were
to confront the executors of American diplomacy: "Can Germany
be held against the Soviet Union, except perhaps by German
troops? Does that mean the rearmament of Germany? Will France
consent, and what dependence can be placed on rearmed Germans? Can we be sure that they will shoot in what we think is
the right direction?" [3] These uncertainties suggest several factors
important for a consideration of the political-military relationship of the United States with Europe, involving on the NATO
side a comparison between commitments and capabilities, and
on the Eastern side capabilities and intentions. No attempt is
made to treat in detail the conception and birth of the Atlantic
Alliance,[4] but it is appropriate to outline the degree to which

military assistance to Europe to provide for the possibility of an attack, which
NSC-68 (memorandum of April, 1950) had suggested would probably not become
imminent prior to 1954, when it was anticipated the U.S. deterrent would have
been substantially neutralized by Russian nuclear weapons. Samuel P. Huntington, *The Common Defense: Strategic Programs in National Politics* (New York:
Columbia University Press, 1961), pp. 314–15; Paul Y. Hammond, "NSC-68: Prologue
to Rearmament," in Warner R. Schilling, Paul Y. Hammond, and Glenn H. Snyder,
Strategy, Politics, and Defense Budgets (New York: Columbia University Press,
1962), p. 306. In 1950 the NATO Standing Group looked to 1954 as the hypothetical
year for strategic planning for war, and although "purely academic" this indicates
an expectation of a considerable time cushion. Lord Ismay, *NATO: The First Five
Years, 1949–1954* (Paris: NATO, 1955), p. 102.

[3] John Foster Dulles, *War or Peace* (New York: Macmillan, 1950), p. 157.

[4] Among the many works which cover this are the following: Harry S Truman,
Memoirs: Years of Trial and Hope, Vol. II (Garden City: Doubleday, 1956); Ben T.

the members had by mid-1950 provided themselves with the capability to implement their defense objectives, the strategic plans which had been formulated, and what strength the potential enemy was thought to possess.

The communiqué and the resolution of the May, 1950, North Atlantic Council meeting had been "couched in general terms, breathing a spirit of leisurely deliberation and cautious enterprise." [5] Germany, central to the strategic question, was still not to be considered in discussing military plans, Secretary Acheson recalled. Balanced collective forces and a progressive build-up were called for, but no time table was settled, nor were these rather ambiguous phrases rendered meaningful by specifying which member was to provide how much of what, apart from a somewhat primitive division of labor.

That there was no particular sense of urgency, despite the fact that the Berlin blockade had (or should have) implied a need for more conventional strength, and despite the Russian atomic explosion in August, 1949, is understandable not so much for military as for economic and psychological reasons. Western Europe in 1950 had only barely begun to recover from the enormous damage of the war, and had small inclination to prepare for another. Fundamentally, morale remained low; the European Recovery Program's beneficial effects had not yet been manifested in much higher living standards; and the outlook of many Europeans was not such that the future seemed to be worth very much additional sacrifice.[6]

Western military strength at the time bore practically no relation to the announced determination of the alliance members

---

Moore, *NATO and the Future of Europe* (New York: Harper, 1958); Royal Institute of International Affairs, *Atlantic Alliance: NATO's Role in the Free World* (London: Royal Institute of International Affairs, 1952); Dirk U. Stikker, *Men of Responsibility: A Memoir* (New York: Harper and Row, 1966); Robert E. Osgood, *NATO: The Entangling Alliance* (Chicago: University of Chicago Press, 1962); George F. Kennan, *Memoirs 1925–1950* (Boston: Little, Brown, 1967); Dean Acheson, *Present at the Creation: My Years in the State Department* (New York: Norton, 1969).

[5] R.I.I.A., *Atlantic Alliance*, p. 16.

[6] Cf. Laurence Wylie, *Village in the Vaucluse* (Cambridge: Harvard University Press, 1961), pp. 33–34.

to defend Western Europe, even if the criterion of adequacy is taken as capabilities which would have been sufficient only to check the advance of Communist troops until the effects of American atomic strikes against the Soviet Union had been felt, and even after taking into consideration the misleading character of numerical comparisons of divisional strength.[7] This weakness was not the result of an allied shortage of manpower or other physical resources necessary for defense. It reflected the unwillingness of European political leaders to impose additional burdens on their peoples in the absence of a genuine conviction that survival was at stake and that greater efforts would bring unequivocal results.

Estimates of the East-West military balance in Europe prior to the Korean War have varied, and in recent years official studies have indicated that Soviet ground strength might have been considerably less than was thought from 1950 on.[8] But apart from the details of comparative division or aircraft numbers, the salient point was that the Eastern military machine was believed to be quantitatively superior by a ratio of something like 10 to 1. According to General Matthew Ridgway, when the Korean War began American troops in Europe were "not ready for battle either mentally or physically."[9]

On paper, Western forces amounted to some twelve to fourteen divisions; qualitatively, they were poorly equipped and even more poorly trained, having been prepared and organized not for combat but for administrative tasks of occupation. In the key central area, "only 4 weak Anglo-American divisions and practically no air force stood between the Channel ports and the 22

[7] Even though American divisions were much larger than Soviet (18,000 and 10–12,000 respectively) the latter had a higher proportion assigned to combat duties, with the result that there may have been no significant difference in fire power. *New York Herald Tribune*, December 2, 1950.

[8] See for example C. L. Sulzberger's remarks about the Pentagon's 1963 estimate of only sixty Soviet divisions. *The New York Times*, December 2, 1963. Also Louis J. Halle, *The Cold War as History* (London: Chatto and Windus, 1967), pp. 185–86, where seventy-five to eighty divisions are suggested.

[9] Matthew B. Ridgway, *Soldier: The Memoirs of Matthew B. Ridgway* (New York: Harper, 1956), p. 190.

Soviet divisions poised a few miles from our zonal boundary." [10]
Soviet troops in East Germany were thought to be backed up by
forces of enormous proportions. To the frequently given figure
of 175 ready Russian divisions was added another of 125 in re-
serve, plus estimates of some sixty or more satellite divisions.
There existed an additional 50,000 or more men in an East German police force which, according to American officials, had, by
reason of its extensive military training and sophisticated equipment, the character of an army.[11] This lopsided balance in ground
forces was accompanied by a similar if somewhat less unfortunate
ratio of air power for their support. There is little question that
the capacity for successful local defense simply did not exist in
Western Europe in 1950, and that the value of the Atlantic Alliance was psychological and political, but hardly military.[12]

In strategic capabilities the country with superiority in atomic
weapons and means for their delivery by heavy bombers was the
United States. In late summer, 1949, the Russians had detonated
their first nuclear device, but prior to the Korean attack there
seems to have been an assumption that the Strategic Air Command would deter a Communist military adventure. Secretary of
Defense Johnson's announcement in May that the United States
had greatly improved its atomic capabilities, and the existing op-

---

[10] Ivone Kirkpatrick, *The Inner Circle: Memoirs of Ivone Kirkpatrick* (London:
Macmillan, 1959), p. 239. Sir Ivone was British High Commissioner to Germany,
1950–53. See also Roger Hilsman, "NATO: The Developing Strategic Context," in
NATO and American Security, ed. Klaus Knorr (Princeton: Princeton University
Press, 1959), p. 14.

[11] Andrew J. Goodpaster, "The Development of SHAPE: 1950–1953," in Edgar
S. Furniss, Jr., *American Military Policy: Strategic Aspects of World Political Geography* (New York: Rinehart, 1957), p. 308; Ismay, *NATO,* pp. 29, 112; Osgood,
NATO, p. 48; Peter Calvocoressi, *Survey of International Affairs, 1949–1950* (London: Oxford University Press, 1953), pp. 87–88, 235, 241; Richard P. Stebbins, *The
United States in World Affairs, 1950* (New York: Harper, 1951), p. 121; *Department
of State Bulletin,* June 5, 1950, pp. 918–19.

[12] General J. Lawton Collins, Army Chief of Staff, who estimated that the 175–
200 Soviet divisions would amount to about 110 American divisions, said that
"Without adequate army forces on the ground, backed up by tactical air forces,
it would be impossible to prevent the overrunning of Europe by the tremendous
land forces of the police states no matter what air and sea power we could bring
against them." U.S. Senate, Hearings, *Assignment of Ground Forces of the United
States to Duty in the European Area,* 82nd Cong., 1st Sess., 1951, p. 169.

position to further financial sacrifices for rearmament, led many Europeans to conclude that a greater conventional effort was unnecessary. In short, the military "balance" was no balance at all: if deterrence failed, Soviet land forces could have taken continental Europe without great difficulty, and American strategic air forces could have moved against the Russian homeland and inflicted severe damage on urban centers.[13]

American strategy, which in effect was the strategy of NATO, was one of massive retaliation (but without that label).[14] Such a strategy, oriented toward air-atomic power, did not encourage lower-level alternatives. Moreover, a strategy which seemed to be beneficial all around and which demanded little of the members was easily accepted; the commitment to local defense actually relied upon the strategic threat. Although later a source of disagreement, "this contradiction between declaratory strategy and actual capabilities . . . was regarded as the price of allied cohesion in the initial phase" of NATO, up to the Korean crisis.[15]

Prior to this time, the European defense question had two aspects: an understanding on force contributions and a plan for operational matters. The distinction between the two is noteworthy. The North Atlantic Council in January, 1950, had agreed upon plans for the integrated defense of the North Atlantic area, and in May upon the principle of balanced collective forces as a guide to the defense contributions of the members. Secretary Acheson told Congress on May 31 that the alliance would look "to each country to contribute what it is best able to contribute to the common defense in accordance with a common plan," and

[13] Raymond L. Garthoff, "On Soviet Military Strategy and Capabilities," *World Politics*, Vol. III (October, 1950), p. 124; *L'Annee Politique, 1950* (Paris: Presses Universitaires de France, 1951), p. 115; James E. King, Jr., "NATO: Genesis, Progress, Problems," in *National Security in the Nuclear Age*, eds. Gordon B. Turner and Richard D. Challener (New York: Praeger, 1960), pp. 150–51; Herman Kahn, *On Thermonuclear War* (Princeton: Princeton University Press 1961), pp. 417–28.

[14] The earlier NATO period has been referred to as one of "enforced collaboration," during which the European allies "had felt compelled to accept United States decisions about important aspects of their defense." William T. R. Fox and Annette B. Fox, *NATO and the Range of American Choice* (New York: Columbia University Press, 1967), p. 222.

[15] Osgood, *NATO*, pp. 31–32.

another high U.S. official wrote of "the assignment of military tasks to those nations whose capabilities lie primarily in certain directions." The original NATO formula envisaged a form of interdependence: "European ground and tactical air power were to be rapidly reconstructed with American help to provide for the actual *defense* of Western Europe, while American air and sea power, based on an invulnerable North America, was held in the background as a *deterrent* to any Soviet move against Europe." [16]

The expectation in the United States was that the Europeans would willingly furnish the bulk of the ground forces and America for her part would, in addition to the atomic airborne force, contribute financial aid and materiel through the Mutual Defense Assistance Program. The European failure to balance the U.S. contribution was one of the factors which underlay the American decision to demand German ground forces, as it became increasingly obvious that the formulas of the North Atlantic Council were agreements in principle, unfulfilled in practice.[17]

The other aspect of the European defense question in 1950 involved military planning for war. This planning assumed the unanimous view of the NATO foreign ministers that there was no immediate threat of war, and their impression that it would take the Soviet Union until about 1954 (the year mentioned in NSC-68) to produce enough nuclear weapons to "neutralize" the American deterrent. Allied plans were reported to have called for no more than thirty-six divisions in Western Europe by 1955, one year later than the projected danger point; in Britain, the military were working on the official assumption that no major war was likely for ten years.[18] The lack of an expectation of imminent hostilities complemented the failure of military plans to include the utilization of German manpower or other potential.

[16] Dennett and Turner, *Documents, 1950*, p. 212; Charles M. Spofford, "Toward Atlantic Security," *International Affairs*, Vol. XXVII (October, 1951), p. 434; Alastair Buchan, *NATO in the 1960's: The Implications of Interdependence* (rev. ed.; New York: Praeger, 1963), p. 43.

[17] Stebbins, *United States, 1950*, pp. 121ff., 262–63.

[18] Schilling, Hammond, and Snyder, *Strategy*, pp. 306, 354; Osgood, *NATO*, pp. 61, 65; Denis Healey, "Britain and NATO," in Knorr, *NATO*, p. 210.

The early strategic context was not greatly affected by the Soviet atomic explosion in August, 1949: "The view that the small and unorganized forces of NATO plus the atomic deterrent would meet all defense needs without greater contributions by the NATO powers—and without the addition of German forces —was so appealing that the many voices of Cassandra found no effective audience in Europe." [19] In theory the Western allies should have begun to plan immediately for what later was thought to be an increased chance of conventional conflict due to the advent of the nuclear balance of terror, but apparently a continuation of American nuclear superiority was considered sufficient. Moreover, some American officials never felt the Soviet leaders considered war a useful means to achieve their objectives; others held that even after the loss of the atomic monopoly the very presence of nuclear weapons and the possibility of their employment would be enough to make a direct attack on a NATO member highly unlikely. These considerations partially explain why ground forces were not increased before the Korean attack; until then, what might happen in combat was rather like a bad dream.

When Foreign Minister Dirk Stikker of the Netherlands first saw NATO's defense plans, based on the Rhine-IJssel line, he was shocked to learn that the northern provinces of Holland and all Germany east of the Rhine were to be abandoned. In addition, these plans included preparations for complex movements of civilian and military personnel back and forth between parts of Germany and Holland in such fashion that the situation created could only have been chaotic. Field Marshal Montgomery had said in mid-June there would be "appalling and indescribable confusion" if Russia attacked. But before the shock of hostilities in the Far East had led to second thoughts about its attractiveness, NATO strategy looked to a possible holding action from positions somewhere west of the Rhine. Even this plan, however,

[19] Laurence W. Martin, "The American Decision to Rearm Germany," in *American Civil Military Decisions*, ed. Harold Stein (Birmingham: University of Alabama Press, 1963), p. 664, editorial comments.

was something for the future, when allied forces would be stronger. The immediate plan simply envisaged another Dunkirk, with NATO troops leaving the Continent pending American nuclear retaliation on the Soviet Union and later, perhaps, an allied liberation of Western Europe.[20]

The question of whether to hold at the Rhine or the Elbe was unrelated in 1950 to military reality, since for even a holding action military men thought in terms of 100 allied divisions (a figure not widely advertised for political and psychological reasons). Indeed, with respect to the Elbe, there was doubt that such a defense line existed. Article 6 of the North Atlantic Treaty stipulated that an armed attack under Article 5 was "deemed to include an armed attack . . . on the occupation forces of any Party in Europe," which in effect meant that Germany was geographically "protected" by the treaty.[21] Military leaders generally favored defending Europe on the ground as far east as possible, but in the absence of major augmentations in ground strength, arguments about whether the defense line should be the Rhine or the Elbe were inconclusive. The demand for a German military contribution had already been made by the time the North Atlantic Council at the September meeting agreed upon the "forward strategy" concept, and while German rearmament and the question of the defense line were not necessarily inseparable, they were considered together and one was thought to imply the other.

[20] Stikker, *Memoir*, pp. 297–98; Ismay, *Nato*, p. 30; Hilsman in Knorr, *NATO*, pp. 14–15.
[21] General Douglas MacArthur later confirmed a shortage of American troops for holding any line at all. U.S. Senate, Hearings, *Military Situation in the Far East*, 82nd Cong., 1st Sess., 1951, p. 210. R.I.I.A., *Atlantic Alliance*, p. 19; Martin in Stein, *Decisions*, p. 647; Report of the Senate Committee on Foreign Relations on the North Atlantic Treaty, June 6, 1949, in Francis O. Wilcox and Thorsten V. Kalijarvi, *Recent American Foreign Policy: Basic Documents 1941–1951* (New York: Appleton-Century-Crofts, 1952), p. 882.

THE STATUS OF GERMANY

A brief review of Germany in 1950 relevant to American diplomacy and the rearmament question involves several factors, due to the international status of the Federal Republic as an occupied country still technically in a state of war with the Big Three Western powers as well as the Soviet Union. Attention should be given to the policy goals not only of the allies who exercised sovereignty over Germany but of the German leaders who desired to regain it and achieve political equality, since the failure of U.S. diplomacy to achieve the goal of German rearmament was related to both.

Even before the Korean War further accelerated the return of Germany to an active role in international politics, the great power competition for European zones of influence had led to the creation, in 1949, of a Federal Republic of Germany in the Western occupation zones and a German Democratic Republic (GDR) in the Soviet zone.[22] The new West German state was administered at the national level by a federal government and parliament at Bonn, but ultimate sovereignty was vested in the Allied High Commission, composed of representatives of Britain, France, and the United States, the three Western occupying pow-

[22] A partial list of sources which cover aspects of the status of Germany prior to 1950 includes: John C. Campbell, *The United States in World Affairs, 1945–1947* (New York: Harper, 1947), pp. 191–98; Calvocoressi, *Survey, 1949–1950*, pp. 174ff.; Edgar McInnis, Richard Hiscocks, and Robert Spencer, *The Shaping of Postwar Germany* (New York: Praeger, 1960); Robert Murphy, *Diplomat Among Warriors* (Garden City: Doubleday, 1964); Edward H. Litchfield *et al.*, *Governing Postwar Germany* (Ithaca: Cornell University Press, 1953), esp. Chap. 5; Konrad Adenauer, *Memoirs, 1945–1953* (Chicago: Regnery, 1966), esp. Chaps. 6–8, 12; U.S. Department of State, *Germany, 1947–1949, The Story in Documents* (Washington: Government Printing Office, 1950); *Department of State Bulletin*, July 24, 1950, p. 154, lists the record of participation in international bodies of the Federal Republic; Harold Zink, *The United States in Germany, 1944–1955* (New York: Van Nostrand, 1957); Wilcox and Kalijarvi, *Policy*, pp. 299ff.; William Reitzel, Morton A. Kaplan, and Constance G. Coblenz, *United States Foreign Policy, 1945–1955* (Washington: Brookings Institution, 1956), pp. 141–61; Alfred Grosser, *The Colossus Again: West Germany from Defeat to Rearmament* (New York: Praeger, 1955).

ers. The commissioners controlled all legislation, conducted the foreign affairs of Germany, and were, in short, ultimately responsible for everything which was done in the country.

The broad American concern with continental stability which had begun with the Marshall Plan, and which looked toward the economic recovery of Western Europe, had included consideration of Germany from the outset. Britain and France, sometimes reluctantly, followed the American lead in the inclusion of Germany in the European Recovery Program, and in general, the Western occupying powers were in agreement that restrictions imposed after the close of hostilities should gradually be eased. Fears of German economic revival were probably not absent from the considerations of the occupying powers; while France had apprehensions about the military implications of German recovery, the United States seemed to be more concerned with relieving the American taxpayer of the burden of supporting the Germans.[23] Yet prior to 1950 German economic revival was not considered dangerous since there was unanimous official agreement on continued demilitarization. The allied controls which were retained when the Federal Republic was established were considered temporary, with the exception of security matters: on the policy level, disarmament was to be permanent.[24]

The occupying powers agreed that there was a German problem and that it had to be managed somehow. Indeed, one of the American reasons for sponsoring, and one of the French justifications for joining, the North Atlantic Pact was the conviction that NATO would be beneficial in this respect (although how this would be done was perceived differently). For the United States one of the most important functions of NATO included its role

[23] France continued to be suspicious and resentful of close Anglo-American relations and afraid of being left out of them. Kennan, *Memoirs*, pp. 398, 456; Edgar S. Furniss, Jr., *France, Troubled Ally: DeGaulle's Heritage and Prospects* (New York: Praeger, 1960), p. 38; Zink, *United States*, p. 170; Acheson, *Present at the Creation*, p. 338.

[24] John C. Campbell, *The United States in World Affairs, 1948–1949* (New York: Harper, 1949), pp. 490–91. The U.S. High Commission did not envisage that the disarmament of the Germans would last forever, but the point remains that no policy reversal was anticipated prior to mid-1950. Interviews.

in "bringing Germany back into the fold." [25] France would not have ratified the treaty had the National Assembly not been unequivocally assured that there was no possibility of German adherence; the French government announced as early as 1949 that it would renounce its own membership rather than accept Germany.[26]

The Occupation Statute, signed by the three High Commissioners and Chancellor Konrad Adenauer on November 22, 1949, contained reciprocal agreements to maintain the demilitarization of the Federal Republic and to prevent the recreation of armed forces of any kind.[27] But behind this facade of formal guarantees and in contrast to the United States and Britain, whose policies tended toward the return of Germany to an equal position in other than military affairs, France was "in the grip of an inferiority neurosis." [28] Washington had substituted the Soviet Union for Germany as the major threat to European stability, but the same change had not taken place in Continental and especially in French thinking. France was concerned with the more distant time when the Russian danger might diminish and a stronger Germany would again have to be faced in closest geographical proximity. The French sense of inferiority, sometimes referred to as the French search for security, was deeply grounded in historical and psychological reality, even if exaggerated in the conditions of postwar Europe.[29] In the absence of a more encom-

[25] Fox and Fox, *NATO*, p. 44. Britain apparently agreed. Kirkpatrick, *Memoirs*, p. 220. The report of the Senate Committee on Foreign Relations on the North Atlantic Treaty said: "While Germany is not a party to the North Atlantic Treaty the impact of the treaty upon Germany's future will be highly important. The committee believes it may make possible a solution of the German problem and a constructive integration of Germany into Western Europe." U.S. Department of State, *American Foreign Policy, 1950–1955: Basic Documents* (Washington: Government Printing Office, 1957), I, 850.

[26] Furniss, *France*, p. 38, and see Chaps. 2 and 3 *passim* for French foreign policy generally; *Christian Science Monitor*, November 23, 1949; Osgood, *NATO*, p. 363, n. 11.

[27] C. G. D. Onslow, "West German Rearmament," *World Politics*, Vol. III (July, 1951), p. 450.

[28] Dean Acheson, *Sketches from Life of Men I Have Known* (New York: Harper, 1961), p. 33.

[29] The U.S. designation of the Soviet Union as the enemy has been dated from the pronouncement of the Truman Doctrine on March 12, 1947. David S. McLellan

passing political framework, "equality" for Germany would mean the end of superiority for France.

In these relative terms, any step toward rearmament, particularly coming in the wake of a German economic revival, would take on a threatening character even though not so intended. It was because of this that French policy planners who favored reconciliation with Germany looked to the creation of European institutions as the solution to the German problem. But even then, France remained apprehensive, as reflected in the Schuman Plan in the spring of 1950, and in the Pleven Plan in the fall. For France caution and even intentional delay were considered appropriate, as the rearmament question exemplified.[30]

American policy, long considered suspicious by many Frenchmen, seemed fairly constant prior to the Korean War, as indeed it was on the official level. The highest U.S. officials had often repeated their commitment to a disarmed Germany, and repeatedly denied rumors to the effect that they were considering rearming the Germans. High Commissioner McCloy said, "our fixed policy has been to impose and maintain effective controls against the revival of a German war machine. . . . there is no gainsaying the fact that Germany still gives evidence of the need for restrictions and controls." [31]

American diplomacy, before the decision was made to press for German rearmament, was sensitive to the need for a Franco-German rapprochement. When French Foreign Minister Robert Schuman wrote in May, 1950, to Chancellor Adenauer about the basically political purpose of the proposal for a coal and steel pool, he mentioned as the first item the calming of French fears

---

and John W. Reuss, "Foreign and Military Policies," in *The Truman Period as a Research Field,* ed. Richard S. Kirkendall (Columbia: University of Missouri Press, 1968), pp. 55–57. See also Reitzel, Kaplan, and Coblenz, *Foreign Policy,* pp. 292–93; *The Times* (London), October 27, 1950; William T. R. Fox, *The Super-Powers* (New York: Harcourt, Brace, 1944), p. 104; Arnold Wolfers, *Britain and France Between Two Wars: Conflicting Strategies of Peace Since Versailles* (New York: Harcourt, Brace, 1940), esp. Chap. 1.

[30] Karl W. Deutsch and Lewis J. Edinger, "Foreign Policy of the German Federal Republic," in *Foreign Policy in World Politics,* ed. Roy C. Macridis (2nd ed.; New York: Prentice-Hall, 1962), p. 120; Stikker, *Memoirs,* pp. 299–300.

[31] *Department of State Bulletin,* April 17, 1950, pp. 587–88.

of Germany. His objective, he stated, was "to eliminate all risk of war and substitute for a ruinous rivalry an association founded upon common interest," and "to join in a permanent work of peace two nations which for centuries have faced each other in bloody rivalries." [32] The American response was affirmative. President Truman welcomed the Schuman Plan as "the basis for establishing an entirely new relationship between France and Germany." [33] Secretary Acheson similarly greeted it as a major step toward reconciliation.

German rearmament was not officially urged by any state before the fall of 1950, but since the signing of the North Atlantic Treaty it had been widely mentioned. In Eastern Europe there was an impression that once the West began to construct a political and military bloc every means of strengthening it, including German remilitarization, would seem justified.

Allied military leaders, faced with the problem of confronting a vastly superior Russian army in Central Europe, were extremely interested in German assets—human, material, and geographical—and began early to pursue them. "The Nuremberg trials were hardly over before German soldiers were traveling to the Pentagon as 'consultants' [who] were consulted, of course, because they had fought against the Russians. . . ." [34] In West Germany, "a great number of former righ-ranking officers of the Third Reich's armed forces had been drawn directly by the Western allies into what was called research work on the Second World War." [35] Although "political sentiments still impeded strategic considerations," American and British soldiers were the first to advocate the rearmament of Germany because of its great military potential, which French officers also favored.[36] For the French

[32] Adenauer, *Memoirs*, p. 257; *L'Annee Politique, 1950*, pp. 114, 139.

[33] *Department of State Bulletin*, May 29, 1950, p. 828.

[34] Gordon A. Craig, "NATO and the New German Army," in *Military Policy and National Security*, ed. William W. Kaufmann (Princeton: Princeton University Press, 1956), p. 215.

[35] Julian Lider, *West Germany in NATO* (Warsaw: Western Press Agency, 1965), p. 31.

[36] Alfred Vagts, *Defense and Diplomacy: The Soldier and the Conduct of Foreign Relations* (New York: King's Crown Press, 1956), pp. 154, 161. See also Hanson W. Baldwin in *The New York Times*, December 29, 1949.

army, "Germany no longer represented any danger, either immediately or in any foreseeable future." [37] The result was that military leaders of all three occupying powers were advocates of German rearmament well before the Korean crisis.

Among civilian leaders the question had also arisen. Notwithstanding the fervent assurances of Foreign Minister Schuman, *Le Monde* declared simply that "the rearming of Germany is contained in the Atlantic Pact like the yolk in the egg." Konrad Adenauer was similarly impressed, and saw in the very signing of the treaty the chance of future German membership and the recovery of German equality.[38] Officials at Senate hearings on the North Atlantic Treaty testified to the lingering European fear of a German military threat and to American determination to maintain demilitarization. One senator said he did not favor rearmament either, "unless it got to the point where we needed some of those Germans to help us defend against an aggressor." [39] Western political leaders differed in their perspectives by mid-1950, but had not yet diverged in their policies.

Of great importance to American diplomacy were the desires of the Federal Republic, which as a practical matter were those of Chancellor Adenauer himself. These embraced a number of overlapping and not always consistent objectives. All, however, touched upon the supreme goal of the recovery of sovereignty. They included the following: the revision and termination of the status of Germany as an occupied country, including the release of most war criminals and the end of war crimes trials; recovery

[37] Paul-Marie de la Gorce, *The French Army: A Military-Political History* (New York: Braziller, 1963), p. 366; see also Calvocoressi, *Survey*, p. 155; Furniss, *France*, p. 62; Drew Middleton in *The New York Times*, April 2, 1950; *Herald Tribune*, November 30, 1949; *The New York Times*, April 2, 1950. Field Marshal Montgomery was probably the most outspoken prominent military leader to argue (in 1948) that West Germany should be brought into defense plans. By early 1949, he favored German association with Western Union and later NATO, and argued that only through German rearmament could there be a "forward strategy." Bernard L. Montgomery, *The Memoirs of Field Marshal Montgomery* (New York: New American Library, 1958), pp. 457–58.

[38] Furniss, *France*, p. 62; Adenauer, *Memoirs*, p. 133.

[39] U.S. Senate, Hearings, *North Atlantic Treaty*, 81st Cong., 1st Sess., 1949, p. 282. See also Eric Willenz, *Early Discussions Regarding a Defense Contribution in Germany* (RAND Research Memo. No. 968, October 15, 1952).

of influence in international affairs and restoration of confidence in Germany in the eyes of other countries, including acknowledgment of the Bonn regime as the only legitimate government of Germany; military security for the Federal Republic, whether by means of a domestic effort or by arrangements with the allies for more troops in Germany, a stronger commitment to defend the Federal Republic at its eastern frontier, or membership in NATO (or *all* of these); reconciliation with France, particularly within a European institutional framework looking toward cooperation, integration, and perhaps unification; and the restoration of equality and independence which, depending on the political context, would amount to "sovereignty."[40] Reunification of East and West Germany does not seem to have been a goal of German policy (as conceived by Adenauer) to a degree sufficient to alter the commitment to any of the other goals.[41]

The chapter of Adenauer's memoirs which deals with the background of the German rearmament question is called "On the Road to Full Sovereignty." Unlike other areas of concern where ends and means were mingled and somewhat interchangeable, the remilitarization of Germany was probably not in itself a goal of policy. It remained a means, primarily a diplomatic gambit, intended to enhance the defense of the Federal Republic by securing the dispatch of additional forces to Germany, and eventually to lead to agreements which would completely restore equality and independence.[42] In mid-1950 German "foreign" policy was perhaps less concerned with the threat from the East than with restrictions maintained by the Western powers, with the

[40] Adenauer, *Memoirs*, pp. 37, 193–94, 202, 220–21, 272 and *passim*. James L. Richardson, *Germany and the Atlantic Alliance: The Interaction of Strategy and Politics* (Cambridge: Harvard University Press, 1966), Chap. 1 *passim*.

[41] Helmut Schmidt, *Defense or Retaliation: A German View* (New York: Praeger, 1962), p. 162, put reunification at the bottom of Adenauer's list. See also Charles Wighton, *Adenauer—Democratic Dictator: A Critical Biography* (London: Muller, 1963), Chap. 2; and Rudolf Augstein, *Konrad Adenauer* (London: Secker and Warburg, 1964), pp. 65–128.

[42] Gordon A. Craig, "Germany and NATO: The Rearmament Debate, 1950–1958," in Knorr, *NATO*, pp. 37–38; Deutsch and Edinger in Macridis, *Foreign Policy*, p. 119; Franz Josef Strauss, *The Grand Design: A European Solution to German Reunification* (New York: Praeger, 1966), pp. 94–95.

shock of the Korean attack modifying but not reversing this order of priority.

Adenauer wanted a West German police force and gave the High Commissioners a memorandum to this effect at the end of June, 1950, mentioning the danger of the East German force and the thirty Soviet divisions which he estimated were stationed in the GDR. On August 17 the Chancellor met with the High Commissioners, and among other requests (such as additional allied troops in Europe) repeated his demand for a police force, which he said could be ready by the spring of 1951 and reach a total of 150,000 men. In two memoranda to the High Commissioners at the end of August, the Chancellor in one message again demanded a West German police force and in the other political equality for the Federal Republic based on new contractual arrangements.[43]

There is some disagreement about Adenauer's real desire; in spite of appearances, the Chancellor may not have wanted a German army but only a police force to match in size and strength that of the GDR. Adenauer often reiterated his opposition to German rearmament as such, but failed to make clear what the difference might be between this and a force of 150,000 heavily armed men, which would have amounted to remilitarization whatever the label.[44] His interest in the possibility of German military collaboration with the occupying powers is traceable to late 1948, when at his request former General Hans Speidel prepared a secret memorandum on what kind of contribution might be offered.[45] In late 1949 Adenauer in a highly publicized newspaper interview suggested that Germans should contribute to defense in a European army. This was apparently intended as a trial balloon, and was met with strong opposition in Germany as well as abroad. It was reported early in 1950 that a group of German

[43] Adenauer, *Memoirs*, pp. 272, 274, 281; *L'Annee Politique, 1950*, p. 182.
[44] Kirkpatrick, *Memoirs*, p. 240; Onslow, "West German Rearmament," p. 459. Schuman apparently consented to an increase in German police forces, but not to a German army, and felt that what Adenauer was asking for looked very much like an army to the French. *L'Annee Politique, 1950*, p. 197.
[45] Augstein, *Adenauer*, p. 24. Interviews supported this.

generals had given Adenauer a list of rearmament requirements, and by mid-1950 the Chancellor's readiness to commit the Federal Republic to an apparently unpopular course was clear.[46]

Adenauer wrapped the rearmament ploy in a covering of other considerations, which he thought could be realized in conjunction with a revision of American policy. These included a firmer U.S. commitment to German defense; an assurance that war planning would attempt to avoid making the territory of the Federal Republic a battleground; and a rapid recovery of German sovereignty. One way of pursuing these objectives was by offering a German contribution to Western defense; rearmament was a way of forming a link with the Western allies which would commit them to defend Germany in case of a war with Russia (hopefully on or beyond what became the forward line), and it was a way to move toward political sovereignty with Germans not serving as mercenaries.[47] But these possibilities would perhaps not have materialized for years, if at all, without the Korean catalyst.

THE IMPACT OF THE KOREAN CRISIS

The event which brought the German rearmament question to the action level and prompted a new examination of NATO's defense efforts was the North Korean attack on the South on June 25, 1950.[48] Security was transformed from a theoretical to a concrete problem, and America's political role as leader of the alliance was sharply altered. The impact of the Korean crisis is important because its effects were different in the United States and Europe, and because American statesmen during the long disagreement on the German rearmament question apparently did not stop to ask whether the European analogy (suggesting the

[46] Deutsch and Edinger, in Macridis, *Foreign Policy*, p. 119. The interview appeared in the Cleveland *Plain Dealer*, December 3, 1949; *The New York Times*, January 14, 1950.

[47] Gerhard Wettig, *Entmilitarisierung und Wiederbewaffnung in Deutschland, 1943–1955* (Munich: Oldenbourg, 1967), pp. 306–41.

[48] Roger Hilsman, "On NATO Strategy," in *Alliance Policy in the Cold War*, ed. Arnold Wolfers (Baltimore: The Johns Hopkins Press, 1959), pp. 147–48.

possibility of a similar event in Germany) was valid, even though the other assumptions of 1950 were later revised.

It is unlikely that when Secretary Acheson said, early in 1950, that the United States considered Korea outside the perimeter of American defense, this was an "invitation to aggression," as critics were to charge.[49] In any case, the attack came as a surprise to all, diplomats and soldiers, from Seoul to Washington. There were different reactions, but the immediate impression was that the international situation had taken a dangerous turn and could deteriorate rapidly.

In 1950, and for years thereafter, few distinctions were made between Soviet intentions and Communist intentions. The potential enemy of the West was seen not as a loose grouping of independent states with separate policies but as a more or less coherent bloc, operating if not as a unit then as a semi-organized alliance (or "conspiracy") under the over all control of Moscow. The North Korean military assault on South Korea was a Communist move, which in 1950 meant a Russian move. A discussion of the meaning of the attack is inseparable from its origin, since it was assumed that the aggression in the Far East was but part of a program for world domination. "The Communists of North Korea struck hard and suddenly with strong forces well-equipped with Russian tanks, Russian planes and Russian heavy artillery. . . . One thing is certain, they did not do this purely on their own but as part of the world strategy of international communism." [50] President Truman referred to the Korean attack in terms of "international communism," "communist imperialism," and "the international communist movement." Clearly, he thought of the Soviet Union as the instigator.[51] Secretary Acheson

[49] For example, Senator Styles Bridges asked Secretary Acheson at the MacArthur hearings whether Acheson's January 12, 1950, statement was not "sort of an invitation . . . to attack in Korea." Senate, *Military Situation in the Far East*, p. 1740. Acheson himself dismisses the idea. *Present at the Creation*, p. 358.

[50] *Department of State Bulletin*, July 10, 1950, p. 49, John Foster Dulles.

[51] "From the very beginning of the Korean action I had always looked at it as a Russian maneuver," Truman wrote, which Moscow used in an attempt to divert the United States from the defense of Europe. Truman, *Memoirs*, p. 437. The President also called it a "war by proxy." State of the Union message, *Department of State Bulletin*, January 22, 1951, p. 124.

used similar language, and later said Russian instigation was virtually certain.[52] Although doubts about the leadership role of Moscow were later suggested, there was little to disturb the certitude of the moment.

The Korean attack, above all, meant that Communism was willing to use force to achieve its aims. International politics in the postwar period had until June, 1950, evolved in a context of tension and confrontation, but the absence of large-scale hostilities led many to believe that a cold-war era had indefinitely succeeded one of hot wars. Secretary Acheson's prognosis that there was nothing to indicate an immediate danger of war was based on the assumption of an East-West struggle conducted politically, economically, and psychologically but not militarily. The Korean attack convinced most American policymakers that a basic shift in Soviet intentions had been revealed, and that it was "plain beyond all doubt that communism has passed beyond the use of subversion to conquer independent nations and will now use armed invasion and war."[53] Reaction was at first the same in other NATO countries. The attack "brought Europe to its feet," according to High Commissioner McCloy.[54]

It has been said with only slight exaggeration that "German rearmament was the product of the war in Korea."[55] It was now obvious that American nuclear-weapons superiority might not be

[52] See for example Dennett and Turner, *Documents, 1950*, pp. 146–49, 235–38. Asked whether he thought the attack was "inspired by Russia," Acheson replied, "I think the Soviet Union has complete domination over the Government of North Korea." Senate, *Military Situation in the Far East*, p. 1936. See also his remarks at the troops-to-Europe hearings, Senate, *Assignment of Ground Forces*, pp. 77–78, and *Present at the Creation*, p. 405.

[53] Kennan said virtually no one in the Department of State agreed with him; he considered the attack a Soviet reaction to American moves elsewhere (such as preparing a separate peace with Japan) and not proof that Moscow had otherwise shifted from the nonuse of military force. *Memoirs*, pp. 497–99. Kennan was apparently one of the few to distinguish between the origin of the crisis and its meaning. U.S. Dept. of State, *American Foreign Policy 1950–1955: Basic Documents*, II, 2539–40 (quote by President Truman).

[54] John J. McCloy, *The Challenge to American Foreign Policy* (Cambridge: Harvard University Press, 1953), p. 29.

[55] Calvocoressi, *Survey, 1949–1950*, p. 168.

a complete deterrent to a local Communist war. This possibility was recognized at least from the time of the signing of the North Atlantic Treaty, but until mid-1950 Western policymakers did not consider it an immediate one.

Secretary Acheson called the Korean attack a "cynical, brutal, naked attack by armed forces upon an undefended country." [56] The parallel of the undefended country in the NATO area which came to mind at once was the Federal Republic, faced across a line of political demarcation with what was thought to be a heavily armed East German force. The analogy between Korea and Germany—both divided, each with a government aligned with one of the sides in the cold war, with the Communist part militarily superior and supplied with Soviet weapons—was superficially persuasive and deceptively neat. Reports from Germany mentioned the German apprehension about their own "38th parallel," the Elbe. Since the military balance in Europe was a lopsided equation with Western nuclear superiority confronting Eastern conventional superiority, and since it was believed the former no longer deterred the latter, a rearmament effort seemed manifestly appropriate. It was in this context that Adenauer himself raised the question of German defense.

When in late 1949 the Chancellor mentioned German rearmament, he later wrote, "it belonged to the realm of fantasy." [57] A German military contribution as a means to achieve political objectives would at best have been possible only as the result of a gradual process over time. In June, 1950, German leaders received an unexpected political bonus: "the war in Korea was a veritable gift from the gods, satisfying their wildest dreams." [58] But West Germans were apprehensive about what the Korean War might mean for their security. Adenauer by his own account "was firmly convinced that Stalin was planning the same procedure for Western Germany as had been used in Korea," an im-

[56] *Department of State Bulletin*, July 3, 1950.
[57] Adenauer, *Memoirs*, p. 269.
[58] Heinz Abosch, *The Menace of the Miracle: Germany from Hitler to Adenauer* (New York: Monthly Review Press, 1963), p. 33.

pression which was underlined early in July when East German leader Walter Ulbricht said the Federal Republic was about to share the same fate as South Korea.[59]

Adenauer developed the argument for a West German police force from this uncertainty of events. He reasoned that this force, if capable of meeting an attack by the GDR, might avoid general war by allowing the Federal Republic to defend itself sufficiently well that the United States would not be forced to regard East German aggression as an attack by the Soviet Union itself.[60] As noted, the Chancellor did not distinguish between his proposal and rearmament, and he did not mention the improbability that the super-powers might simply stand by as observers, while hundreds of thousands of East and West German "police" conducted a civil war. Adenauer emphasized instead that he wanted the armed force as a deterrent and believed that this, combined with a reinforcement of allied occupation troops, would suffice to reassure West Germans and to convince East Germany that the price of aggression would be too high.[61]

While of doubtful value as a practical solution to the risk of attack in Europe, the Chancellor's proposals did amount to something which the Western allies could consider when they convened in New York in September, 1950. In terms of German policy goals, they were directed especially toward obtaining political concessions from the occupying powers. Adenauer's use of the international situation depended on his diplomatic skill, particularly since Germany's ambiguous status as half-enemy and half-ally (and really neither) made caution essential. The Korean crisis allowed him openly to link his goal of sovereignty to a defense contribution. Thereafter, "the successful pursuit of political re-

[59] Adenauer, *Memoirs*, p. 273; Perry Laukhuff, "German Reaction to Soviet Policy, 1945–1953," *Journal of International Affairs*, Vol. VIII, No. 1 (1954), p. 69.

[60] This reasoning was not shared by U.S. military leaders. General Collins specifically rejected the Korean analogy as to limited conflict in a limited area: "Certainly if Western Europe is invaded by aggressive forces from the east it means war, general war." Senate, *Assignment of Ground Forces*, p. 174.

[61] The Chancellor also failed to explain how a reinforced NATO contingent could have kept itself apart from hostilities in a German civil war while the country remained occupied. Adenauer, *Memoirs*, pp. 271–83.

covery at crucial points ran parallel to the developments that led to the rearmament of Germany." [62]

Once the German analogy had been widely accepted, the concept of a massive Soviet attack as the most likely danger was altered. Europeans believed thereafter that an attack by the satellites was the most probable military danger.[63] Yet while there was general European agreement on increasing the scale and speed of defense efforts, priorities were at issue, and even at the moment of greatest apprehension American initiatives were followed only with hesitation. France pledged the production of fifteen divisions, but only conditionally: financial aid was requisite and America and Britain must send more troops to Europe. It was also pointed out that the disintegration of economic and social conditions within Europe would be just as dangerous as the external threat.

The time factor was an additional part of the European rearmament problem, especially for Washington. Acheson warned that "the epitaph of freedom, if it is ever written, would be 'too little and too late.' We must have enough, and we must have it soon enough." [64] Under this impression of immediacy, the U.S. priority was shifted away from economic recovery and toward military strength. Both at the time and later, the greater sense of urgency was felt in Washington, not in London or Paris. As the Far Eastern situation increasingly appeared to be a limited conflict and not a prelude to attacks elsewhere, concern about aggression in Europe began to fade. But by then the American decision on German rearmament had been made.

THE U.S. DECISION TO REARM GERMANY

The crucial period of choice for NATO's future occurred in "the crowded and crisis-ridden months of July and August 1950." The

---

[62] Wolfram F. Hanreider, *West German Foreign Policy 1949–1963: International Pressure and Domestic Response* (Stanford: Stanford University Press, 1967), p. 50.

[63] Jean-Jacques Servan-Schreiber, "Europe and America: Views on Foreign Policy," *Journal of International Affairs*, Vol. V (Winter, 1951), p. 19.

[64] Dennett and Turner, *Documents, 1950*, pp. 148, 149.

Washington atmosphere in mid-1950 had ample reason to be chaotic, as many of the major assumptions on which American policy had rested were questioned or seemed false. The Korean War made a new set of operational premises valid even if they had not been proven correct. Among these were: the Soviet Union would expand militarily if not checked by visible countervailing power; local imbalances which favored Russia or a satellite would lead to further "Koreas"; and the most inviting local imbalance was in Central Europe.[65]

President Truman, looking back at NATO's early weakness and discussing the major problem of German participation, concluded that "Without Germany, the defense of Europe was a rearguard action on the shores of the Atlantic Ocean. With Germany, there could be a defense in depth, powerful enough to offer effective resistance to aggression from the East. The logic behind this situation is very plain. Any map will show it, and a little arithmetic will prove what the addition of German manpower means to the strength of the joint defense of Europe." [66] From the summer of 1950, official American acceptance of this "logic" and "arithmetic" was such that U.S. diplomacy was from then on firmly committed to German rearmament.

When the Pentagon raised the point that Western Germany must be part of a unified defense of Europe, Acheson later wrote,

This was indisputable. But there could be and was a difference of opinion on how to bring it about. The Pentagon insisted on making German participation a condition to a unified command, on the logically persuasive ground that the command would be an American responsibility and should not be assumed until it was made feasible by German participation. The State Department argued that only the logic of demonstrated necessity would gain French agreement to German rearmament. German participation was bound to follow the establishment of the unified command.[67]

[65] Coral Bell, *Negotiation from Strength: A Study in the Politics of Power* (London: Chatto and Windus, 1962), p. 47; Brown, *Faces of Power*, pp. 54–55.

[66] Truman, *Memoirs*, p. 253.

[67] Acheson, *Sketches from Life*, p. 26.

Notwithstanding his reluctance to do so, the secretary, without obtaining French agreement, accepted the linking of German rearmament, as demanded by the Department of Defense, with the other elements of what became known as the package agreement. These elements, as called for by the State Department, included the provision of an American as Supreme NATO Commander, increased financial aid, the integration of alliance forces, and the sending of more U.S. troops to the European area. The secretary considered it a mistake to proceed in this manner because of the rigidity of the agreement, but explained afterwards that the events which led to it came at a time of multiple crises and a great sense of danger. The President's approval was also given in haste.[68]

Believing time to be short, American policymakers considered the arguments for and against a reversal of the official U.S. commitment to permanent German demilitarization. The reasons why Germany should have been permitted to rearm fall into broad military-strategic and political-economic categories. All have been mentioned in public sources; many continued to be debated up to (and even after) the time when agreement was finally reached in 1954. The U.S. decision raised, but did not settle, the question of whether the Federal Republic should rearm. Its presentation as American policy meant an answer had to be worked out one way or another; the demand did not make any particular solution inevitable.[69]

What first led to U.S. insistence on a German defense contribution was the strictly military consideration of NATO's need for troop strength.[70] Other military-strategic factors were related to this necessity: the desire to balance defensively the conventional superiority of the Soviet Union before American atomic superi-

[68] Acheson, *Present at the Creation*, pp. 435–40.
[69] An excellent summary of the U.S. decision on German rearmament may be found in Lewis J. Edinger, *West German Armament*, Air University, Maxwell Air Force Base, Alabama, 1955, pp. 4–11. See also Wesley B. Truitt, "The Troops to Europe Decision: The Process, Politics, and Diplomacy of a Strategic Commitment" (unpublished Ph.D. dissertation, Columbia University, 1968).
[70] Hans Speier, *German Rearmament and Atomic War: The Views of German Military and Political Leaders* (Evanston: Row, Peterson, 1957), p. 8.

ority could be neutralized; to counter the rearmament of the Communist satellite states, and in particular to deter an attack by the GDR People's Police; to tap the German manpower resources, considered not only quantitatively adequate but qualitatively impressive both as fighters and as experienced veterans of Russian campaigns; and generally to make up for deficiencies when material did not seem to be forthcoming elsewhere rapidly enough to meet the urgency of the situation. Another factor among the military-strategic reasons for German rearmament was the geographical position of Germany in NATO strategy, and the establishment of a forward line of defense to avoid liberating occupied areas in the event of attack. The new Supreme Allied Commander of Europe (SACEUR), American officers felt, should not be given a task beyond his abilities and resources. German rearmament within a reasonable time would permit him to accomplish his mission.

American military leaders who favored rearmament for these reasons, incidentally, did not naively believe that German soldiers would spring forth like dragons' teeth. Some Pentagon officials might have had this impression, but those on the higher planning levels were aware that time would be required to recruit, train, and equip a new German army. They were also aware that the question had a domestic aspect in the Federal Republic which would have to be resolved. There was, however, probably more optimism in the Pentagon, and in the State Department, about the willingness of Germans to rearm than the reports from High Commissioner McCloys' office warranted.

There were several political arguments for German rearmament. One, shared by allied military leaders, was that Germany was no longer a danger. Related to this was the likelihood that German demands for equality would eventually include the right to rearm, and that it would be politically advisable to concede readily and with grace what would in any case be extorted later.[71]

---

[71] Calvocoressi, *Survey, 1949–1950*, p. 152. High Commissioner McCloy apparently accepted this view. Martin in Stein, *Decisions,* 647; Hilsman in Knorr, *NATO,* p. 17; and interviews.

It is difficult to judge the weight assigned such views by policy-makers in Washington. While American treatment of Germany had already moved away from the punitive, the failure to place any noticeable emphasis on whether the Germans themselves wanted remilitarization, and the failure of the American proposals to provide for either political or military German equality (not to mention farther reaching concepts such as reunification), suggest that to a significant degree *this* aspect of relevant political considerations may not have been persuasive. Allied unwillingness to rearm was probably the key political factor.

Another consideration which in its effect was political was the ideological, or perhaps the psychological, factor. American opinion tended to favor the Germans over the French. The Germans were thought to be strongly anti-Communist and not susceptible to hostile propaganda, in contrast to the "unreliable" French with their large Communist party (or at least numerous voters) and chronic governmental and financial instability. This bias was to persist in the coming years.[72] In addition, some U.S. officials felt that morality dictated that the Federal Republic be allowed to defend itself, but this was probably secondary to the American impression that the French were unreliable.[73]

Other reasons for German rearmament touched upon American diplomatic goals. A German military connection with other Western European countries might further the integration of the Federal Republic into the Western political system; it might serve as a device to prod the other NATO allies into greater defense efforts; and it might contribute to American diplomatic strength through augmentation of Western power generally and thereby

[72] Speier, *German Rearmament*, p. 7. Zink, *United States*, p. 118, noted that the Americans in Germany preferred the Germans to the French "despite their enemy status." See also Halle, *Cold War*, p. 243. Some Americans wondered whether France, even with a large army, might prove to be a disappointment, based on the memory of the 1940 collapse. See, for example, Senate, *Assignment of Ground Forces*, p. 25.

[73] McCloy, *Foreign Policy*, p. 30. General Gruenther and the other U.S. military leaders shared the view that a key reason for German rearmament was that the French military would not fight very well. C. L. Sulzberger, *A Long Row of Candles: Memoirs and Diaries (1934–1954)* (New York: Macmillan, 1969), pp. 598–99.

bring closer an East-West settlement. Negotiations might then be undertaken (in Acheson's view) without the drawback of a militarily weak position.

Economic considerations were also important. There was concern, especially in Britain and France, that the Federal Republic would obtain unfair advantages in international commercial competition if all resources were to be free for the production or purchase of nonmilitary goods. Moreover, the time element affected the economic picture, since the longer German military spending was deferred the greater would be its differential advantage in the trade sphere. The British High Commissioner saw German economic revival without German rearmament as a special threat.[74]

Arguments against the rearmament of Germany were put either in the form of an affirmative statement ("rearmament is contrary to the will of the German people") or as a question ("would the Germans be willing to rearm?").[75] The other side of the coin of the military necessity of German rearmament was its political and psychological distastefulness. Memories of suffering in the war were still fresh in the Federal Republic, as well as in France and elsewhere, and many thought that too little time had passed to warrant the acceptance of the risk of another German danger.[76] Included in fears of a "new danger" was the apprehension that even if a rearmed Germany were unlikely to turn against the West, its territorial claims might drag the NATO allies into a revisionist struggle to remove the Oder-Neisse line and recover the lost areas. And if rearmament did not lead to this at once, then it would foster future instability by making the division of Germany more or less permanent, prolonging the cold war, and

[74] Alistair Horne, *Return to Power: A Report on the New Germany* (New York: Praeger, 1956), p. 28. Kirkpatrick wrote that without German rearmament the Federal Republic would be "hoisted . . . into a position of economic preponderance in Europe. A Germany in that situation would be a greater nuisance to us than a Germany with an army and an armaments industry limited by treaty and by her own economic and manpower capacity." *Memoirs*, pp. 242-43.

[75] Jules Moch, *Histoire du rearmement allemand depuis 1950* (Paris: Laffont, 1965), p. 15; Adenauer, *Memoirs*, Chap. 15 *passim*.

[76] Henry Byroade, Director of the Bureau of German Affairs in the Department of State, emphasized this. *Department of State Bulletin*, September 11, 1950, pp. 426-29.

preventing agreement on a general European settlement. Meanwhile, there was the chance of a violent Russian reaction if Soviet leaders decided their interests would be so threatened by a remilitarized Germany that preventive measures were worth the risk of intervention. Other Eastern European states, especially Poland and Czechoslovakia, in addition to the GDR, would be driven toward even greater dependence on the Soviet Union. Less likely but not beyond possibility, a resurgent Germany might be later tempted to reach a new Rapallo agreement and, once rearmed, join the Eastern camp.

Less dramatic, but no less important, reasons against German rearmament were based in part upon the awareness of the traditional German problem: the European balance might again find itself unable to accommodate a Germany which, after commencing rearmament with only a small force, sooner or later would become preponderant. Moreover, Bonn might later look toward the acquisition of sophisticated modern weapons instead of remaining a supplier of cannon-fodder, as the original American formula seemed to imply.[77] This possibility would be all the more unsettling if German rearmament for one or another reason led to an American political-military withdrawal from the Continent, a contingency which Europeans had little difficulty imagining and one which some American spokesmen had even offered as one of the advantages of German remilitarization.[78]

Other arguments against German rearmament included the concern that military expenditures would delay the economic recovery of the Federal Republic and prolong the burden of outside aid; the apprehension among allied leaders that equipping German armed forces would divert scarce military resources from their own armies, still acutely short of materiel; the fear that

[77] Cf. Catherine M. Kelleher, "The Issue of German Nuclear Armament," *Proceedings of the Academy of Political Science*, Vol. XXIX, No. 2 (1968), pp. 95–107.

[78] Eisenhower in 1966 said that the sending of troops to Europe in 1951 was an emergency measure on the strict understanding that as soon as the Europeans raised their own ground forces U.S. troops would be brought back, leaving only air and naval units permanently in Europe. He said this was later "shelved or forgotten," especially with the admission of the Federal Republic to NATO. *The New York Times*, May 22, 1966. See also Stikker, *NATO*, pp. 303-4.

the infant of German democracy would be strangled by the return to militarism which rearmament would impel; the argument that Europe could be defended without any German involvement in practical military affairs, or that conventional rearmament was pointless when the United States held a virtual monopoly of nuclear weapons; the chance that the alliance that was sought to be strengthened might instead be damaged or even ruined by the withdrawal of France and the resentment of the other allies; the preference for binding Germany to Europe economically as a beginning step on the difficult road toward integration, since rearmament might well damage the process if attempted prematurely and without a prior foundation of mutual trust and confidence; and the consideration that the decision to permit Germany to rearm was not an American decision at all, and could only be made with the other Western occupying powers if not with the Russians. These arguments almost without exception were concerned with matters which would and should have been more disturbing to European than to American sensitivities, so that there was a rough division between the arguments for German rearmament and those against it, which corresponded to a somewhat vague but still significant U.S.-European dichotomy of perspectives.

The American decision to demand a German military contribution was impelled by international pressures, particularly those generated by the crisis in Korea. If measured by results it was not a decision at all but a suggestion, which was not acceptable for a considerable time period. Unlike the troops-to-Europe decision, which was implemented without allied resistance, German rearmament was a policy reversal incapable of unilateral American enforcement, in part because the consent of other states was indispensable, and in part because even after such consent was granted political unwillingness to act upon it persisted. In a sense the American package was a European product: a central command for the Western European Union (WEU) had been urged since the signing of the Brussels Treaty; the British and the French had long desired a supreme NATO commander, preferably an American, and the reinforcement of American troops in Europe; Adenauer had conceived to use remilitarization as a diplomatic gambit; allied military leaders had called for utilization of German military potential; and France wanted a defense east of the Rhine. In retrospect it seems logical that all these elements should have been placed together, since each made more sense when linked with the others. The allies' anxiousness for all the ingredients except German rearmament allowed the United States to bargain for this, when otherwise it would have been opposed too firmly to be considered. The basic equation involved an assumed need for German troops versus a probable alienation of at least some allies and a possible German refusal to cooperate; on balance, the United States chose the former.

In the postwar years, having rejected the notion of a rigid Draconian solution, American leaders were sensitive to the German problem in international politics as an area of U.S. choice. The rearmament decision of 1950 was neither right for the wrong reasons nor wrong for the right reasons. The American goal of remilitarizing the Federal Republic, however, could have been presented and pursued differently, and might have been realized more quickly (although not necessarily more propitiously) had American diplomacy been otherwise. As it was, something of a metamorphosis occurred as the caterpillar of German rearmament was temporarily transformed into the butterfly of supranational European unification. How diplomatic endeavors to implement a politically unacceptable decision seemed to lead to an ever expanding scenario for the place of Germany in the future European system, and how U.S. policy objectives mushroomed from rearming the Germans into uniting Western Europe, form the substance of the rest of this study.

CHAPTER II

The Period of Deadlock

IN September, 1950, Secretary Acheson announced that in the judgment of the U.S. government the defense of Europe required a direct and immediate military contribution from the Federal Republic. In the ensuing period of Franco-American deadlock, and for the remainder of the time that the German rearmament question persisted, this basic commitment never wavered.[1] What did change was the framework within which German rearmament might be made palatable to the states most concerned, particularly France and the Federal Republic. The events of the latter part of 1950 were important to the German rearmament question both in their own right and because many of their essential elements continued in the following months and years.[2] The battle lines which were drawn by Paris, Bonn, and Washington—with the single exception of the American shift from a preference for national German rearmament to the EDC —assumed characteristics of tenacity approaching permanence. To American policymakers, the combination of Communist willingness to use force and Soviet development of nuclear weapons meant that as American strategic air power was neutralized an

[1] Harold Zink, *The United States in Germany, 1944–1955* (New York: Van Nostrand, 1957), p. 99.

[2] Jules Moch, *Histoire du rearmement allemand depuis 1950* (Paris: Laffont, 1965), *passim*.

34

effective European system of ground defense was essential if deterrence was to be preserved.[3]

Prior to the fall of 1950, the United States had—without notable success—urged its allies to augment their rearmament efforts, but not until after the German rearmament demand was there an intra-allied disagreement so sharp that it could not be resolved, even at a time when "enforced collaboration"[4] remained. French unwillingness to agree to German rearmament led, in October, to the European army proposal as an alternative suggestion in place of the U.S. demand for what, in effect, would have been national German rearmament. Attempts to reconcile Franco-American differences were soon complicated further by the inclusion of the Federal Republic's somewhat different view of the question.

American diplomacy on the German rearmament question was, of course, the product of many ingredients, personal and institutional, official and unofficial. It was, however, to a great extent conceived and guided by the secretary of state. One of the hallmarks of Acheson's approach to East-West matters was his conviction that the intense political competition which characterized the cold war could only end when there existed the ability in the West to negotiate with the East from a position of strength.[5] From early 1950 on, the secretary's hope for less aggressive Soviet behavior was based not upon an anticipation of Russian do-

[3] Secretary Acheson testified in February, 1951, that "the best use we can make of our present advantage in retaliatory air power, is to move ahead under this protective shield to build the balanced collective forces in Western Europe that will continue to deter aggression after our atomic advantage has been diminished." U.S. Senate, Hearings, *Assignment of Ground Forces of the United States to Duty in the European Area*, 82nd Cong., 1st Sess. (Washington: Government Printing Office, 1951), p. 79.

[4] This phrase is used by William T. R. Fox and Annette Baker Fox, *NATO and the Range of American Choice* (New York: Columbia University Press, 1967), p. 222.

[5] See Coral Bell, *Negotiation from Strength: A Study in the Politics of Power* (London: Chatto and Windus, 1962), pp. 12ff. and *passim* for a discussion of the concept; Dean Acheson, *Power and Diplomacy* (Cambridge: Harvard University Press, 1958), affords a general overview of Acheson's outlook upon and approach to diplomacy and international relations, as does McGeorge Bundy, ed., *The Pattern of Responsibility* (Boston: Houghton Mifflin, 1952), pp. 23ff. and Chap. 3, *passim*. See also Dean Acheson, *Present at the Creation: My Years in the State Department* (New York: Norton, 1969), pp. 274–75, 727.

mestic evolution but on the belief that political adjustments would flow from Western power so impressive that the Soviet Union would realize its inability to upset the international balance.[6] Acheson went out of his way to denigrate calls for "negotiation" with the Russians, and expected little of such occasions.[7] Since President Truman shared Acheson's skepticism, U.S. diplomacy was mainly focused upon achieving policy goals *within* the Western camp rather than on the other side of the cold-war fence.[8] This was especially true of the German rearmament question. In addition, many policy decisions about the Federal Republic were equally directed toward the Soviet Union, just as they often reflected the demands of the American, French, and German domestic political arenas.[9]

Acheson apparently looked to strength which would be enough to discourage a full-scale Russian attack, not to the creation of defensive forces in Europe which would be capable of meeting an all-out assault by the huge Soviet military machine. This distinction is important, since whether or not German rearmament was deemed worthwhile in the early 1950's often depended upon whether the analyst thought in terms of deterrence or defense—a dozen divisions from the Federal Republic would hardly make Europe defensible, but could well give an adversary second thoughts about the attractiveness of initiating hostilities. What Acheson sought in the long run was to make Europe capable of handling its own affairs.[10]

[6] Cf. David S. McLellan and John W. Reuss, "Foreign and Military Policies," in *The Truman Period as a Research Field,* ed. Richard S. Kirkendall (Columbia: University of Missouri Press, 1968), p. 65.

[7] Norman A. Graebner, "Dean G. Acheson (1949–1953)," in *An Uncertain Tradition: American Secretaries of State in the Twentieth Century,* ed. Norman A. Graebner (New York: McGraw-Hill, 1961), p. 274.

[8] Cf. Peter Calvocoressi, *Survey of International Affairs, 1949–1950* (London: Oxford University Press, 1953), p. 17.

[9] Royal Institute of International Affairs, *Atlantic Alliance: NATO's Role in the Free World* (London: Royal Institute of International Affairs, 1952), p. 108.

[10] David S. McLellan, "The Role of Political Style: A Study of Dean Acheson," in *Foreign Policy in the Sixties: The Issues and the Instruments,* eds. Roger Hilsman and Robert C. Good (Baltimore: The Johns Hopkins Press, 1965), p. 245.

Beginning in mid-1950, what has been called the militarization of U.S. foreign policy occurred. American officials had been privately urging Western rearmament since the Soviet bomb in mid-1949, but not until the Korean attack was there an opportunity to adopt this openly, although Western rearmament did not necessarily include German rearmament. Military planners as early as 1947 doubted that the allies' promises to produce more divisions would ever be kept, but they had to wait until the Soviet Union did something to make it possible politically to ask for German troops. In the United States, there was a "strengthening of every policy trend that was identifiable with straight-forward anti-Communism." Scruples about the rehabilitation of "anti-Communist" nations such as West Germany were dropped. The State Department under Acheson became "even more hardboiled, power oriented, and realistic" than the Pentagon; its military viewpoint was "by and large the uncoerced product of its own thinking on foreign affairs." [11]

German rearmament fitted easily into this, and became a fixed American goal which in later periods was not altered as the cold-war temperature went up or down.[12] Acheson believed that the basic source of international tensions lay not in such matters as German rearmament but in the Russian attitude itself, which was characterized by a lack of any real desire or intention to reach basic agreements.[13] He refused to play up the role of ideology or to embark upon crusades against Bolshevism; the cold-war threat

[11] Samuel P. Huntington, *The Soldier and the State: The Theory and Politics of Civil-Military Relations* (Cambridge: Harvard University Press, 1957), p. 381. See also George F. Kennan, *Memoirs, 1925–1950* (Boston: Little, Brown, 1967), pp. 356ff., and Richard P. Stebbins, *The United States in World Affairs, 1950* (New York: Harper, 1951), p. 251, and see pp. 249–55 for a discussion of the shift to the military emphasis.

[12] Cf. Alfred Vagts, *Defense and Diplomacy: The Soldier and the Conduct of Foreign Relations* (New York: King's Crown Press, 1956), p. 161.

[13] *Department of State Bulletin*, January 15, 1951, pp. 90, 92. President Truman held similar views: "There was never a day during the four years of Dean Acheson's secretaryship that anyone could have said that he and I differed on policy." Harry S Truman, *Memoirs: Years of Trial and Hope* (Garden City: Doubleday, 1956), Vol. II, p. 430.

was Russian imperialism, not Communism (the latter being but an instrument of the former). "In foreign affairs, only the end can justify the means," he said.[14]

American officials at first refrained from embellishing the German rearmament question; military necessity was sufficient. But even in Washington there was an awareness of an inherent danger; because of this there persisted a distrust as to what Germany might do if given a new opportunity to act independently. The policy of the United States thus had to adapt to a somewhat ambiguous situation: it was decided to make Germany an ally at a time when American opinion at the highest official level was *not* yet prepared to terminate, legally or psychologically, the status of the Federal Republic as a defeated enemy.[15]

The United States and France, while differing on almost every other aspect of the German rearmament question, agreed that some form of supervision was essential (a view shared by Adenauer, although the Chancellor was aware that supervision and political recovery went hand in hand).[16] Washington and Paris both desired to bring Bonn firmly into the Western camp, but differed as to the speed and the method with which this should be attempted. They also agreed that because of the peculiar situation where Germany had lost everything and could gain much by change, German friendship could not be taken for granted.[17] Acheson's basic view was that German resources must be denied the Soviet Union, and that the Federal Republic must become

[14] Dean Acheson, "Ethics in International Relations Today," in *The Puritan Ethic in United States Foreign Policy*, ed. David L. Larson (Princeton: Van Nostrand, 1966), p. 137.

[15] Germany was, under the original American formula, to be rearmed *before* it was independent. Cf. Lewis J. Edinger, *West German Armament*, Air University, Maxwell Air Force Base, Alabama, October, 1955.

[16] As one analyst noted, "it would have been much more difficult for Bonn to extract concessions from the western powers if the restored elements of sovereignty had not been subject to international surveillance." Wolfram F. Hanreider, *West German Foreign Policy 1949–1963: International Pressure and Domestic Response* (Stanford: Stanford University Press, 1967), p. 83.

[17] R.I.I.A., *Atlantic Alliance*, p. 110. See also, Louis J. Halle, *The Cold War as History* (London: Chatto and Windus, 1967), p. 243.

a part of the Atlantic community, both because Germany—as history and geography showed—would otherwise be a danger, and because German strength was necessary as an addition to Western strength.[18] It is consistent with this that EDC was later accepted as the solution to the German rearmament problem.

German rearmament as a political question had to be resolved without offending the Germans themselves, in a manner acceptable to France and America's other European allies, in a framework which would minimize the risk of a future German military adventure, and which would avoid provoking a violent Russian response. These circumstances produced in late 1950 a three-cornered relationship between the United States, France, and Germany in which the containment of the Soviet Union was to be achieved through the cooperation of a state which itself had to be contained. One review remarked that although the German rearmament dispute seemed to be a duel between Washington and Paris, "in reality, however, the issue was enmeshed in a dense tangle of political and technical interests that prevented its being considered in isolation or solely on its own merits." [19] The German rearmament question was never so considered, and indeed could not have been, since the states which were in fundamental disaccord could neither isolate the problem nor agree on a criterion of what the merits were.

THE U.S. DEMAND FOR GERMAN REARMAMENT

Not until September was the American attempt to obtain a German defense contribution—which had begun somewhat haphazardly during the summer of 1950—made pursuant to official U.S. policy. The presentation to the allies of the package proposals marked only a beginning of a new approach to the German

[18] Bundy, *Responsibility*, p. 102, and see also pp. 291–92. Cf. also Graebner, *Uncertain Tradition*, p. 272.

[19] Stebbins, *United States, 1950*, pp. 258–59. See also *The Times* (London), October 27, 1950.

problem.[20] Especially in France it triggered "profound instinctive fears."[21] The French knew in their bones that German rearmament was something they could not embrace, whatever the military necessity.

Agreement on the German rearmament question might have been possible had the unstable international situation and the degree of external threat (as then perceived) been the controlling factors. These were *not* determinative, however, and American diplomatic efforts were frustrated even though the Atlantic Alliance was enjoying the "youth and vigor" generated by the Korean War and its implications drawn from European analogies.[22] The alliance leader could not implement a major policy decision in spite of an international situation which should have made the NATO allies more rather than less responsive to Washington's demands.

Secretary Acheson could hardly have thought that the "bomb" he was to drop at the meeting of the Big Three foreign ministers on September 12, 1950, would come as a complete surprise to his colleagues. In addition to the numerous references by American officials to the effect that German rearmament was in some form indispensable, there had been a flurry of press reports saying that the United States had already decided on it—reports corroborated by Acheson himself in a press conference during the week preceding the meeting.[23]

Nevertheless, several factors were important concerning the presentation of the German rearmament demand, even though there

[20] The phrase "the German problem" in September, 1950, and thereafter meant, for Washington, how to get German rearmament and, for Paris, how to prevent it. Walter Millis, Harvey C. Mansfield, and Harold Stein, *Arms and the State* (New York: Twentieth Century Fund, 1958), p. 343; Moch, *Histoire, passim.*

[21] Walt W. Rostow, *The United States in the World Arena* (New York: Harper, 1960), p. 220.

[22] James E. King, Jr., "NATO: Genesis, Progress, Problems," in *National Security in the Nuclear Age*, eds. Gordon B. Turner and Richard D. Challener (New York: Praeger, 1960), p. 149.

[23] See Raymond Dennett and Robert K. Turner, eds., *Documents on American Foreign Relations, 1950*, Vol. XII (Princeton: Princeton University Press, 1951), p. 552; *L'Année Politique, 1950* (Paris: Presses Universitaires de France, 1951), p. 197; *The New York Times*, September 7, 1950. See also C. G. D. Onslow, "West German Rearmament," *World Politics*, Vol. III (July, 1951), pp. 450ff.

had been unofficial "warning" that it was coming and even though there was no further question concerning whether or why this should become U.S. policy. The factors included what should be called for; when this should be done; and how the demand was to be presented. These elements of form, timing, and style were part of the substance of American diplomacy. Perhaps "the difference between the Pentagon and the State Department had dwindled to one of method and timing" on the German rearmament question before the September meeting, "but insofar as success depended on the active cooperation of other nations it was of the essence that the new policy be presented to them in an acceptable form and at a favorable moment." [24]

Acheson seemed to overcome his own better judgment in his initial approach to the German rearmament problem vis-à-vis the allies. He later wrote that "everything was wrong: the plan itself, the attempt to bring it forward without preparation," and that doing so was an "error." [25] But the secretary's hesitation, however genuine, did not prevent him from presenting the demand as an integral part of the American package proposal, at a time and in a manner not conducive to optimism that agreement could be reached.

Later disclaimers, clarifications, and communiqués to the contrary notwithstanding, the U.S. government had made the decision to seek with no delay *national* German rearmament in the form of military units of divisional strength from the Federal Republic, with no particular control arrangement other than that which would have resulted simply by virtue of the German troops being under NATO command and without their own general staff.[26] The substance of the American proposal, worked out by

[24] Laurence W. Martin, "The American Decision to Rearm Germany," in *American Civil-Military Decisions*, ed. Harold Stein (Birmingham: University of Alabama Press, 1963), p. 659.

[25] Dean Acheson, *Sketches from Life of Men I Have Known* (New York: Harper, 1961), pp. 26, 41, and *Present at the Creation: My Years in the State Department* (New York: Norton, 1969), pp. 442ff.

[26] The United States joined with Britain and France to state in the communiqué on Germany of September 19, 1950, that a German national army would not serve the best interests of any of the parties. Dennett and Turner, *Documents, 1950*, p. 556.

the first days of September, to a great degree dictated the diplomatic style with which it was presented at the New York meetings.

The German rearmament portion of the package agreement, which also included the reinforcement of American troops in Europe, an American Supreme Commander, the integration of NATO forces, and increased aid to the allies,

. . . did not go very far in dealing with the technical details involved, although there was mention of some limitations on the kinds of weapons the Germans might possess, on the arms they might manufacture, and the staff organization they might establish. Probably the unified command also seemed to be an effective control. The plan was quite definite, however, in calling for an immediate start of the formation of German units large enough for operational requirements, which, in the eyes of the Joint Chiefs of Staff, meant divisions directly incorporated in the NATO force. Removing all doubt on this point had been the chief concern of the Pentagon representatives at the joint discussions.[27]

Jules Moch, then French minister of national defense and one of the strongest opponents of any kind of German rearmament, later explained that the United States did not demand an "independent" German army: "What Acheson asked for during these days was not, as has been claimed, the creation of an autonomous German army of ten divisions juxtaposed in Germany with diverse allied armies. . . . What he wanted was an integrated army, under a single commander, obviously American, with an international command which would include, in addition to allied forces, a number to be determined of German divisions." [28]

While Acheson may not have demanded an independent or autonomous German army, he did demand a national German army. This distinction, sometimes ignored both in official pro-

[27] Martin in Stein, *Decisions*, p. 657.
[28] Moch, *Histoire*, p. 47. Edinger wrote that the substance of the American demand was for national German rearmament. Edinger, *West German Armament*, p. 10.

nouncements and in the literature, is important to later Franco-American misunderstandings on such questions as whether or not there had somehow been agreement on the principle of German rearmament.[29]

The American proposal did not, apparently, include detailed mention of such factors as whether the Germans would agree or what conditions Bonn might impose. Acheson told the British and French foreign ministers "that it was quite possible to deal with the German Government on the issue, not as supplicants, but merely as agreeing to proposals already made by Adenauer to contribute units to European forces and to force him to accept conditions to our acceptance of his proposal." In other words, a change amounting to a termination of the status of the Federal Republic as an occupied country was not formally part of the American demand for that country's remilitarization, although the two questions turned out to be inseparable.[30] The omission of the political element from the substance of the American proposal was perhaps unavoidable; a definite and permanent control arrangement, and a termination (not simply a limited easing) of Germany's inferior status, respectively the basic minimum conditions precedent of Paris and Bonn to agreement on German rearmament, were at this time irreconcilable.

What the United States demanded was a military contribution which would really have amounted to the modern equivalent of cannon-fodder.[31] This was underscored by the fact that there was

[29] See, for example, *Department of State Bulletin,* November 6, 1950, p. 727.

[30] Personal telegram from Acheson to the President, September 15, 1950, in Truman, *Memoirs,* p. 255. The ministers did agree to terminate the state of war with Germany, and further to relax occupation controls, as indicated in their interim communiqué of September 14, 1950. Dennett and Turner, *Documents, 1950,* p. 532.

[31] Additional discussions relevant to the substance of the U.S. demand include: Lord Ismay, *NATO: The First Five Years, 1945–1954* (Paris: NATO, 1955), p. 32; Sir Ivone Kirkpatrick, *The Inner Circle: Memoirs of Ivone Kirkpatrick* (London: Macmillan, 1959), p. 240; Ben T. Moore, *NATO and the Future of Europe* (New York: Harper, 1958), p. 36. See also Royal Institute of International Affairs, *Britain in Western Europe: WEU and the Atlantic Alliance* (London: Royal Institute of International Affairs, 1956), p. 26; Acheson, *Sketches from Life,* pp. 25–26; and Truman, *Memoirs,* p. 254.

to be no German high command or general staff. German rearmament was to begin immediately. German military contingents were to consist of approximately ten West German divisions directly incorporated into the forces of NATO. No alternative was offered.[32]

Three weeks before the meeting of the foreign ministers of the three occupying powers, Henry Byroade, the director of the State Department's Bureau of German Affairs, appeared on national television to discuss the German problem in the world context. On August 20, he said the Federal Republic was in a very formative stage; the bulk of the German people had strong feelings against remilitarization; and "in this, above all fields, the Allies must remain in common unity." He did not accept the Korean analogy, which suggested that the Communist half of a divided country might decide on aggression against the other half. Any attack in Europe, he said, would amount to "a direct attack on the combined armies of the West." Referring to the Schuman Plan as the greatest development since the war, he stressed that at the very heart of Europe's problems lay Franco-German rapprochement. For all these reasons, Byroade concluded, great caution would have to be exercised concerning any German rearmament.[33]

By September 12 these views had been lost in the making of the package agreement. Perhaps the impending date of the meeting dictated that Acheson present the entire American package, since a policy had to be ready before then. But if the secretary *had* postponed presentation of a disruptive question, this might only have been temporary. On the day of the opening session, the President had asked for and received the resignation of Secretary of Defense Louis Johnson. With this change, the Departments of

[32] Edinger, *West German Armament*, p. 10; Robert E. Osgood, *NATO: The Entangling Alliance* (Chicago: University of Chicago Press, 1962), p. 85; Martin in Stein, *Decisions*, p. 654; Wesley B. Truitt, "The Troops to Europe Decision: The Process, Politics, and Diplomacy of a Strategic Commitment" (unpublished Ph.D. dissertation, Columbia University, 1968).

[33] *Department of State Bulletin*, September 11, 1950, pp. 426–29.

State and Defense might have eased the rigidity of the package formula as George Marshall began to exercise his considerable influence, which indeed happened later on.[34]

The assumption that the United States needed a definitive plan for the alliance is questionable. While the international situation seemed to call for something more than ambiguous communiqués expressing agreements in principle by the NATO Council (such as was the case in May, 1950), there was no reason apart from the exigencies of the domestic situation in Washington which dictated so rigid a policy as Acheson announced. There was an unusually strong connection in this case between the substance, and the timing and style, of American diplomacy; distinguishable in retrospect, they were then so closely related that the former tended to dictate the latter.

Assuming the inviolability of the package agreement between the Departments of State and Defense, then once what to offer had been determined, little flexibility remained as to how and when. The call for German rearmament could, given these assumptions, be made *only* in conjunction with the other elements of American troops-commander-aid (and conversely the latter could not be offered to the allies unless the former were asked in return). This was inherent in the State-Defense compact and could have been altered only by changing the agreement itself. Apparently no one was in a convenient position to do this once the President had given his blessing to the newborn arrival. To have thrown out the bath would have meant throwing out the baby as well, and under these circumstances they both remained, until after Marshall's return to the Pentagon had ended the "absurd situation" [35] which had so much to do with the emergence of the package in the first place.

Once it was clear, on the eve of the Big Three meeting, that the proposals, in addition to being ill-conceived, might be ill-

[34] Samuel P. Huntington, *The Common Defense: Strategic Programs in National Politics* (New York: Columbia University Press, 1961), p. 318; Acheson, *Present at the Creation*, p. 444.
[35] Acheson, *Sketches from Life*, pp. 26–27, 162.

timed as well, there were a number of factors for and against postponing their presentation. President Truman on September 8 approved the package agreement; on the next day he made the troops-to-Europe announcement. He did not mention that the decision had been made at the highest level to permit Germany to rearm.[36]

Although the State Department had informed the Joint Chiefs of Staff of its acceptance of what amounted to "a speedy, frontal assault on the problem of a German armed force" by August 18, the time factor was pressing. There were only a few days between Truman's decision and the scheduled opening day of the foreign ministers' meeting, September 12. This meant that there could be no prior consultation with the allies on the reversal of the demilitarization commitment, nor could even "the respectable minimum" of two weeks' advance notice be given to France and Britain. Because of this, and since German rearmament was bound to be a slow process, a key reason for reconsideration of the timing would have been to prepare a diplomatic approach which would lessen rather than aggravate political difficulties. In the event, the only formal U.S. notification that the German rearmament question would be raised in New York was sent in telegrams to Bevin and Schuman on September 9 or 10.[37] Even if the question to be placed on the table had been less of a surprise, this would have suggested the propriety of a delay. In these circumstances, the abrupt demand for German rearmament could only assume the character of an ultimatum.

This point is underscored by another: in contrast to the "offer" part of the package, which the European allies had themselves requested and were expected to receive with enthusiasm, U.S. officials knew that the "demand" part would be opposed, particularly by France, but also by Britain and the Federal Republic itself, both for reasons of state and because of the domestic political situations in these countries. German rearmament had not

[36] Calvocoressi, *Survey, 1949–1950*, p. 161; Acheson, *Present at the Creation*, p. 439; *Department of State Bulletin*, September 18, 1950, p. 468.

[37] Martin in Stein, *Decisions*, pp. 656–58. Allied views on German rearmament had not been formally sought prior to September 12.

been discussed with enthusiasm (other than in military circles) or even with guarded approval in Paris, London, or Bonn. A "speedy, frontal assault" on the question would entail grave diplomatic risks of alienating those whom the American reversal of the disarmament policy was intended to protect.

There were many reasons why Acheson decided to go ahead with both the meeting and the policy.[38] It was an election year and the administration was under severe domestic political attack for failure to press the Europeans to do more at once for their own defense. Also related to the allies' limited effort was the assurance which the Joint Chiefs of Staff wanted that they could count on German rearmament if the United States was to assume responsibility for command of an integrated force. It was, moreover, feared that news of the decision would leak out soon and create a situation suggesting the existence of a U.S. ultimatum. Within the alliance, the next stage of NATO planning had to be begun at once, and if German rearmament were to be a part thereof, related decisions had to be taken without delay. Acheson personally felt that since the President had approved the package, its nonpresentation would have amounted to conducting a meeting on a false basis. The elements of the package other than German rearmament had been requested by the allies, and if nothing was done the Korean stimulus might have been dissipated beyond recall.[39] Finally, an immediate attempt to get German rearmament under way would have the dual advantage of commencing what, given the material and psychological extent of demilitarization in the Federal Republic, would of necessity be a long process, and if agreed to soon might forestall what could later become a sharp rise in Bonn's price for compliance. In this context, American diplomacy was to proceed

---

[38] These points are largely taken from Martin's account. See also Acheson, *Present at the Creation*, pp. 439ff.

[39] Huntington said that if the package had not been put on the table at once then American policy would have been more leisurely, with the result that "the August apprehension over who would take the first step might well have hardened into firm mutual reluctance to act." Huntington, *Common Defense*, p. 318. Implicit in this, however, is that the magnitude of the external threat was less than crystal clear.

without delay. What was demanded, and when it was asked—in terms of allied interests—were inseparable from how German rearmament was presented, first to the other two occupying powers and then to the full NATO Council.

The September 12 meeting occurred when the possibility of a general war in Europe was taken more seriously than at any other time after 1945. There was no question that European security involved the defense of the Federal Republic,[40] and it was not out of the question that the Bonn government should itself contribute to this. What was not expected by the allies was the American insistence on the integrity of the package, which was presented in a manner "too serious to be shrugged off." [41]

Secretary Acheson, in his last official remarks to the North Atlantic Council on December 18, 1952, recalled how German rearmament was introduced into the situation in 1950:

Then we had the meeting in September in New York, and there our delegation put forward a suggestion which was that there should be a real unified command with troops, a staff, a commander, and supply arrangements so that there would be in Europe an army which could grow and be effective. At the same time it was pointed out by our military advisers that in order to have any effective defense in Europe it had to be a defense as far east as possible, and that was particularly important to the northern members of this Organization—the Netherlands, Denmark, and Norway. And so we worked in September on a plan for a forward defense, and in working on that plan it became perfectly clear that it was not workable unless Germany took part in its own defense and in the defense of Europe. But the problem was how to do that and we adjourned that meeting without coming to a conclusion.[42]

This account inaccurately gives the impression that the German rearmament decision emerged at the meeting rather than well

[40] This was formally agreed to when the North Atlantic Council adopted the forward strategy concept, and was explicitly stated in the communiqué issued by the three foreign ministers on September 19. U.S. Department of State, *American Foreign Policy, 1950–1955, Basic Documents*, Vol. II, pp. 1711–13.
[41] Sir Anthony Eden, *Full Circle* (Boston: Houghton Mifflin, 1960), p. 34.
[42] *Department of State Bulletin*, January 5, 1953, p. 6.

before it; that German rearmament appeared militarily necessary only as plans for a forward defense were developed; and that there was no particular connection between German rearmament and the elements related to the "suggestion" of a unified command.

What shocked the British and French, perhaps even more than the German rearmament demand itself, was that the other elements of the package were made dependent upon their acceptance of it. Acheson, no believer in tactics of heavy-handed persuasion, on this occasion applied what everyone agreed was enormous pressure, which included the allies being "told politely that we were only fabricating arguments against the rearmament of Germany." [43] The secretary himself, in a telegram to the President on September 15, reported he had stressed that a defense of Europe as far east as possible was "not possible without facing squarely and deciding wisely the question of German participation," and that as the meeting progressed without agreement "the British and French will become increasingly uncomfortable on their seats." [44] The American insistence on German rearmament was as firm as it could have been without adding to the ultimatum an even greater penalty for noncompliance than forgoing the other package ingredients. The degree of inflexibility U.S. diplomacy reached was reflected in the responses which followed, while by the same token America's energetic negotiation produced agreement among all allies but France—and Germany.

ALLIED REACTIONS TO THE U.S. DEMAND

Since the American decision was revealed first to the other two Western occupying powers, it was British Foreign Secretary Ernest Bevin and French Foreign Minister Robert Schuman who first responded to the U.S. demarche. Apart from the troops-to-Europe, integrated force, and supreme-commander proposals,

[43] Kirkpatrick, *Inner Circle*, p. 240; McLellan in Hilsman and Good, *Foreign Policy*, p. 255; Paul-Marie de la Gorce, *The French Army: A Military-Political History* (New York: Braziller, 1963), p. 368.
[44] Truman, *Memoirs*, pp. 254, 255.

which at least as a matter of form all the NATO allies would have to agree to, the German rearmament question was legally as well as politically the special concern of Britain and France.

Bevin, who had sailed for New York without cabinet instructions on the German rearmament question, but who was reported to be prepared to oppose any suggestion for the creation of a West German army, was, like Schuman, receptive to Adenauer's requests for a strong police force.[45] He was probably not, contrary to Acheson's assertion that the British foreign secretary "really agreed with me," in favor of German rearmament as conceived and presented by the American delegation.[46] The British High Commissioner, who was present at the meeting, wrote that Bevin agreed with him that "it seemed wiser to grant a German request than to seek to impose on them a repugnant proposal," and that Bevin "fought hard" for the police force and against a German army.[47]

Why did the United States ignore these considerations? Acheson apparently did not consider militarily relevant the possibility of a strong Federal police which would balance the GDR force, even though the latter was reported to be building up to a projected strength of 360,000.[48] He seems to have retained this view even after the package had fallen apart, despite the fact that, except for the label, German rearmament would have been begun simply by acting upon the German Chancellor's request, since

[45] Acheson's report (Truman, *Memoirs*, p. 254) that "the British and French . . . had flatly refused to face in any way the question of German participation" is somewhat misleading, since both allies had shown willingness to increase Federal police strength, and is probably explained only by Acheson's notion of "German participation"—which was the Pentagon's definition. The distinction is vague but significant; early in September Premier Pleven had agreed to an increase in Federal police forces, but "opposed vigorously the recreation of a German *army*." Cf. Moch, *Histoire*, p. 46; *L'Annee Politique, 1950*, p. 197; R.I.I.A. *Britain in Western Europe*, p. 26; *The New York Times*, September 7, 1950.

[46] When Churchill raised the German rearmament question earlier in the year and Prime Minister Attlee called this irresponsible, Bevin said "We are all against it." Onslow, "West German Rearmament," p. 455.

[47] Kirkpatrick, *Inner Circle*, p. 240.

[48] Martin in Stein, *Decisions*, p. 647. For an earlier report on the GDR force see *Department of State Bulletin*, June 5, 1950, pp. 919–20.

the other two occupying powers had already expressed their consent.[49] Acheson's rejection of this solution is noteworthy, since it would at a single stroke have disposed of what were to become under the "German rearmament" label almost insoluble problems: French insistence on prior agreement to German military inferiority, and German insistence on political and military equality. A police force rather than an army would, perhaps more than has been realized, have met both these demands, since France would not have considered it as remilitarization and the Federal Republic would not have been required to participate in an international military organization as a mere source of cannon-fodder.[50]

Acheson later said that Bevin, who shared his concern for military strength but disagreed with the U.S. approach, was personally sympathetic and helpful. He added that the British government had "extensive doubts" about German rearmament, and elsewhere reported that Bevin had been "put under wraps" not to say anything, although even before this it was believed in Washington that the British would yield.[51] But at the outset Bevin's support was at best personal, rather than representative of the view of his government, the latter having been persuaded to go along with the U.S. demand apparently only after Bevin had assured the cabinet that France would in no case agree. Kirkpatrick said the British, after attempting to convince the Americans otherwise, "gave way in order to secure the appointment of General Eisenhower and the massive reinforcement of the United States Army in Germany." [52] Thus in spite of London's view that

[49] "The American purpose was to bring about a degree of German rearmament as quickly and effectively as possible. They would have achieved their aim more quickly if they had simply acceded to Dr. Adenauer's request." Kirkpatrick, *Inner Circle*, p. 241.

[50] Acheson later explained *(Present at the Creation*, p. 442) that the American rejection of the police force idea was based on the fear that it could develop into a separate army—hardly a convincing point when U.S. spokesmen were assuring the French that German divisions would not be dangerous since they would not have their own general staff!

[51] Acheson, *Sketches from Life*, pp. 25–26; Truman, *Memoirs*, p. 255.

[52] Kirkpatrick, *Inner Circle*, p. 240.

German rearmament was premature, both politically and militarily, Britain "had to bow, like the other European powers, to the American ultimatum." [53]

French reaction to the idea of German rearmament has been compared to that of a bank president asked to place a notorious thief in charge of the vault.[54] For obvious historical-psychological reasons there was an abiding antipathy in France to the very existence of German military power; but even in the immediate situation of the summer of 1950 France did not share the sense of urgency felt by the United States, and the "lesson of Korea" was not so clear in Paris as in Washington.[55] Whatever the previous trends, the American demand was a shock to the French, to whom the gradual easing of restrictions on the Federal Republic was quite distinguishable from a reversal of the demilitarization policy.[56]

Schuman was calm but firm: he agreed that German rearmament did present a problem but said this must be carefully examined and no premature decision taken in the meanwhile, since the raising of German troops at that stage would do more harm than good. His position was one of refusing to take any decision whatsoever, based on instructions from Paris "to oppose any arrangement that would bring about the creation of a German army or of anything that could serve as the framework for such an army." [57] He told Acheson in private that even if he were to agree with the American demand his government would not support him, and even if it did the National Assembly would not support the government.[58] Schuman said France was simply not ready for German rearmament, even if over time the reasons for

[53] Denis Healey, "Britain and NATO," in *NATO and American Security*, ed. Klaus Knorr (Princeton: Princeton University Press, 1959), pp. 211, 212.

[54] Edgar S. Furniss, Jr., *France, Troubled Ally: DeGaulle's Heritage and Prospects* (New York: Praeger, 1960), p. 62.

[55] Alexander Werth, *France: 1940–1955* (London: Hale, 1956), p. 472; and see Edinger, *West German Armament*, p. 11.

[56] Alfred Grosser, "France and Germany: A Confrontation," in *France Defeats EDC*, eds. Daniel Lerner and Raymond Aron (New York: Praeger, 1957), p. 56.

[57] Truman, *Memoirs*, p. 254. See also Ismay, *NATO*, p. 33.

[58] Acheson, *Sketches from Life*, p. 42. This was confirmed by Moch, *Histoire*, p. 80.

wanting the Federal Republic to participate in European defense were sound; the United States "had not thought the problem through, particularly the political setting essential to any German rearmament." [59]

American officials seemed to believe that the basis for French opposition to German rearmament stemmed from fear of a future German attack, or from fear that it would provoke a preventive war by the Russians, but the more basic concern of France was political even more than military: German rearmament threatened France's opportunity to recover its status as a great power. French security was, with the Brussels Pact, the North Atlantic Treaty, and the presence of Anglo-American forces on the Continent, as well assured as it could be: "Only France's notions of independence and European supremacy were really at stake. A Western Alliance in which an armed Western Germany participated might come under the domination of the strongest country —Western Germany." [60]

Acheson noted but did not seem fully to appreciate this French concern. He described Schuman as unable or unwilling to take any decision, even in principle, on German rearmament, "until the forces of the Allies had been so strengthened in Europe that the French Government could face the psychological reaction to the creation of German armed force." The secretary, nevertheless, felt that in the course of the discussions he had "blown out of the water the practicality of leaving the beginning of the formation of German military units until the Allied forces were completely supplied with equipment," and had destroyed the "logical basis" to the fear of a Russian preventive move.[61] The problem was essentially one of disagreement between U.S. officials looking to practical and logical aspects of German rearmament, and French representatives reflecting their countrymen's repugnance to accept it, based upon quite different criteria of

[59] Acheson, *Sketches from Life,* p. 42.

[60] Roy C. Macridis, ed., *Foreign Policy in World Politics* (New York: Prentice-Hall, 1962), p. 67.

[61] Acheson telegram to Truman, Truman, *Memoirs,* p. 255.

practicality and logic, which seemed to Washington imaginary and emotional.

Schuman countered with a series of questions intended to challenge the American case. He asked whether the Germans themselves would raise divisions; whether German troops could be integrated into an Atlantic command without Germany being admitted to NATO; what the effect would be if German rearmament pushed the East European countries more tightly into the Soviet embrace; and what impact remilitarization would have on the endeavor to democratize the Federal Republic.[62] Disagreement on the rearmament aspect of the German question was complete, with the French representative declining to agree even to the "principle" of an eventual German military force, which Acheson sought when the American demand appeared unacceptable as originally presented. The opening meeting of the three occupying powers ended on September 14 in deadlock, with (in Acheson's words) Britain and France "prepared to accept what we offered but . . . not prepared to accept what we asked." [63] The interim communiqué released on this date mentioned that the ministers had "a preliminary exchange of views" on what amounted to the ingredients of the package, and added that other German matters had been discussed, such as measures relating to internal security and steps looking toward a quicker restoration of Germany in the family of free nations, including ending the state of war and further easing occupation controls. Acheson, while acknowledging that the results of the meeting were "immediately discouraging," was still optimistic that the American demand would be met.[64]

The members of the NATO Council met on September 15, having, of course, already learned that the Western Big Three had discussed without agreement the German rearmament question. The first to raise the issue within the council was the foreign minister of the Netherlands, Dirk Stikker, who expressed

[62] Moch, *Histoire*, pp. 48ff.

[63] Acheson telegram to Truman, Truman, *Memoirs*, p. 255. See also *L'Année Politique, 1950*, p. 198.

[64] Truman, *Memoirs*, p. 256; Dennett and Turner, *Documents, 1950*, pp. 531–32.

his country's vital interest in a defense of Germany at a point as geographcially remote from Holland as possible.[65] Stikker, before leaving for New York, had obtained his government's support for a German contribution, probably due less to Dutch enthusiasm for a new German army than to the military argument that a forward strategy was not conceivable without the participation of the German Federal Republic.[66] Yet Stikker said, concerning a defense east of the Rhine-IJssel line: "I noted to the Council that this could be done either by stationing American, British and Canadian troops in Europe—in addition to those to be furnished by the Continental countries—or by Germany assuming its share of Western European defense." [67] The alternative expressed in this statement, apart from its accuracy as a military judgment, is significant in its recognition of the political limitation on the defense effort of the alliance. German rearmament was necessary not because there could not have been a forward strategy without the participation of the Federal Republic, but because the countries whose interests were supposed to include the defense of the territory of the Federal Republic did not consider this so vital that they were themselves willing to provide the required troops.

It was known that opinions in NATO about rearming the aggressor of only a few years past would be mixed, but first things came first: "American security was in issue and the susceptibility of allies could not be allowed to override the exigencies of the situation." [68] On September 16, Acheson argued that it was a simple question of principle—there would be no German high command and the allies would get full preference on arms delivery. By September 17, Schuman was supported only by Belgium and

[65] R.I.I.A., *Britain in Western Europe*, p. 26.
[66] Ismay, *NATO*, p. 33.
[67] Dirk U. Stikker, *Men of Responsibility* (New York: Harper and Row, 1966), p. 298–99.
[68] Calvocoressi, *Survey, 1949–1950*, p. 22. After informing the President that he had no intention of "imposing specific conditions," Acheson did just this by stating to the allies that the United States could go no further without "a definite commitment from the Europeans both on their own contributions and on German rearmament." Martin in Stein, *Decisions*, p. 658.

Luxembourg in his view that the question was wholly premature since allied rearmament had hardly begun.

At the time the Big Three meeting was adjourned to allow Bevin and Schuman to ask their governments for instructions, it was reported that representatives of the "little nine" said they, too, should be consulted.[69] Support for the U.S. proposal of a unified force for Europe to include German participation was mixed.[70] In spite of what seemed a general trend toward acceptance of the American position, the council was unable to agree. After three days the meeting was adjourned so that the representatives could consult their governments, ostensibly concerning the best method of creating an integrated force. "It was, however, no secret at the time that the chief reason for adjournment was the French opposition aroused by the unexpected American proposal that Western Germany should be rearmed. . . ."[71]

By September 18, France was the only member of the council still unwilling to accept the principle of German participation. The adjournment, Lord Ismay wrote, was intended to allow the Big Three time (before the council reconvened) to re-examine the German rearmament question, which rested motionless between Acheson's demand for German military units and the use of German productive resources to supply them, and Schuman's willingness to consider a German contribution in the fields of production and military construction, but not the raising of troops. The council communiqué covering the meeting disregarded German rearmament, but said the proposal for an integrated NATO military force had been "warmly welcomed." [72]

[69] *The New York Times,* September 15, 1950.
[70] Onslow, "West German Rearmament," p. 464; *The New York Times,* September 24, 26, 30, 1950; Werth, *France,* pp. 484–85; *News of Norway,* September 28, 1950, Norwegian Information Service, Washington, D.C.
[71] R.I.I.A., *Atlantic Alliance,* p. 53.
[72] Ismay, *NATO,* pp. 32–33, text of the communiqué, p. 185.

THE OUTCOME OF THE SEPTEMBER, 1950, MEETINGS

On September 19, the foreign ministers of the three occupying powers issued a separate communiqué on the Federal Republic expressing views on many important matters of a political nature, including the following: their intention to terminate the state of war with Germany (without, however, ending the occupation); to extend the authority of the Federal government through amendment of the Occupation Statute; to authorize the establishment of a ministry of foreign affairs and allow diplomatic relations with foreign countries "in all suitable cases," that is, not with themselves; to ease controls over legislation and economic matters, and remove shipbuilding and steel production limitations where it would facilitate the defense effort of the West.

The ministers also included military matters in their statement, expressing concern about "the security of the Federal Republic in both its external and its internal aspects." They stated that any attack against the Federal Republic or Berlin from any quarter would be treated as an attack upon themselves. They then "fully agreed that the re-creation of a German national army would not serve the best interests of Germany or Europe." [73] This might appear to represent a change in the American position, but because the United States did not consider that German forces under NATO command would be "national," this was not the case.

Finally, of some interest but little notoriety, was the attention paid to the internal security of the Federal Republic. The ministers announced their agreement for this purpose on the establishment of "mobile police formations organized on a land basis but with provisions which would enable the Federal Government to have adequate powers to make effective use of all or part of this force in order fully to meet the exigencies of the present situa-

[73] Dennett and Turner, *Documents, 1950,* pp. 555–58; *Department of State Bulletin,* October 2, 1950, pp. 530–31.

tion." Had it not been for the German rearmament question overshadowing other matters, this agreement might have led to recruitment of forces which could later on have become part of the integrated command. As suggested above, the "police" solution seemed feasible as an allied-German as well as an interallied matter. What precluded its utilization was apparently the insistence of the U.S. representatives that German units of military character be recruited in divisional strength and placed under NATO command. As it turned out, even the police forces agreed to were delayed as deadlock persisted on the nature and extent of the German forces.

The next meetings, on September 21 and after, included the defense ministers of the occupying powers. Prior to Moch's departure for New York, the French cabinet had spent several days going over the Acheson proposals "sentence by sentence." By September 20 the French cabinet was unanimously hostile not only to immediate German rearmament but even to an immediate declaration accepting in principle eventual German rearmament, although opinion was divided on whether the principle of German rearmament might later be accepted. The cabinet resolved that Moch on his arrival in New York should congratulate Schuman on his successful resistance of American pressure.[74]

On the evening of September 21, when Moch met privately with Emanuel Shinwell, the British defense minister said he was "terrorized by the American position: it is veritable blackmail. I am convinced we shall not receive any financial aid unless we accept a declaration agreeing in principle to German rearmament." Schuman had said substantially the same thing to Moch earlier in the day. But, Shinwell said, Bevin had decided to cooperate with Acheson, and he could not oppose the foreign secretary because of Bevin's strong position in the government and in the party.[75]

When the foreign and defense ministers came together, Ache-

[74] Moch, *Histoire,* pp. 52–59; *The Times* (London), September 21, 1950; *The New York Times,* September 21, 1950.

[75] Bevin had actually agreed to German rearmament several days before, after Acheson repeatedly stressed that it was only a "principle." Werth, *France,* p. 484.

son noted that there was agreement on "creation of an integrated force under a single command." What remained to be done was to make a decision in principle on German rearmament; the allies would have full priority on equipment for their own rearmament and all precautions would be taken to prevent a rebirth of German militarism. "What the American government wants," Acheson said, "is, essentially, that France accept the principle of [German] participation." [76] This defense participation would not be "German rearmament" since all German units would be under a Supreme NATO Commander and outside the control of the Bonn government. According to this logic, there would be no new "national" German army; German units would be part of an "integrated" allied force.

The French replied that the twenty divisions France had promised should first be completely armed, and not until then should any consideration be given to German units. Meanwhile, Schuman said, the Federal Republic could contribute industrially and in other material ways. These elemental differences stemmed from domestic realities in both cases: the package agreement made prior action on German rearmament a part of the condition for an integrated force for the United States, while for France only a pre-existing NATO force could open the door to possible favorable parliamentary consideration of the German rearmament question. Acheson's insistence on agreement "in principle" did not manifest an appreciation that for the French there was really no difference between agreement in principle and agreement in practice: the National Assembly would not have accepted either in the fall of 1950. The French government hence thought any decision on the question premature, since it would have no practical value, and a vote of confidence on it would have brought the fall of the Pleven cabinet.

By the next meeting, on September 22, the British endorsed an immediate decision in principle since German troops eventually would be necessary. The United States assured the allies that American productive capacity was such that German forces could

[76] Moch, *Histoire,* p. 64.

be equipped simultaneously with French and others. Acheson urged French acquiescence on the ground Congress would otherwise not vote funds for aid and troops to Europe would be opposed. French reaction to this "double threat" of reduced aid and a later return to isolationism was that it was "too big to be sincere," which turned out to be the case.[77] Moch stated there were three questions, the answers to which France had to know before any decision on German rearmament could be made: How many German divisions were contemplated? How many American divisions would be sent to Europe? How and when would this be done? [78] Marshall's reply to the first question, that the number of German divisions would depend on how many the allies furnished, was itself a kind of threat in French eyes.

The meeting of September 23 apparently brought a note of flexibility in the U.S. approach, as Acheson said that while President Truman had hoped for NATO Council approval of the entire American proposal, it had become clear that the question would have to be put aside to avoid winding up in a blind alley. But, the secretary said, "If, in October, the French government notifies us that it is irrevocably opposed to German rearmament, we shall have to reconsider our whole plan and look for another solution." [79] This statement showed an awareness that France did have a veto on the German rearmament question, but it suggested that if Paris exercised this then the price might be the loss of the other elements of the package which the French had long desired. In these circumstances, Truman wrote, Marshall sought a compromise which might avoid saying anything specific, either in answer to Moch's questions or on what German rearmament would consist of. The President added that the United States promised financial support at a later session, and "With this assurance, the French were now willing to agree to the general principles of the proposal that Acheson had originally placed

[77] Moch, *Histoire*, pp. 68–69. The French tended not to be impressed so much by American diplomatic threats as by the fear that the United States might take hasty action.

[78] Truman, *Memoirs*, p. 256.

[79] Moch, *Histoire*, pp. 77–78.

before Bevin and Schuman. On September 26 a communiqué from New York announced that the NATO Council had agreed on the establishment of a unified force for the defense of Europe. This left a great many things still to be agreed on." [80]

The latter included German rearmament. Neither the language of the communiqué itself nor later research supports Truman's impression that an understanding on this question, however limited, had been reached. The other elements of the original package were unanimously approved, as expected. As to the omitted ingredient, there was no agreement on German rearmament among the allies, nor was there mention of whether the Germans would be willing to rearm.[81] The communiqué reported that

The utilization of German manpower and resources was discussed in the light of views recently expressed by democratic leaders in Germany and elsewhere. The Council was in agreement that Germany should be enabled to contribute to the build-up of the defense of Western Europe, and noting that the occupying powers were studying the matter, requested the Defense Committee to make recommendations at the earliest possible date as to the methods by which Germany could most usefully make its contribution.[82]

President Truman's account notwithstanding, the most that can be said to have been agreed to was that the Federal Republic should make *some* contribution to the defense effort. The basic French stand was unchanged: no German troops should be permitted to appear, even semantically, whatever else might be allowed.[83]

As Acheson later wrote, "the Pentagon's plan had been tried on and produced a Donnybrook, in which many heads were bro-

[80] Truman, *Memoirs*, pp. 256–57.

[81] On September 19, Chancellor Adenauer had demanded complete equality for the Federal Republic and full restoration of German sovereignty. This was all but ignored at the New York meetings.

[82] For the text of the communiqué, see Dennett and Turner, *Documents, 1950*, pp. 213–14.

[83] For example, the phrase "German army units" was deleted from the text of the communiqué at French insistence. Moch, *Histoire*, p. 86.

ken and tempers and time lost." The French, he said, had been adamant, and only when General Marshall had joined him in New York (September 19) had it been agreed "that we should break off the effort and try another approach." Acheson, looking back at these sessions, was gratified that they produced "no small record of achievement." [84]

For their part, the French were satisfied that they had, concerning German rearmament as defined in Paris, agreed to nothing at all. While the forward strategy concept accepted by the allies in the meetings may have been tantamount to agreement on a plan which could only be carried out with the help of a West German army, this did not mean that France agreed, whether or not military logic made agreement imperative, even though French army leaders did not oppose the idea of German troops.[85] Indeed, the defense committee during October agreed on other matters, but not as to the method by which Germany could make its most useful contribution.

FRENCH COUNTERPROPOSAL: THE PLEVEN PLAN

After Washington's adoption of a more measured approach to German rearmament, the center of the activity shifted to Paris, where the French government sought some escape from the dilemma imposed by the U.S. ultimatum. Pleven was certain that the German rearmament issue would be brought up soon again, with even greater insistence, and that the only way France could get ahead of a new American demand was by advancing its own "original project." The American demand compelled the French government, as usual resting on a fragile base, to produce a policy "which could be simultaneously represented to the United States and to Great Britain as permitting German rearmament, and to

[84] Acheson, *Sketches from Life,* pp. 26–27; Acheson, *Present at the Creation,* pp. 444–45.

[85] Edgar S. Furness, Jr., *American Military Policy: Strategic Aspects of World Political Geography* (New York: Rinehart, 1957), p. 281.

the National Assembly and the French people as preventing just that." [86]

From the outset of the duel between Washington and Paris over whose approach to the problem of a German defense contribution should prevail, there was a basic dichotomy with respect to the linking of German rearmament and European unification. The original U.S. demand for German rearmament was made without reference to its effect on the political future of Western Europe, and with very little concern for its impact on Franco-German reconciliation efforts; EDC later became the reverse, intended to solve *all* the problems of both these questions. But for France the search for security against a revived Germany and French interest in European integration were inseparable, and had been officially so proclaimed from the time of the announcement of the Schuman Plan in May, 1950.

After one of the September meetings, Acheson was told by Luxembourg's Foreign Minister Joseph Bech that in Paris Jean Monnet was working on a plan to bring the Germans into a military arrangement analogous to the Schuman Plan, and that Schuman himself did not know this yet. The immediate goal of the French political leaders was to advance the European army idea "in order to avoid having to give a clear answer of yes or no regarding German rearmament." [87] What emerged as the Pleven Plan for a European army was "hastily and ingeniously concocted by M. Monnet and his associates." Acheson's urgings had compelled Paris "to pull a rabbit from a hat quickly," and since the magician in both cases was the same, it was "little wonder that Pleven's animal was a close relative of Schuman's *lapin*." [88]

The Pleven Plan must be considered a masterpiece, if for no other reason than because it sounded so attractive on so many

[86] Furniss, *France, Troubled Ally*, pp. 64–65; *L'Annee Politique, 1950*, p. 222; Moch, *Histoire*, pp. 92–93; *The New York Times*, September 29, 1950.
[87] Acheson, *Sketches from Life*, p. 42; Raymond Aron and August Heckscher, *Diversity of Worlds: France and the United States Look at Their Common Problems* (New York: Reynal, 1957), p. 10.
[88] Eden, *Full Circle*, p. 34; Furniss, *France, Troubled Ally*, p. 75.

counts—it would bring military strength, Franco-German reconciliation, European unification, and so forth. What was envisaged was a supranational framework intended to avoid the "disaster" of national German rearmament, which would "inevitably lead to a revival of German militarism," as Pleven told the National Assembly. In place of this, the Premier said, "the French government proposes the creation of a European Army attached to the political institutions of Europe." [89]

In outline terms, the French cabinet proposed that the question of German rearmament be solved by merging European armed forces into a single army which would include Germans and which would form a single entity along with the European Coal and Steel Community (ECSC), with these military and economic entities under a common *pre-existing* institutional European political framework. The Pleven Plan, announced in the National Assembly on October 24 but widely discussed beforehand, included a proposal for the raising of small German units which would be incorporated into larger "integrated" units. The European army would be under a European minister of defense, who would receive instructions from a supranational council of ministers, which would be responsible to a European parliamentary assembly, the latter to have the power to vote a common European defense budget. The Federal Republic was not to recruit a national army or establish a general staff or a ministry of defense. The European army was not to interfere in any way with the creation of Supreme Headquarters Allied Powers Europe (SHAPE); all free countries of Western Europe, especially Britain, were to be invited to join; and these steps were not to be begun until agreement in the form of a treaty embodying the Schuman Plan was signed.[90]

[89] For accounts of the Pleven Plan, see F. Roy Willis, *France, Germany and the New Europe, 1945–1963* (Stanford: Stanford University Press, 1965), Chap. 6, *passim;* *L'Annee Politique, 1950,* pp. 222ff.; Stebbins, *United States, 1950,* pp. 270ff.; Calvocoressi, *Survey, 1949–1950,* pp. 163ff.; Moch, *Histoire,* pp. 93ff.; Werth, *France,* pp. 486–87.

[90] See, for example, *The New York Times,* October 20, 1950; *Christian Science Monitor,* October 23, 1950. The Pleven Plan was never intended as a separate device,

The French Premier expressed his conviction that the European authority he proposed—not German rearmament—was the proper method of building Europe's future, and that with faith and imagination the technical and psychological obstacles could be overcome, especially if the United States would give its active sympathy to the project. He stressed repeatedly that there would be no new German army; Germans would take part on the level of the smallest possible unit—which was taken to mean regimental combat teams. The European army was to be a complete fusion of forces, not "a mere juxtaposition of national military units which, in reality, would only be a mask for a coalition of the old type." [91]

The National Assembly accompanied its approval in principle of the Pleven Plan by a declaration that the deputies especially approved the government's declaration against the creation of a new German army. The assembly vote (which was 343 to 225) was not a vote to approve the Pleven Plan or to accept, even in principle, what the French understood to be "German rearmament." It was, probably, hardly more than a vote that the Premier should attempt, by pursuing the proposals he had suggested, to fend off the American thrust. Schuman, a few weeks later, defined the meaning of German rearmament as envisaged under the Pleven Plan: "Now what does the rearming of Germany really mean? To arm a country means to make freely available to it— to its government—a national armed force capable of becoming the instrument of its policy. . . . If Germany is prepared to authorize or compel her people to enlist in a European Army, that does not mean that she is rearming herself." [92] With this distinction the keynote of French diplomacy, France embarked upon

---

but instead sought to link German rearmament's framework with other European schemes. Edinger, *West German Armament,* p. 13; *The New York Times,* October 25, 1950.

[91] Ambassade de France, Service de Presse et d'Information, Document, October 23, 1950; this contains the full text of the Pleven Plan. *The Times* (London), October 25, 1950. Combat teams were thought of as having from 800 to 1,200 men, while divisions had at least 12,000, and if on the American model up to about 18,000.

[92] Willis, *New Europe,* p. 130, quoting Schuman's remarks to the Council of Europe, November 24, 1950. See also Moore, *NATO,* pp. 38–39.

the long, futile attempt to "rearm the Germans without rearming Germany."

Pleven's statement that the proposal for a European army should in no way interfere with the establishment of the integrated NATO force sought to gain the benefits of the American package proposal minus German rearmament. The French Premier said his plan was neither a delaying maneuver nor a means of permanently imposing discrimination on the Federal Republic, but instead the only way to avoid the danger of a new conflict which the recreation of a German army would bring.[93] One analyst, who considered the Pleven Plan "shrewdly calculated to prevent the emergence of any German army," wrote:

In its provisions regarding Germany Pleven's plan was not very far from the original American proposal. Neither would have permitted Germany an armaments industry or a general staff. The largest German unit envisaged by the United States had been a division; Pleven hoped to limit it to approximately combat-team strength. *Where Pleven's plan differed from those of the Council of Europe and of the American government was not in detail but in its broad conception. It would have delayed German rearmament until after the political unification of Europe* [emphasis added].[94]

The timing envisaged by the Pleven proposal cannot be overemphasized: the overriding goal of French foreign policy, concerning any German rearmament at all, was maximum delay. By presenting the European army plan in such fashion that it could be undertaken only after the many details of the Schuman Plan had been agreed to, and only after the supranational European political edifice had been erected, the French government sought to assure itself that considerable time would pass before a German in uniform could appear—and if he did, he would not be in a German but a European uniform. The original Pleven Plan was the most "supranational" of all the European army schemes,

[93] *The Times* (London), October 30, 1950.
[94] Furniss, *France, Troubled Ally*, p. 65.

before or after, and was understood by the National Assembly to mean that German rearmament would never occur at all, since the political unification of Europe would precede the military resolution of the German question.

The reaction in France to the proposal was hesitant. It was reported from Paris that Frenchmen were confounded by the idea of "handing any German even a popgun, in whatever federated wrappings," yet they found the plan appealing as a creative approach to a new relationship with Germany under French leadership. It was not clear whether the Premier was trying to say "no" by cleverly wrapping German rearmament in an unlikely supranational garb, or whether he was using this same cloak to say "yes" to the United States in a manner palatable to the French.[95] Whichever the case, neither the American proposal nor the French counterproposal had been made with the consent of the Germans, without whose cooperation the Federal Republic could be neither rearmed nor included in a political framework for a European army.

RESPONSE IN THE FEDERAL REPUBLIC

The question of how the Germans themselves might feel about remilitarization was apparently not seriously considered in allied circles prior to the fall of 1950, although McCloy told Adenauer when he returned to Bonn after the New York meetings that the views of the Chancellor had been fully considered.[96] Until the official reversal of U.S. policy, German governmental reaction to

[95] Janet Flanner (Genet), *Paris Journal, 1944-1965* (New York: Atheneum, 1965), p. 132; Werth, *France*, p. 488.

[96] Onslow, "West German Rearmament," p. 472. Adenauer had discussed a German defense contribution with the High Commissioners earlier, but when asked about this just before the New York meeting he replied that the Bundestag's views could be sought only if the Federal Republic were first officially approached by the occupying powers. This was perhaps done to force the allies to make the initial formal move. Julian Lider, *West Germany in NATO* (Warsaw: Western Press Agency, 1965), p. 58. Cf. also *L'Annee Politique, 1950*, p. 200; Konrad Adenauer, *Memoirs, 1945-1953* (Chicago: Regnery, 1966), p. 285.

the rearmament question was necessarily in the realm of suggestion. Although "trial balloons" had been floated by the Chancellor since late in 1949, there is little reason to assume that Adenauer consented in advance to what Acheson outlined in New York.

The German situation included public opinion, the position of the government, and the views of the opposition. This threefold distinction is useful because popular preferences were often not demonstrably connected with this contest otherwise "dominated by the dictates of political expediency." [97]

Public opinion on the rearmament question can be described almost summarily: with the exception of a small minority, many of whom were former Wehrmacht officers and members of veterans' groups, there was no popular call for remilitarization. After the American and French plans had been announced, it was reported that "The French aversion to arming the Germans appears to be matched only by the German aversion to being rearmed." [98] Not even the North Korean attack made remilitarization more attractive, even though the analogy with East Germany was almost universally accepted.

The first popular reaction, instead, was a demand that the allied forces be increased, and that they defend the Federal Republic on its eastern borders. After the United States in September gave the impression that German rearmament would be forthcoming, some Germans feared that the Russians would not tolerate this; others showed a negative attitude reflected in the *ohne mich* comment which was widely expressed when the subject of military service was discussed. Recent wartime and postwar events had led the people psychologically to reject the use of force, and in view of the extensive allied re-education campaign to remove all vestiges of militarism from German life, the sudden American call for rearmament was greeted with considerable cynicism. Newspaper polls showed figures such as 67 percent op-

[97] Gordon A. Craig, "Germany and NATO: The Rearmament Debate, 1950–58," in *NATO and American Security*, ed. Klaus Knorr (Princeton: Princeton University Press, 1959), p. 238.

[98] *The New York Times*, November 5, 1950.

posed to any participation in Western defense matters or service in any army.[99]

These feelings were especially reinforced by the impression that German rearmament would bring two highly undesirable results. If war came, the Federal Republic would be the battlefield, and if it did not, reunification would be indefinitely put off. On the military side, there was little interest in Germany's becoming part of a force of a dozen "rather rickety divisions." [100] Not even the former military accepted German rearmament as proposed in the competing French and American plans of 1950. One officer said:

It should be stated openly that German soldiers of a Federal Republic with no full rights, considered as a strengthening of the Western defense force, might multiply the number of little pennants on the operational maps of Western general staffs, but in conditions of such dual policy their striking force would be out of all proportion to the costs involved. Like mercenaries they would be children of shortsightedness, and their use would as much resemble military reality as a gimmick resembles art.[101]

Religious groups, trade unions, and youth organizations were generally opposed to German rearmament, although there was a certain tendency to accept such proposals as the Pleven Plan because of its emphasis on French-German reconciliation and European cooperation. Generally, it was said that there could be no German rearmament until the consent of the people had been gained.

Yet, unlike the French case, the leadership of the German government was not closely tied to popular opinion, and was capable of operating in foreign-policy matters quite independently, even

[99] Hanreider, *West German Foreign Policy*, p. 105; T. W. Vigers, "The German People and Rearmament," *International Affairs*, XXVII (April, 1951), pp. 152–53; Heinz L. Krekeler, "The German Defense Contribution," *The Annals*, CCCXII (July, 1957), 84–88.

[100] Alistair Horne, *Return to Power: A Report on the New Germany* (New York: Praeger, 1956), pp. 78–80; Brigadier A. H. Head, "European Defense," *International Affairs*, XXVII (January, 1951), pp. 5–6.

[101] Lider, *West Germany in NATO*, pp. 35–36, n. 18

on a question as sensitive as remilitarization. The German political elite of the Christian Democratic Union (CDU) under Adenauer's leadership supported consistently the European army proposals, even though each of ten opinion polls between 1950 and 1954 showed more opponents than supporters for the plan. For this reason the German government and the German people are differentiated from one another. The ultimate test of whether the people would, in this time period, have supported the government, had German rearmament been formally agreed to by all sides, cannot be known.[102]

The degree to which the Bonn regime was dominated by the Federal Chancellor was shown when the one minister who opposed Adenauer's willingness to undertake German rearmament was reportedly expelled from the cabinet.[103] Adenauer believed "We had to join one or the other side if we did not want to be ground up between them," and used this judgment as a partial basis for his attempt to regain the Federal Republic's political equality. His willingness to cooperate with the occupying powers caused the Social Democratic Party (SPD) leader Kurt Schumacher to brand him in the parliament as "the Chancellor of the allies," which was both correct and incorrect. In the sense that he was willing—in the face of popular disapproval—to go along with the allies (especially the United States), Adenauer was "their" Chancellor; but in the sense that he skillfully maneuvered as the leader of a defeated and occupied country to restore Germany to an equal place among nations, he was the servant of the Federal Republic.

[102] James L. Richardson, *Germany and the Atlantic Alliance: The Interaction of Strategy and Politics* (Cambridge: Harvard University Press, 1966), p. 22. Adenauer in his *Memoirs* candidly stated that "the overwhelming majority of Germans were entirely hostile towards the notion of reestablishing German armed forces, a German Wehrmacht" (p. 279), although he felt that the idea of a strengthened Federal police force had been favorably received (p. 282).

[103] *Herald Tribune,* October 11, 1950. Adenauer (*Memoirs*, pp. 291–92) said he resigned. This official, then minister of the interior, was Gustav Heinemann, who early in 1969 was elected President of the Federal Republic. *The New York Times,* March 6, 1969.

Adenauer saw German rearmament as (in this order) a way to regain sovereignty, to achieve security vis-à-vis the East, and to further Western European integration. His demands that the state of war be ended, the Occupation Statute replaced, and various restrictions (especially economic) on Germany removed having been partially met by the September 19, 1950, proclamation of the occupying powers, the Chancellor then argued not only that his policies would lead to restoration of German sovereignty but that German rearmament was a necessity in itself. Adenauer never publicly questioned the Korean analogy.[104]

The Bonn government, following the emergence of the rival American and French approaches to the problem of a German military role, made it clear that it had little interest in consenting to either Washington's cannon-fodder demand or the second-rate status implicit in the Paris formula. The feeling was strong that Germans should not serve as mercenaries, and Adenauer said that if German forces were to be recruited it must be on a basis of "complete equality with all other contingents."[105] This in effect amounted to a rejection of both the U.S. plan and the Pleven Plan.

Specifically, the Chancellor in the Bundestag debate said that Germany should provide for its own defense. He welcomed the Pleven Plan—adding that the Federal Republic would expect equal rights, which the French scheme was intended permanently to preclude. He said further that the Pleven Plan as it stood denied the equality to which the Federal Republic considered itself entitled. On November 8, the Chancellor stated the position of the government as follows: "If the request [for German participation in the defense of Western Europe] is made by the western Powers, then, in the Government's opinion, the Federal Republic must be ready to make an appropriate contribution. . . . The prerequisite of such a contribution is the complete equality of the rights of Germany with other Powers taking part; and, fur-

---

[104] Adenauer, *Memoirs*, pp. 78–79, 193, 290, 293; Willis, *New Europe*, p. 154.
[105] *The Times* (London), October 30, 1950.

thermore, the strength of the defense front must be adequate to render any Russian aggression impossible." [106]

Once more, troops-to-Europe and German rearmament were linked together. In a statement on November 24, 1950, Adenauer asked the Western powers for a security treaty as a substitute for the existing Occupation Statute. The Chancellor also explained what he meant by the "complete equality" prerequisite in the November 8 statement: the same equipment for German as for other units; equality of size of German units with others (although not necessarily the same number); and the same participation in leadership for Germany as for other participating nations. Those were the very elements of German rearmament which both the United States and France had ruled out. Not only were the French disturbed by the prospect of extensive German demands, but there were numerous American complaints about the lack of military spirit in Germany; McCloy's office even issued a sharp criticism of German hesitation in military matters.[107]

By late 1950, each of the participants in the German rearmament triangle of Washington-Paris-Bonn was at odds with the other two, in addition to having internal differences.[108] Even when it was announced that the Spofford Plan (discussed below) had brought a measure of compromise between the United States and France, this was rejected by the Chancellor on the ground it denied equality to German forces in both weapons and command authority. Adenauer said "Our troops must definitely not be intended merely as cannon fodder," which would have been the case without heavy weapons or representation in a high command. While exploring how to use the remilitarization issue vis-à-vis the occupying powers, the Chancellor had to be domestically careful; German rearmament was the link which held together

[106] Dennett and Turner, *Documents, 1950*, p. 553; and see *The New York Times*, November 17, 1950.

[107] *The New York Times*, November 5 and 7, 1950.

[108] The Chancellor complained that he received very little information on an official level from either Washington or Paris, and "had to rely to a large extent on what was published in the newspapers" to follow developments in the German rearmament exchange between the French and the Americans. Adenauer, *Memoirs*, pp. 302, 307.

the government's foreign-policy program, which (although popularly not a critical issue) was under sharp attack by the opposition.[109]

The SPD position embraced a number of arguments, the most important of which was that reunification would be precluded by German rearmament. This was one telling point which the Chancellor's "negotiating from strength" approach could not match. Even if the Socialists were not fundamentally opposed to German rearmament, "The essential difference between Adenauer's view and that so tenaciously held by Schumacher was a matter of diplomatic timing: the Socialists and other nationalist groups wished to give first priority to the unification question and reproached Adenauer for sacrificing German unity to a policy of pleasing the Western powers." [110] Whether the real difference was one of substance or timing, the result was the same: the penalties of remilitarization were out of proportion to the rewards it might bring.

The SPD's other criticisms included rejection of the "blackmail" of the allies which was implicit in the offer to restore sovereignty in return for German rearmament. They argued that Germany should not be rearmed against its will. Also, the legal point was made that under the Basic Law the Bundestag did not have the constitutional authority to decide the question (as the CDU said it did), and politically it was said that German rearmament would increase international tensions and make the Russians more hostile (a denial of the negotiation-from-strength rationale).

In terms of domestic political considerations, the Socialists complained that German rearmament would lead to a revival of militarism and in other ways threaten the development of German democracy. They argued further that the German forces envisioned at the time would not be strong enough to liberate the Eastern zone should war occur. Similar to the CDU, the SPD

[109] Hanreider, *West German Foreign Policy*, pp. 95, 100–1.
[110] Ferenc A. Vali, *The Quest for a United Germany* (Baltimore: The Johns Hopkins Press, 1967), p. 29.

position thus rejected both the U.S. formula for German divisions without the restoration of sovereignty, and the French formula based on German inferiority. "No one will die for an occupation statute. That is why equality of rights should be granted to Germany . . . otherwise the German contingent would be only a Foreign Legion. It is for this reason that we do not accept the Pleven plan, since it is based on the principle of German inequality, even in its purely military aspects." [111] SPD criticisms of the Bonn government's approach to the German rearmament issue assumed an importance in Adenauer's bargaining with the occupying powers which increased with time. The Chancellor is generally regarded as having used the Socialist attacks against his position in order to extract greater concessions from the allies than would otherwise have been forthcoming.[112]

In this situation of popular opposition to (or at least apathy toward) German rearmament, and agreement between the major political groups in Bonn only that inequality for the Federal Republic was intolerable, Adenauer sought to utilize the American demand. Even if German rearmament did not occur for the indefinite future, at least part of the price the allies would have to offer for German consent could be paid much sooner. The Chancellor perceived and exploited the basic contradiction between converting Germany from a defeated enemy into a rearmed ally while still keeping it in the inferior status of an occupied state. This was only slowly realized, or perhaps conceded, by the allies, who had not yet acknowledged that whatever was eventually done could only be with the compliance of Bonn. Meanwhile, Washington had been presented with the Pleven Plan.

[111] Carlo Schmid, "Germany and Europe," *International Affairs*, XXVII (July, 1951), pp. 310–11. See also Alfred Grosser, *The Colossus Again: West Germany from Defeat to Rearmament* (New York: Praeger, 1955), pp. 209–11.

[112] Karl W. Deutsch and Lewis J. Edinger, *Germany Rejoins the Powers: Mass Opinion, Interest Groups and Elites in Contemporary German Foreign Policy* (Stanford: Stanford University Press, 1959), p. 64.

U.S. REACTION TO THE EUROPEAN ARMY PROPOSAL

Following the adjournment of the New York conferences, Franco-American differences persisted as the ministers of finance and defense met in Washington. During the mid-October sessions with the French, Marshall told Moch that the rearmament plan for twenty new French divisions by 1953 was quite acceptable to the United States; but he soon returned to the German rearmament question and repeated that German divisions were a necessity for an effective defense east of the Rhine.[113] This belief was reinforced by a deep suspicion in Washington that Paris would simply not produce.[114] The reverse was also the case, with U.S. officials giving the French the impression the latter were dealing with colleagues who were not above what Acheson later called "a rather shabby descent into sharp practice." These Franco-American meetings ended on October 17 in complete disagreement and with serious misunderstandings. In the next week, German rearmament was debated in the French parliament and the European army approach approved "in principle" by the deputies.

The first U.S. reaction to the new French démarche, in spite of its bold approach to the long-held American goal of European unity, was distinctly cool. Secretary Acheson's statement was polite but noncommittal:

The United States Government welcomes the initiative taken by the French Government in proposing a method for organizing armed forces in Western Europe, including those of Western Germany to deter and if necessary to resist aggression. This represents a further approach toward the objective of bringing the common interests of the

[113] This account of the Washington meetings is based on Moch, *Histoire,* pp. 111–22, and Acheson, *Present at the Creation,* pp. 457–59.

[114] Senator Tom Connally, for example, said about the French promise: "When, and only when, the men to fill the ranks are recruited, France will have demonstrated her determination to do her part." *Department of State Bulletin,* October 9, 1950, p. 564.

free nations of Europe more closely together within the framework of the North Atlantic community.

This proposal, which contains many far-reaching concepts, deserves and requires further study, which the United States Government will undertake to give it.[115]

It was immediately apparent that the United States had serious misgivings about the plan, especially on such points as the proposed European defense minister.[116] Unlike the Schuman Plan, which Acheson considered a practical, commonsense approach, the secretary found the Pleven proposal a hopeless idea—an impression in which the President and Marshall concurred. The language of the Acheson statement seemed concerned only with German rearmament—it did not mention at all the many aspects of the plan concerned with the political framework within which the military organization was to be realized. The promise to give the proposal further study amounted to an expression very close to outright disapproval, especially in comparison with the enthusiastic language with which the Schuman Plan had been greeted less than six months before.

Perhaps one reason why Acheson paid so little serious heed to the French plan was because he expected it to be dropped rather quickly, as France realized it would have to give in to the U.S. demand. There was also, perhaps, an American tendency to downgrade what seemed to be a delaying tactic on the part of Paris because "the Anglo-Saxon partners had grown accustomed to a certain amount of French obstruction, followed by resigned acceptance, to see anything unusual in her initial refusal of German rearmament." [117] Acheson later said much the opposite; he recalled that the French were "united and dug in" and he considered threats too dangerous. Instead, he anticipated dropping the "one package" proposal which he had never liked in the first place.

Reaction in the Pentagon tended to lean toward a view that

[115] *Department of State Bulletin,* November 13, 1950, p. 777.
[116] *The Times* (London), October 26, 1950.
[117] Grosser in Lerner and Aron, "France and Germany," p. 56.

the Pleven Plan for German participation on the level of regimental combat teams was ridiculous as a military formula, and that it really amounted to an attempt to keep the Federal Republic from a capability for independent action by isolating one German unit from another. Not only was it organizationally impractical and incomplete as a method of using German manpower, but even if it could be made to work, military critics argued, the delay involved would be enormous at a time when troops were needed at once. Marshall informed the President that there was only a single U.S. army division in the country in December and "it would be spring before any other divisions would be trained and ready for action." [118] In addition, the U.S. military had increased their estimates of what was necessary since summer, 1950, and were now more convinced than ever of the view that without German help their needs could not be met.

American disdain for the Pleven Plan was illustrated by Marshall's announcement, on the same day Acheson promised to study the proposal, that the United States planned to arm at least two German divisions by the end of 1951. Also illustrated by this, however, was the American willingness to ignore the realities of the bargaining situation, as neither Paris nor Bonn would have agreed to German rearmament in the absence of a drastically revised position. But this was susceptible to exploration. For the moment, the Pleven Plan was rejected by the United States as "a politically impossible and militarily unfeasible subterfuge for preventing German rearmament," a proposal which Acheson considered "designed for infinite delay." [119]

Other allied reactions tended to follow the American one. Within ten days it was reported that in all the NATO countries the proposal was opposed by both military and civilian people, as technically unrealistic, "surrounding" every German with a Frenchman, Dutchman, and so on; militarily ineffective, since the units would be too small when only divisions were operationally appropriate; and politically impossible, with "a Defense Min-

---

[118] Truman, *Memoirs*, p. 421.
[119] Acheson, *Present at the Creation*, p. 457; Osgood, *NATO*, p. 85.

ister who represents nobody and reports only to a phantom." The British, for example, were anxious to proceed with the creation of integrated NATO forces, including Germans, and did not want to be diverted from this. London was not interested in joining any federal-type European project, and thought the Pleven Plan itself impractical and nebulous.[120] The Netherlands' foreign minister considered it simply one among a series of "French moves to retain discrimination against Germany," and apart from this believed it could not work because "Europe was not yet ripe for such far-reaching concepts." [121]

On October 28, 1950, Moch returned to Washington, where he presented the already well-known provisions of the Pleven Plan to the allied defense ministers as an alternative to the U.S. proposals. Ismay found the positions of the United States and France "too divergent to be reconciled." [122] The result, he added, was that decisions could not be taken either on German rearmament or on such other matters as NATO's military organization in Europe and on the command structure—in other words, the package was still being preserved as a single diplomatic bargaining position by the United States, even if Acheson had decided to ease the U.S. stand. An earlier suggestion by Moch that the alliance proceed with what was already agreed upon, that is, the rest of the package, and postpone the German rearmament question while the delay was used to explore chances of agreement with the Soviet Union, had been rejected by Marshall on the ground it would mean a loss of perhaps several months.[123] The United States, apparently, would thenceforth ease the rigidity of the package, but would do so not with a dramatic stroke but more indirectly in the forum of subministerial exchanges. As

[120] Arthur Krock, *The New York Times*, November 3, 1950. See also *The New York Times*, October 25, 1951. Field-Marshal Montgomery considered it "utterly impracticable." Bernard L. Montgomery, *The Memoirs of Field-Marshal The Viscount Montgomery of Alamein* (New York: New American Library, 1958), p. 458.

[121] Stikker, *Memoir*, p. 300.

[122] Ismay, *NATO*, p. 34.

[123] Moch, *Histoire*, p. 121. This occurred on October 17.

Acheson later admitted, "It was a relief to get myself unstuck, if only briefly, from the cloying problem of German participation in defense." [124]

The failure of the defense committee meetings of late October led to the French plan, plus the U.S. package, being passed along to the council deputies and the military committee for further study. Washington's attitude at the time was said to be characterized by displeasure, irritation, and impatience—but the diplomacy it led to did not bring success in spite of a different line. It was reported that the United States assured the French that many of their fears were imaginary, and added the reminder that "since Uncle Sam is paying for this show, he damn well has a right to say who will play what parts." [125] The contrasting and so-far irreconcilable scenarios of Washington and Paris (both, in effect, rejected by Adenauer in his address to the Bundestag of November 8) were given to the council deputies to work on—without the Germans. The now somewhat modest goal of American diplomacy was French agreement "in principle" on German participation, but even this was elusive.

Finally, U.S. reaction to the political parts of the Pleven Plan was important, especially since the very elements which in late 1950 were cited as extremely difficult were later referred to with bland optimism after the shift in favor of EDC. For example, Acheson said the French scheme raised very hard questions about how institutions would actually work in a European federation; what, he asked, would be the authority of the various parts in relation to each other? The secretary later wrote that he was "continually baffled" by the work of the Monnet group and the various proposals looking toward European unification. He found a lack of orderliness and clarity which made him skeptical of what was being attempted, and wondered how there could be unity when the parts could secede or when decisions of the organizations could not be enforced. He realized that "it was the essence

---

[124] Acheson, *Present at the Creation*, p. 459.
[125] *The New York Times*, November 12, 1950.

of the Schuman method not to attack the question of sovereignty head-on," [126] but from his own account he was not really convinced.

The noteworthy point here is that Acheson in late 1950 rejected the French approach to European unification which he accepted in mid-1951. The distinction can only be that in the former time period the United States was interested not in a European army, but in German troops; the later decision to postpone insistence on the principle of German rearmament, while the supranational defense scheme was explored, was only because there was no alternative.

FRANCO-AMERICAN DEADLOCK
AND THE SPOFFORD COMPROMISE

The American diplomatic attempt to gain French consent to German rearmament by making the other elements of the package conditional on this part had been met with a French counterproposal on the German question and a suggestion to proceed with the *rest* of the package. It was the latter aspect of the deadlocked confrontation which gradually convinced American policymakers that because of the interest of the United States in strengthening European defense, it would not be wise to hold out for what might eventually become maximum strength, if this meant that minimum strength would be bypassed in the interim. But before this commonsense conclusion could be formalized at the Brussels NATO Council meeting, there was required a great deal of effort to lay the groundwork for what would give the impression of a compromise between Washington and Paris. Until this could be done, the reciprocal rejection of the two approaches persisted.

Premier Pleven had given his solemn promise to the National Assembly that if the United States refused the European army

[126] Acheson, *Sketches from Life,* pp. 43–44; *The New York Times,* November 2, 1950.

plan, France would refuse to sanction German rearmament. Although it was later denied that Moch had been instructed to present the Pleven proposal in the United States on a "take it or leave it" basis, there was complete deadlock when the French in effect said "take it" and the Americans declined.[127] Moch told the defense committee: "I came here to recommend vigorously the adoption of the French plan and only for that." [128] The split was 11 to 1, with France defiant in her refusal to accept the judgment of her partners in NATO that the Pleven Plan was unworkable. The French position was explained and defended November 24 by Schuman before the European Assembly. The military problem as part of the effort to create European institutions, he said, arose "sooner than we thought and sooner than we desired." France would have preferred to leave until last "the construction of the military edifice," but the German issue had raised this now. No one wanted a new Wehrmacht, but this need not be feared under the French scheme—the Pleven Plan would bring not *German* rearmament but the armament of *Europe*. Finally, he said, it should be appreciated that France saw its approach as a permanent one, leading to a permanent European army, whereas the American plan for a NATO "Atlantic army" was only temporary.[129]

The vital differences between the U.S. and French conceptions were illustrated, both before and after the Spofford compromise plan, by the long dispute about the size of the units which were to be recruited in the Federal Republic. While the French were disturbed that the American government was demanding the creation of two German divisions before the end of 1951, the United States, for its part, was shocked to learn that Moch envisaged German units of 800–1,200 men, while it considered combat groups of 5,000–6,000 barely adequate. When in mid-November American representatives were gaining French agreement to the "principle" of combat teams of 5,000 or 6,000 men,

[127] *Manchester Guardian Weekly*, November 30, 1950.
[128] *L'Annee Politique, 1950*, p. 224.
[129] *L'Annee Politique, 1950*, pp. 381–82.

the French simultaneously demanded that the principles of the Pleven Plan be accepted by the United States if there was to be any German rearmament at all. In other words, to a certain extent there was a failure of communication (or perhaps a willful refusal to understand) between the adversaries: in practical terms the size of the unit made no difference whatsoever, because the French did not conceive of these units other than in the framework of the European army, to which the United States had not agreed.[130]

After the October defense committee meetings Moch stated in a press conference that France would never agree to a new German army or "anything that appears to be the origin of a new German army."[131] The United States, which considered Moch's objections based on emotional rather than on rational military considerations, in private was attempting to convince the French that many of their worries were imaginary. The French countered with criticism of Washington's "too zealous wooing" of Germany, which they said had caused the latter to become overly hard to please, and had led to *de facto* independence for the Federal Republic, when it was not yet even clear whether the Schuman Plan would be signed. The United States saw no reason to link the Schuman Plan with German rearmament, but for France they were inseparable.[132] The French view was that American policy leading toward a too rapid restoration of German power would undermine the approach to European integration based on the surrender—not the restoration—of part of the sovereignty of the members.

[130] Since November 4 the United States had been proposing the immediate raising of German combat teams, which could then have been incorporated into an Atlantic army, a European army, or into various national armies. In return for agreeing to the prohibition of a German general staff, the United States had asked France to stop requesting a European defense minister. The deputies discussed these matters November 13–30. *L'Annee Politique, 1950,* p. 247; Werth, *France,* pp. 496–97; Willis, *New Europe,* p. 133.

[131] Ambassade de France, Service de Presse et d'Information, Document 24, November 2, 1950.

[132] Pleven said, "Above all, the Plan is bound to the coal-steel pool." *L'Annee Politique, 1950,* p. 222.

An indication of the easing of American pressure was Acheson's statement on November 15, 1950:

We have been wrestling, as you know, throughout the North Atlantic Treaty Organization with the question of German participation. This raises very difficult questions for the Germans. These questions have got to be dealt with soberly and quietly without getting exasperated because everyone does not see the problem in exactly the same way. We must find a solution which can be acceptable to all so that we may move forward with very considerable speed in building up that military strength. It is our judgment here that time is most important, that if this strength can be built up quickly then many dangers can be averted which would not be averted if too much time has to be occupied with preliminary adjustments.[133]

Concern with the time factor was implicitly a rejection of the Pleven Plan, which in Washington had become synonymous with delay, but it was also the clue to the breakup of the package proposal, since delay on one part had come to mean delay on the rest, as long as a solution "acceptable to all" did not exist.

The NATO committees met through November and into December, working separately but keeping each other informed, at a time when the negotiations were delicate. The major problem was what safeguards were necessary for a German contribution, with the French holding out for the European army. The meetings were long and difficult, with the representatives' capacity to reach compromise tested to the utmost. One reason for this situation was that the French had no support for the Pleven Plan from other allied representatives. In spite of their protestations that the proposal was "neither a dilatory maneuver nor an involved subterfuge to prevent German rearmament, but the only possible solution to a problem which was as political as military, there was a strong feeling outside France that the European nations were not ready for the supranational entity implied in the plan and the French knew it." [134]

[133] *Department of State Bulletin,* November 27, 1950, p. 854.
[134] Edinger, *West German Armament,* p. 14; R.I.I.A., *Atlantic Alliance,* pp. 54–55.

The allies apparently thought that the great sacrifices which the United States had made for Europe, and the new American willingness to undertake the far-reaching commitments involved in sending additional troops and providing a supreme commander for an integrated force, gave Washington the right to insist on a defense plan which only France—perhaps in bad faith —opposed.[135] This combination of willingness to accept American leadership (albeit with an awareness that aid funds and military supplies depended on cooperation with the super-power ally), and unwillingness to accept an alternative which was considered impractical, made the isolation of France striking. At the same time, however, unequivocal statements by U.S. officials, to the effect that a new national German army would *not* be created, necessarily set the stage for at least the temporary pursuit of some kind of alternative. The French seemed to have agreed that Germans might have guns in their hands again *if* the proper framework could be erected, and the Americans seemed to have agreed that these German hands should not be national ones.

By late 1950, an approach which would more convincingly avoid national German rearmament had at least to be considered. Once this became clear, a compromise became possible—not because either Washington or Paris had had a change of mind, but because the United States wanted to go ahead with the other aspects of establishing an integrated force, and because the French had decided they could not persist with pure and simple refusal concerning German rearmament.[136]

The council deputies, in early December, heard British arguments that the French accept the propositions of Chairman Charles Spofford for the immediate creation of German units— that is, before the European army plan could be implemented. Under the combined pressure of London and Washington, the French cabinet on December 7 sent instructions to Hervé Alphand (the French deputy) to the effect that France *would* consent

[135] *Herald Tribune*, November 5, 1950.
[136] Cf. Acheson's remarks in *Department of State Bulletin*, December 18, 1950, pp. 964–65; Moch, *Histoire*, p. 132.

to the raising of German units ("combat teams") of 5,000 to 6,000 men. But, these instructions continued, Alphand was to state at the same time that by so doing France did *not* renounce its commitment to the actual initiation of either the Schuman Plan or the Pleven Plan. Paris added that the German combat teams should not be independent in either supply or arms; should have no heavy weapons; should not be capable of coming together to form larger units; and should not amount to more than one-fifth of the allied total. Further, no German ministry of war should be allowed, and troops were to be raised only by the Federal minister of works under the control of the High Commission.[137]

This French move led to a compromise agreement, the Spofford Plan, largely embodying the terms enumerated above.[138] It provided that the basic unit of the European army should be the combat team; that there should be only one German combat team to five other European ones; and that the European army should contain German units from the beginning. This agreement, announced on December 8, added that the Germans would not have heavy weapons and that there would be no German general staff. On December 11, the Federal Chancellor in reply said German units should enjoy "complete equality" with others, including these matters.[139] On December 12, Schuman again defined the position of France before the National Assembly: "We remain completely attached to our proposal for the creation of a European army because this is the only solution which is possible and acceptable to everyone, especially for Germany. Moreover we do not wish German units to be at any time whatsoever, even during a transitional period, at the disposition of a German government."[140]

While it seems quite clear from these sources that the French

[137] *L'Annee Politique, 1950*, pp. 272, 408. See also Calvocoressi, *Survey, 1949–1950*, pp. 166–67, and *The New York Times*, December 8, 1950.

[138] The Spofford Plan was not a coherent outline at all but one of a number of variations the deputies had been discussing for several weeks.

[139] Adenauer, *Memoirs*, p. 307.

[140] *L'Annee Politique, 1950*, p. 272.

willingness to consent to immediate German rearmament on combat-team level was at no point divorced from France's conviction that German rearmament could only occur within the European army framework, Lord Ismay's account of what followed is partially inconsistent with this. He said a joint meeting in London of the council deputies and the military committee on December 13 produced a report which was forwarded to the defense committee and the NATO Council, which were to meet less than a week hence. "The essence of their recommendations was that 'an acceptable and realistic defense of Western Europe and the adoption of a forward strategy could not be contemplated without active and willing German participation. . . .'" The report recommended that certain provisional measures concerning a German contribution be begun in the immediate future—"for example, 'preliminary work on the military organization.'" It also dealt with the maximum size of future German units and the various limitations and controls which were to apply to the German contribution.

What seems incompatible with the French understanding of the matter are Ismay's next statements: "The report recognized that 'any system of German participation must be within the NATO structure' and mentioned the various solutions which had been discussed—without, at this point, making a choice between them. The broad alternatives were the incorporation of German units either in NATO's integrated defense force (United States proposal) or in the unified European Army (French proposal)." In light of the instructions of the French government to Alphand, and the Schuman statement to the French parliament, even if Ismay's account is correct as to the London meeting's report, there had not been any change in the position of the Paris government. Simply leaving open "the broad alternatives" really left the parties just where they had been before the Spofford compromise and the ensuing report. The United States had not given up pressing for German units incorporated directly into a NATO force, and France had not given up pressing for the European army as the only possible solution to the German rearmament dilemma.

And, since the government of the Federal Republic had, in advance, rejected *both* "broad alternatives," it is apparent that these agreements amounted to no substantial change.[141] The ambiguity of the Spofford Plan and the report which it led to provided an appropriate prelude to the "unanimous agreement" proclaimed at Brussels.

THE BRUSSELS MEETING, DECEMBER, 1950

On December 18–19 the NATO Council and the defense committee met in Brussels and announced agreement on several important matters. An integrated NATO force was at last to be established. General Eisenhower was appointed by President Truman as Supreme Commander at the request of the council, and a production board was to oversee the utilization of Europe's economic resources for defense. As for the German rearmament question:

The Council also reached unanimous agreement regarding the part which Germany might assume in the common defense. The German participation would strengthen the defense of Europe without altering in any way the purely defensive character of the North Atlantic Treaty Organization. The Council invited the Governments of France, the United Kingdom and the United States to explore the matter with the Government of the German Federal Republic.[142]

On December 22, Acheson described in equally discreet, but no more specific, terms the status of the German problem. The council, he said,

took action on the very important question of the relation of Germany to the defense of Western Europe. We cleared away the obstacles which had been in front of German participation. We made it perfectly clear to the Germans that their participation is a matter to be discussed

[141] Ismay, *NATO*, p. 34. Acheson's own account supports this analysis. *Present at the Creation*, p. 486.

[142] Dennett and Turner, *Documents, 1950*, p. 215.

with them. Their will and their enthusiastic cooperation is an essential part of anything which is to be done. We made it clear that, if they take part in this effort, then clearly their relations with the nations of Western Europe and with us in the United States will be and can be on a different basis from what they are now.[143]

These references to Germany's role in European defense are most noteworthy for their expression of allied awareness that these matters could be worked out only through direct dealings with the Bonn government, and that a price would have to be paid for German cooperation in the form of a new basis for relations between the Federal Republic and the allies—that is, either a restoration of German sovereignty or its functional equivalent in a common institutional framework.[144] Equally noteworthy, however, was what the council did not say. The "unanimous agreement on the part which Germany might assume," which presumably resulted after the allies "cleared away the obstacles" hindering German participation, was not further explained. The communiqué did *not* spell out the German role in European defense, or even mention German rearmament. The word "participation" hardly went beyond the language of the September NATO Council's communiqué which mentioned a German "contribution." The reason for this vagueness is not obscure. There had been no agreement at all on the German rearmament issue, and the approval of the Spofford Plan by the NATO Council and the defense committee amounted to no more than the compromise in the plan itself—a papering over of the still irreconcilably different French and American approaches.

What was agreed to was that the occupying powers would for the first time deal formally with the Bonn regime on the question. President Truman's statement of December 21 was more indicative of what was really done than the communiqué or the remarks of the secretary of state. He said that informal conversa-

[143] *Ibid.*, p. 217.

[144] Acheson's statement that "we" made it clear to the Germans that their participation would have to be discussed is curious, since it was the Germans who had been saying just this to the allies for months.

tions between Acheson, Bevin, and Schuman "resulted in full agreement on how the three governments, pursuant to the NATO Council's decision, would take up with the German Government the problem of German contributions to the defense of Western Europe." [145] The crucial point—which was "the part which Germany might assume"—remained unresolved.

The Brussels meeting in effect produced what the President said, not what the communiqué proclaimed. The occupying powers agreed not to German rearmament, but to take up with Bonn the "problem" of German rearmament, and even in this limited sense there was not a meaningful Franco-American accord (as indicated soon afterward by the "rival" conferences at Paris and Bonn). Although the Spofford Plan was "approved," its implementation was necessarily postponed. The allies were in accord that a conference should commence in January in order to study the possibilities of effecting the Pleven Plan. The Spofford Plan could in no case have been followed until Bonn had agreed to it, so that the French acceptance of the combat-group proposal came at the very moment it was by implication admitted all around that it was premature.[146]

Indeed, in the December 19 meeting of the High Commissioners with the German Chancellor immediately following the Brussels conference, it was obvious that an enormous effort would have to be made before German rearmament could materialize. It was reported that Adenauer and the High Commissioners were in accord that discussions should begin concerning the replacement of the Occupation Statute with a treaty, which would establish a new political basis for German-Western relations; that a committee to look into the "scale and manner" of the German defense contribution should be organized; and that the allies would in turn expect to reach agreement with the Federal Republic on such matters as Germany's prewar and postwar debts,

[145] *Public Papers of the Presidents of the United States. Harry S Truman, 1950,* p. 755.
[146] Millis, Mansfield, and Stein, *Arms and the State,* p. 343, noted that "the point was more or less overlooked at the time" that Bonn would not accept what had been agreed to at Brussels.

the distribution of strategic defense materials, a prohibition against traffic in such materials between Western and Eastern Germany, and an understanding that the Federal Republic would avoid any quarrel in connection with the areas east of the Oder-Neisse line.[147]

When the scale and scope of these matters are considered, and when it is realized that they were all to a marked extent interconnected, if not interdependent, and when the French commitment to the European army approach is added to all this, the German rearmament problem appears at once as one which could be resolved only over time if at all.

Finally, the Brussels meeting was of lasting significance precisely because the German rearmament question was *not* agreed upon. The United States, in deciding to allow the ingredients of the original package proposal to be separated, withdrew its ultimatum that German rearmament had to be agreed to if the other elements were to be forthcoming, and thereby took the step which meant that NATO could be "properly launched." [148] It had been more important all along that an integrated force under a single commander be established than that the Federal Republic, a defeated, politically occupied, and psychologically ambivalent country, be pushed into raising troops. In this sense, although partly for distinguishable reasons, the French had been correct in their ordering of priorities.

At Brussels, France consented "in principle" to German rearmament (or so it was thought), and the United States, with the other allies, consented to the French request that a conference be called to explore support for the European army plan. The latter was in the nature of a "hunting license" granted to Paris without the expectation the French "would bag any big game." But this was not the main consideration. What mattered was that American diplomacy had dropped what was becoming a counterproductive approach to European security. Washington's interest in German rearmament had by no means diminished, but the

[147] Dennett and Turner, *Documents, 1950*, p. 553.
[148] Ismay, *NATO*, p. 37, quoting Foreign Secretary Bevin.

United States thereafter pursued this policy goal without the emphasis on its immediate realization which had so belatedly been perceived as impossible. Acheson later wrote that "two simultaneous approaches to German participation" had been authorized—one, by the High Commissioners with Adenauer on the raising of German forces according to the Spofford Plan, and the other to provide the institutional basis for the European army. He did not mention their incompatibility, but indicated the complexity of the problem by noting "we must make no further concessions to the Germans" until they would agree to pay their debts and "shoulder their proper burdens." [149]

The Brussels meeting may be seen as an end to a period which witnessed the manifestation of virtually all the interrelated and overlapping aspects of the German rearmament question. It also marked the conclusion of the period of American inflexibility. The Spofford Plan was not significant as a French concession, but was useful as a device which allowed American diplomacy to save face and turn away from a counterproductive approach. If the approval by the council of the Spofford Plan, which called for an immediate commencement of the raising of German combat teams, cannot be reconciled with the communiqué's invitation to the occupying powers to explore the question with the Bonn government *or* with the proposed exploration of the institutional basis of the European army project, it was because the United States had decided to embrace a superficially acceptable compromise in order to get off the hook of the package proposal. If the German units were to be raised immediately and incorporated into allied occupation divisions in Germany, the agreement to this by the French—who had not dropped their insistence on the European army approach—can only have been based upon the knowledge that its realization was impossible, since Adenauer had already refused it, and only upon the understanding that these units were ultimately to become part of a European army.

While it seemed that France had at last consented to the principle of German rearmament, and that the United States had

[149] Acheson, *Present at the Creation*, p. 487.

consented to the exploration of the European army approach, with both to be undertaken only in conjunction with the German government, the three contrasting scenarios which had been conceived in the fall of 1950 remained. It is probable that the circumstances at the time were such that German rearmament could not have been agreed to in a manner simultaneously acceptable to Washington, Paris, and Bonn, whatever diplomatic approaches might have been employed.

Moreover, the immediate situation was fundamentally incompatible with too-rapid changes. Historical, psychological, and nationalistic forces remained too strong to permit the lingering still-sharp fragments of the wartime years to be swept under the rug of the Soviet threat. The three-cornered situation which the German rearmament issue highlighted was perceived differently from each vantage point, with the national interest of each of the participants the conditioning agent of its outlook. Frenchmen thought the American fear of Russia exaggerated, Americans thought French fear of Germany exaggerated, and Germans, with a mixture of apathy and ambition, reacted with an opportunism which satisfied neither Washington nor Paris. "What the Brussels statement amounted to in fact was an admission that the question, as originally posed, had been wrongly framed. The problem was not, and had never been, how best the supposedly willing Germans might be allowed to rearm, but rather, how best a reluctant Germany could be persuaded to accept her rightful [sic] position in the mutual defense system of the Western world." [150]

Acheson's professed reluctance to treat German rearmament as a military rather than a political and psychological problem is questionable in light of U.S. insistence in the next months (whether by Acheson or Marshall or Spofford) on immediate German rearmament. Nor did the allies at Brussels bow to the insistence on acceptance of the principle of German rearmament without reluctance and a sense of danger: "For however compelling the military arguments, the fact remained that one could not expect a German contribution until the Federal Republic

[150] Onslow, "West German Rearmament," p. 478.

was given complete sovereignty, and a Germany which had regained her sovereignty and her armed strength might find herself tempted, or compelled, to use her new position for purposes other than those envisaged by the members of NATO." [151]

For all these and other reasons, strong opposition to any kind of German rearmament existed throughout Europe, including Germany, in late 1950. European leaders felt that only comprehensive negotiations among the concerned governments could produce a solution which would be politically as well as militarily acceptable, and at this point in time the German rearmament demand, instead of assisting the integration of the Federal Republic into the Western camp, "handicapped it by arousing new fears among the recent victims of German militarism and stiffening German resistance to Western policy." [152]

Such apprehensions created further impediments to projects which might have contributed to European security as well as European cooperation, particularly since the Federal Republic raised the price for cooperation with the West just as the United States began to look upon the Pleven Plan with more interest.[153] The period of Franco-American deadlock gave way to a three-sided confrontation as Germany was at last invited to participate in the exploration of the rearmament question.

[151] Craig in Kaufmann, "NATO and the New German Army," p. 195.

[152] Edinger, "West German Armament," pp. 11–12.

[153] Inept American handling of the rearmament issue had already given Bonn a stronger bargaining position. Onslow, "West German Rearmament," p. 474.

CHAPTER III

The German Rearmament Question in Transition

THE dictum that Western Europe could not be defended without Germany, and in turn that Germany could not be defended without the Germans, had become something of a truism by early 1951. This was not, however, because it was incontrovertible in the sense that no area can be defended without the willing participation of its inhabitants. It was because military plans could not be made solely on the basis of military needs, but depended upon political and economic factors.

At the September, 1950, New York meeting, the North Atlantic Council had unanimously agreed that NATO should defend as far to the east as possible. In the next months, the allies pledged many divisions, but economic conditions were such that an even greater danger than military weakness might have been generated by the socio-psychological trauma of declining living standards. The result, even though the Anglo-Saxon powers were to reinforce their troops in Europe, was that the European allies were unwilling to furnish "even remotely adequate contingents out of their own resources." [1] This left only the Federal Republic

[1] Louis J. Halle, *The Cold War as History* (London: Chatto and Windus, 1967), p. 247. The troops necessary for European defense could have been raised without

as an additional source of troops. Western Germany was hence to become the central forward bastion of European defense.[2] The rebuilding of German power, considered necessary for the containment of Russia, raised the problem of avoiding another German danger. These considerations, which were not new but were better appreciated, began to set the stage for the major 1951 diplomatic development in the Western alliance, the shift of the United States toward a European army.

"The Germans wanted restoration of their full sovereignty before they assumed their place in the scheme of defense, but the French kept insisting that Germany had to be kept under controls. In conference after conference it seemed impossible to break this deadlock."[3] Perhaps the problem was all but insoluble. In addition to the broader issue of how to redress the East-West balance, the problem in NATO was that of developing a German contribution which would bring security vis-à-vis the external danger without giving the appearance of creating a new threat to internal security within the NATO area, "the miracle of making the German armed force stronger than the Russian but weaker than the French"[4] without offending the Germans themselves.

Once the United States decided not to attempt to arm the Germans without the consent of the Paris government, it faced the problem of how to frame a policy simultaneously acceptable to all the parties. Not only would France have to agree, but American desires for German defense participation could be realized only if they were domestically acceptable in the Federal Republic. The ambivalence of the situation was reflected in the diplo-

German rearmament at any time following 1950. Coral Bell, *Negotiation from Strength: A Study in the Politics of Power* (London: Chatto and Windus, 1962), p. 46.

[2] Lewis J. Edinger, *West German Armament*, Air University, Maxwell Air Force Base, Alabama, October, 1955, pp. 84–86. See also U.S. Congress, Senate, *Assignment of Ground Forces of the United States to Duty in the European Area*, 82nd Cong., 1st Sess., p. 141.

[3] Harry S Truman, *Memoirs: Years of Trial and Hope*, Vol. II (Garden City: Doubleday, 1956), p. 253.

[4] Edgar S. Furniss, Jr., *France, Troubled Ally: DeGaulle's Heritage and Prospects* (New York: Praeger, 1960), p. 81.

matic arena, as two rival conferences were for several months held concurrently at Paris and Bonn, each exploring an avenue of approach to the German rearmament question almost as if the other were irrelevant.

During 1951 both the United States and most of the other NATO allies—some of them without conviction—moved toward support of EDC. Washington had for years favored the closer political integration of Western Europe, but had refrained, since the beginning of the Korean War, from pressing for this, as military priorities were overriding. As EDC's attractiveness increased, American policymakers saw in the European army scheme the way to achieve not only German rearmament but also European unification (without downgrading military priorities). Acheson had testified some time before that he did not feel pressure should be put on the Europeans to move more quickly toward integration, but this preceded the mid-1950 deterioration of the international situation.[5]

The period from the Brussels meeting, when the United States consented to an exploration of the European army plan while still opposing it, to July, 1951, when an interim agreement was reached at Paris, was the germination period for the EDC in the American diplomatic imagination. As 1951 began, the three occupying powers, together with their allies, began to explore whether there would be an eventual rearmament of Germans, if not Germany, as a part of free Europe.[6]

U.S.-GERMAN-FRENCH CONFRONTATION

Secretary Acheson said after the Brussels conference that the period of planning for NATO was finished. "From now on it is

[5] U.S. Senate, Hearings, *The Mutual Defense Assistance Program, 1950*, 81st Cong., 2nd Sess., 1951, p. 11.

[6] McGeorge Bundy, ed., *The Pattern of Responsibility* (Boston: Houghton Mifflin, 1952), p. 121.

action which counts, and not further resolutions or plans or meetings, although there will be all of those." [7] On the action side, the three-sided confrontation of American-German-French interest in the question of the remilitarization of the Federal Republic produced a number of collisions and near accidents. In addition to the difficulties present in the bilateral relationships of the three states most directly concerned, there was also an underlying divergence between the United States and Europe, most sharply focused upon the American impression that Europeans were not doing enough and the impression of many Europeans that the United States "was drawing them, in the name of collective security, into a desperate adventure." [8] The opening months of 1951, when the German rearmament question was explored both by the occupying powers with the Federal Republic at Bonn and by states interested in the European army at Paris, were marked by a number of events which tended to intensify doubts in Europe about the direction of American policy.[9] In the United States, the "great debate" concerning the sending of additional troops to Europe had begun; McCarthyism was increasingly pervasive; the State Department was under severe attack; anti-Communism often became hysterical; the Korean War became bitterly divisive; and General Douglas MacArthur engaged in what amounted to open controversy with the President and was recalled. In the cold-war arena, Soviet propaganda against German rearmament was constant and vigorous, and the East-West confrontation remained uncompromisingly rigid, as reflected by the failure of the foreign ministers' deputies to achieve agreement in their prolonged meetings at Paris in the spring. Europeans especially felt a persistent uncertainty about Soviet policy, and,

[7] *Department of State Bulletin,* January 1, 1951, p. 3.

[8] Brookings Institution, *Major Problems of United States Foreign Policy, 1951–1952* (Washington, D.C.: Brookings Institution, 1952), p. 11; Peter Calvocoressi, *Survey of International Affairs, 1951* (London: Oxford University Press, 1954), pp. 13–14.

[9] Ben T. Moore, *NATO and the Future of Europe* (New York: Harper, 1958), pp. 39–40. For a French review of the international situation at the time, see *L'Annee Politique, 1951* (Paris: Presses Universitaires de France, 1952), pp. 18ff.

in the confusion of whether Moscow's apparently peaceful line in Europe could be reconciled with support for aggression in Asia, many felt rearmament either unnecessary or too provocative.[10]

Since the American decision to press for immediate German rearmament was above all based upon the desire to redress disparities in the conventional capabilities of Western forces, and not upon any U.S. plan to link this with European unification projects, it is not surprising that policymakers in Washington continued to perceive the question in terms of an international confrontation in which Communist-led hostilities could occur in Europe. The most likely point of attack in the view of NATO strategists continued to be the central front, and it was to the forces available there that the alliance planners looked in their assessment of the situation.

The creation of forces to withstand a possible Soviet attack was not a matter of controversy among the allies, in the sense that all agreed upon their desirability. The divergence came with the consideration of methods of reinforcing Western strength. The United States wanted German troops to supplement increased allied forces, while France and Germany—for once agreed on something—favored more American and British forces in the Federal Republic. Neither Paris nor Bonn was anxious to see German troops, even though both favored a forward defense (which probably was not militarily feasible without German rearmament).[11] High Commissioner McCloy, when asked whether defense would be on the Rhine or the Elbe, replied only that Western forces would defend as far to the east as their capabilities allowed. The NATO goal was to delay a Soviet attack long enough for the allies to mobilize their full strength, by a "more or less conventional holding action, trading space for time by a 'defense

[10] Richard P. Stebbins, *The United States in World Affairs, 1951* (New York: Harper, 1952), Chap. 2 *passim;* Calvocoressi, *Survey, 1951,* pp. 130–44; Royal Institute of International Affairs, *Atlantic Alliance: NATO's Role in the Free World* (London: Royal Institute of International Affairs, 1952), pp. 22–23.

[11] See Roger Hilsman, "NATO: The Developing Strategic Context," in *NATO and American Security,* ed. Klaus Knorr (Princeton: Princeton University Press, 1959), pp. 14ff.

in depth' of Western Germany," until the full weight of Western power was imposed on the aggressor.[12] This in effect made "forward strategy" a euphemism for a slower withdrawal from the territory of the Federal Republic, a longer time-cushion made possible by the additional room for battlefield maneuvering. But even this goal was then too ambitious; upon Eisenhower's arrival in Europe, Western forces were "totally inadequate" for defense of the Continent.[13]

One report found that the military balance in Europe early in 1951 "was on any view of the risks disturbing," and "on the assumption that it might be difficult to keep the peace in 1951, it was downright alarming." The Supreme Commander himself, in his review of the situation at the time, stated that NATO units "could have offered little more than token resistance to attack." [14] Testimony to the same effect was offered by U.S. military leaders, who said without qualification that Western Europe could not be held in the event of a Russian attack. Secretary Marshall emphasized the American atomic deterrent, but said Russia might nevertheless turn to aggression in Europe "at any moment." He added that the bases the United States had in Western Europe were vital to the operation of America's strategic air force, and the rearmament effort should continue in spite of NATO's immediate vulnerability.[15]

In addition to conventional superiority, the Soviet Union was known to possess an unspecified number of atomic bombs, and by early 1951 was thought to have the ability to deliver them on

[12] Edinger, *West German Armament*, p. 90; *Christian Science Monitor*, July 16, 1951.

[13] Bernard L. Montgomery, *The Memoirs of Field-Marshal The Viscount Montgomery of Alamein* (New York: New American Library, 1958), p. 460.

[14] Eisenhower said this in his report to the Standing Group in 1952. R.I.I.A., *Atlantic Alliance*, pp. 17, 21.

[15] Marshall stressed how long the effort would take; he had earlier testified that "the ground-force procedure moves with almost the slowness of a turtle." Senate, *Assignment of Ground Forces*, p. 70. See also the statements of General Bradley and General Collins at the MacArthur hearings. U.S. Senate, Committees on Armed Services and Foreign Relations, Hearings, *Military Situation in the Far East*, 82nd Cong., 1st Sess., 1951, pp. 592–93, 1094–95, 1212.

U.S. targets.[16] In an article on the military balance, Secretary Acheson said:

> To summarize the evidence so far: the United States has many more atomic bombs at this time, better planes with which to deliver them, and fewer targets which must be hit to achieve a decisive effect. However, the Russians could reach any point in the United States with their existing heavy bombers, and they possess something up to 200 atomic bombs. There is not the slightest reasonable doubt that in the event of war the United States would have to sustain a heavy attack of atomic bombs.[17]

But, he went on, even though the United States would have a relative advantage in an atomic war, Soviet ground forces would still be able to overrun Europe even after Russia had been devastated. As Russia tended toward balancing American atomic strength, NATO must move toward balancing Soviet ground strength—and only the Europeans could provide this. Should the Soviet Union achieve comparable atomic striking power while the Western allies remained inferior in conventional forces, he said, then "the time comes when the Russian land army becomes the decisive weapon in the military balance." At the hearings concerning the sending of additional American troops to Europe, he stressed sharply the inevitable relative decline of the atomic advantage as the Russian nuclear arsenal increased: "If you and I are standing close together and I am pointing a .38 at you and you are pointing a BB gun at me, I have a considerable advantage. But if we are standing very close together and I am pointing a .45 at you and you are pointing a .38 at me, the advantage has declined. . . . I do not think I should go into this any more." [18]

The secretary's analogy, however, did not necessarily imply a

[16] Testimony of General Bradley, Senate, *Military Situation in the Far East,* p. 495.

[17] Anonymous [Dean Acheson], "The Balance of Military Power," *Atlantic Monthly,* CLXXXVII (June, 1951), pp. 24, 25. These estimates by Bradley and Acheson may have been premature, but it was on such assessments as these that policy was being based.

[18] Senate, *Assignment of Ground Forces,* pp. 78–79.

German troop contribution as the solution to the dilemma of declining nuclear superiority. If the United States was so apprehensive that a failure to increase Western troop strength would have meant a dangerously higher risk of war, it could have sent many more troops to Europe than the planned four additional divisions then being debated in Washington. And if this was not feasible for domestic political reasons in the United States, it was even less so in economically fragile Europe. When General Eisenhower on February 1 reported to the Congress on European conditions he stressed that Europe was no more than partially rehabilitated; there was much "pessimism bordering upon defeatism." [19] When the new Supreme Commander asked the allies what they could contribute, their answers "all tripped over one hard, tough fact. This fact was the poverty of Western Europe." Economic considerations, in such circumstances, took precedence over the rearmament effort for Europeans, and one of the key questions facing NATO remained whether the defense effort would bring "dangerous economic and financial disturbances and even political upsets." [20]

The depressing military outlook was compounded by confusion about the moment when—if at all—Russia might turn to hostilities. General Bradley seemed to express this when he testified concerning Soviet plans. "It would be pretty hard to guess what the men in the Kremlin are thinking. They have a timetable. . . . I wouldn't know, and wouldn't profess to know, what the men in the Kremlin will do under any circumstances. They don't think like we do." [21] While Acheson personally did not expect war in the near future, U.S. planning of course had to take into consideration the possibility that an attack might occur, even if rational calculations should dictate to the Russians that they not start a war with an atomically superior adversary. In these circumstances, the need for German rearmament was virtually axiomatic. Acheson said a major accomplishment of the Brussels

[19] *Department of State Bulletin*, February 12, 1951, p. 247.
[20] Truman, *Memoirs*, p. 258; Stebbins, *United States, 1951*, p. 329.
[21] Senate, *Military Situation in the Far East*, p. 942.

agreement on the integrated force was that "it provided the most acceptable basis on which Western Germany might add its strength to our common cause of defending freedom," but did not say what this basis was.[22] In any case, whatever had been agreed to had not made German rearmament acceptable to either Bonn or Paris, in spite of the lopsided military situation.[23]

There was no disagreement that as a military necessity German rearmament was indispensable, if for no other reason than that the troops were not forthcoming elsewhere. The military need, however, was transcended by the political outlook. The Supreme Commander himself affirmed this when he reported to the Congress on his recent tour of Europe:

I am not even going to mention my several conversations in Germany and for a very specific reason. I personally think that there has to be a political platform achieved and an understanding reached that will contemplate an eventual and earned equality on the part of that nation before we should start to talk about including units of Germans in any kind of army. I, certainly, for one commander, want no unwilling contingent, no soldiers serving in the pattern of the Hessians who served in our Revolutionary War, serving in any army I command. Therefore, until the political leaders, the diplomats, and the statesmen find the proper answer, it is not for a soldier to delve in too deeply.[24]

Although by July he was to ignore the latter dictum, the general's statement was important on several counts. It showed his awareness of the reluctance of the Germans themselves to rearm on anything other than a basis of equality; it rejected the cannon-fodder approach without mentioning the European army alternative; it noted that equality could not come instantly, but had to

[22] Senate, *Assignment of Ground Forces*, p. 84; Dean Acheson, *Present at the Creation: My Years in the State Department* (New York: Norton, 1969), p. 487.
[23] It was estimated that early in 1951 there were six allied divisions on the German front, and that the combined Eastern force consisted of 50,000 GDR police, 175 to 200 Soviet divisions (total), and some 60 to 70 divisions of satellite troops. Stebbins, *United States, 1951*, p. 46.
[24] *Department of State Bulletin*, February 12, 1951, p. 247. General Bradley testified to the same effect. Senate, *Assignment of Ground Forces*, p. 141. Cf., however, Colonel Robert J. Wood, "The First Year of SHAPE," *International Organization*, Vol. VI (May, 1952).

be "eventual and earned"; and it showed his awareness that German rearmament was a political problem which would remain militarily irrelevant until diplomatically resolved. His remarks were received with relief in France, where they were welcomed as evidence of an easing of American pressure, and elsewhere Europeans responded approvingly. The London *Times,* for example, commented that the myth had at last been exploded that the Germans were longing to rearm and only French intransigence prevented this.[25] The Supreme Commander's willingness to postpone indefinitely the appearance of German troops did not mean he did not give German rearmament high priority, but only that the alliance should not pause needlessly on this political question while it might proceed on other matters.

The political outlook for the form German defense participation might take was somewhat confused by two events at the end of January which gave a greater impression of Franco-American agreement than in fact existed. On January 27, Acheson sent a letter to Foreign Minister Schuman concerning the proposed European army meeting.[26] The United States warmly welcomed the French initiative in calling a conference of interested states in Paris, he said, and had long supported closer European cooperation and integration. If France, in close consultation with Germany and others, could bring Europe closer together in the spirit of the Schuman Plan, there would be a reasonable hope "for long term solutions of many of our problems, be they political, military or economic." Integration, if worked out in a practical manner, would provide a sound basis on which military and economic strength could be built. The secretary added, "We know you also

[25] C. G. D. Onslow, "West German Rearmament," *World Politics,* III (July, 1951), p. 483. Congressman John F. Kennedy, recently back from a European tour, reported that he found in the Federal Republic "total unwillingness of the Germans to join in this defense effort." Senate, *Assignment of Ground Forces,* p. 444. The folklore that the Germans were "a military people" was still embraced by Senator Stennis, for example, and in general Americans did not realize how genuinely repugnant the rearmament proposal was in the Federal Republic. *Ibid.,* 141, for the Stennis quotation.

[26] The text of the letter is in Raymond Dennett and Katherine D. Durant, eds., *Documents on American Foreign Relations, 1951* (Princeton: Princeton University Press, 1951), p. 246.

agree with us that it is of primary importance to press forward vigorously with the strengthening of the North Atlantic Treaty Organization."

Acheson's indirect reminder to Schuman that the Pleven Plan, from its earliest presentation, had been seen in Washington as both slow and impractical indicated the U.S. view of the European army conference. If French efforts could foster workable agreements, resulting eventually in European integration, this would bring long-term benefits. But meanwhile, the need for a speedy military build-up must be vigorously met. The United States, Acheson concluded, would be happy to send an observer to the Paris meeting, and would do its best to aid the success of the conference. Neither the Pleven Plan specifically nor the European army proposal generally was endorsed, and there was no formal U.S. acceptance of the French approach to the German rearmament issue even though the language of the American statement was comparatively friendly. Some analysts have regarded the Acheson letter as an endorsement of the European army idea, but the secretary himself stated that he did not really develop the "conviction that the United States should plump for this solution" until the summer of 1951, when the President, Marshall, and Eisenhower did so as well.[27] At best, this expression of hope that the conference might succeed was a follow-up to the issuance of the "hunting license" to France by the NAC at Brussels.

The other event which gave the appearance of Franco-American accord was the visit of the French Premier to Washington at the end of the month. With reference to the Spofford compromise agreement and its endorsement at Brussels, the President and the Prime Minister on January 30 somehow found "a fundamental identity of views" between France and America.[28] The chief

[27] Dean Acheson, *Sketches from Life of Men I Have Known* (New York: Harper, 1959), p. 44. See also Hans Speier, *German Rearmament and Atomic War: The Views of German Military and Political Leaders* (Evanston: Row, Peterson, 1957), p. 9.
[28] *Public Papers of the Presidents of the United States. Harry S Truman, 1951* (Washington: Government Printing Office, 1965), p. 129.

executives "were in fundamental agreement that the cause of peace in Europe and the world would be furthered by a progressively closer integration in every aspect of a democratic Germany into a vigorous Western European community." President Truman, as had Secretary Acheson, welcomed the European army conference and expressed hope for its success. Then, with no further explanation, "The President and the Prime Minister reaffirmed their conviction that German participation in the common defense effort as envisaged last month at Brussels would strengthen the security of Europe without altering in any way the purely defensive character of the North Atlantic Treaty Organization." The communiqué concluded—perhaps as a fillip to French public opinion—with a declaration that genuine opportunities to settle international problems by negotiation would not be neglected.

The United States had again deliberately refrained from an endorsement of the European army as such, and the expression of mutual satisfaction with the Brussels formula could only mean that Truman and Pleven had decided to preserve the appearance of agreement. Although the Brussels accord based on the Spofford compromise was to have allowed the immediate formation of German units pending agreement on the Pleven Plan, there had been no attempt to implement the formula, for reasons discussed above, and (after an interval of a single day) the fact that there would be no attempt to do so was conclusively underscored by General Eisenhower's avowal that he would have "no unwilling contingents" in any force under his command. Agreement was lacking—even "in principle"—between Washington and Paris, and between the occupying powers and Bonn.

As 1951 began, the political outlook was such that German rearmament remained no more than "subject to further consideration," and "as time passed Europeans, who had been stunned into endorsing it, grew to like it no more and to object to it more openly." One of the reasons for this was that as Bonn became increasingly discontent with all restrictions involving sovereignty, the Federal Republic's price for cooperating with the West rose. Germany, Acheson recalled, was "beginning to realize her importance and inclined to bargain." [29]

The increase in the German price made some American policy-makers hesitate about the wisdom of continuing to push for German rearmament, but this hesitation never came close to a reversal of the U.S. position. Chancellor Adenauer, apparently unimpressed by High Commissioner McCloy's assurance "that the presence of one American soldier was the greatest security we [Germany] could get," continued to urge a U.S. troop buildup in the Federal Republic. He felt that even if the Soviet Union itself was not likely to turn to war, Communist forces in the GDR were dangerous in their own right. A visible display of American power was indispensable to deter another Korea, and only thereafter could the Federal Republic's remilitarization be pursued.[30] The United States was apparently aware of this, and the point was made in the troops-to-Europe hearings that one reason for reinforcing American forces in the Federal Republic was to provide an indispensable precondition for German rearmament. These security matters, however, represented collateral considerations for the Federal Chancellor. German rearmament, as always, was above all a diplomatic bargaining asset on the road back to political equality: "Adenauer never allowed the connection between rearmament and sovereignty to go unnoticed." [31]

The most obvious reminder of the Federal Republic's position as a defeated and still "enemy" state was the Occupation Statute, regarded at the time of its promulgation in 1949 as a significant step toward German rehabilitation, but by 1951 seen as an increasingly intolerable advertisement of subordinate status. Not only

---

[29] Acheson, *Sketches from Life*, p. 27; Calvocoressi, *Survey, 1951*, p. 3; Acheson, *Present at the Creation*, p. 494.

[30] Konrad Adenauer, *Memoirs, 1945–1953* (Chicago: Regnery, 1966), pp. 352, 319ff.

[31] Wolfram F. Hanreider, *West German Foreign Policy 1949–1963: International Pressure and Domestic Response* (Stanford: Stanford University Press, 1967), p. 96. John Sherman Cooper noted that "the Germans are exposed. They will not arm before there is some assurance of security." *Department of State Bulletin*, March 12, 1951, p. 430. See also Senate, *Assignment of Ground Forces*, p. 583.

should German units receive absolute equality with the contingents of other nations if the Federal Republic was to rearm, but as a matter of intergovernmental relations a contractual agreement should replace the 1949 convention.[32] In addition, the Chancellor said, "defamation" of the German soldier must cease; continued outside financial aid would be indispensable to a defense contribution; no "deal" could be made between East and West which would damage Germany's interests; and he listed other points which "amounted to a prospectus for many weary months of allied-German negotiations in 1951 and on into 1952." Acheson's recollection that in February, 1951, Adenauer "pressed for ten to fifteen divisions as the German contribution to defense" is unsupported by the other available evidence.[33]

The restoration of political equality was a domestic political necessity because of the unpopularity of German rearmament; only concessions could make it palatable to the German people, whose desire for improvements in Germany's international position was pitted against their equally strong wish to avoid the risks and burdens of remilitarization.[34] The contrast between German public opinion and the position of the Bonn government continued.[35] Opposition to German rearmament was such that "The world, for whom the typical German seems to be and to

[32] Adenauer, *Memoirs*, p. 175; Stebbins, *United States, 1951*, p. 63; Calvocoressi, *Survey, 1951*, pp. 61ff. General Clay made this clear; he said "it is not realistic to expect a German contribution until the political atmosphere has been created in which the Germans can make that contribution on a reasonably equal basis. . . . I believe that the political atmosphere in which Germans are no longer under occupation, but are returned to the family of free nations, and received in the North Atlantic Pact organization, is essential, however, before we can expect real fighting support from the German ground troops." Senate, *Assignment of Ground Forces*, p. 748. Statements such as this were recalled when the Federal Republic demanded NATO membership early in 1952.

[33] Stebbins, *United States, 1951*, pp. 62–63 and 57–68 *passim*; Acheson, *Present at the Creation*, p. 552.

[34] Karl W. Deutsch and Lewis J. Edinger, *Germany Rejoins the Powers: Mass Opinion, Interest Groups and Elites in Contemporary German Foreign Policy* (Stanford: Stanford University Press, 1959), pp. 160, 164.

[35] In addition to the Adenauer government, the other source of support for German rearmament was the former military, especially those of higher rank, who believed that remilitarization was justified because "with twelve German divisions and allied assistance, it might be possible to halt a Soviet advance in Europe." Speier, *German Rearmament*, p. 134 and Chap. 7 *passim*.

remain a symbol of barracks and carnage, has been astonished to learn of the German reaction to rearmament—a categorical 'no.' There are many reasons for this, but in fact this refusal is the product of a sentiment, not pacifist but anti-militarist, deeper than Germany has ever known." [36] The domestic German opposition continued to take the form of popular protest and parliamentary controversy. As to the former, Adenauer and the German foreign-policy elite responded in two ways: they made little effort to reveal to the German people the extent of their rearmament plans, and they utilized the German tradition of leaving complex questions of foreign policy to experts and persons of authority. In such circumstances, the Bonn government was able to count on popular acquiescence even when taking unpopular steps. There was never a popular majority for remilitarization in the Federal Republic. The German rearmament agreements "demonstrated the far-reaching and generally uncontested independence of German foreign policy decision makers from the influence of domestic public opinion." [37]

The most sensitive question which German rearmament necessarily raised was what effect participation in Western defense arrangements would have on the possibility of reunification of the two Germanies. It was on this that the Socialists pegged their strongest arguments against the policy of the government. Schumacher and his colleagues argued against rearmament on a number of grounds, but their basic thesis was that the military involvement of Western Germany with the allies would necessarily preclude the Russians from permitting reunification. The Adenauer reply to this was that only through close relationships with the West could there be reunification, which could be sought not by a weak and occupied Germany but only by a strong and independent Federal Republic. This charge and countercharge reflected the two salient goals of German foreign policy, reunifi-

[36] Carlo Schmid, "Germany and Europe," *International Affairs*, XXVII (July, 1951), p. 309. See also Carl J. Friedrich, "Why the Germans Hesitate," *The Atlantic Monthly*, CLXXXVII (April, 1951), pp. 40–41.

[37] Deutsch and Edinger, *Germany*, pp. 29, 31, 161; Calvocoressi, *Survey, 1951*, pp. 67–72. See also Drew Middleton's article, *The New York Times*, June 26, 1951.

cation and recovery of sovereignty. The problem was that the two could not be simultaneously achieved.

The Chancellor's conviction that a strong Federal Republic would be able to induce the Soviet Union to allow German reunification was apparently sincere even though mistaken. Another view is that Adenauer sought to strengthen the Federal Republic deliberately to *prevent* reunification.[38] His utilization of the issue to restore Germany's status took the form of asking a higher price for German rearmament, not because it might mean permanent division, but because of the strong domestic appeal which the Socialist opposition enjoyed. He pointed out that his willingness to take the unpopular step of remilitarization should be rewarded by the political concessions which would make this popularly palatable, and American officials were appreciative of his position. If reunification might not be gained as a result of remilitarization, then at least sovereignty should be. In any case, Adenauer's view was that the Brussels formula had left open the framework for the German defense contribution; but, since all the NATO allies had agreed upon the desirability of German contingents of some sort, this was subject to exploration.[39] The importance of this is that the Federal Republic knew that a Franco-American agreement would require time and that this left ample opportunity to press for specifically German interests.

Perhaps it was only a matter of time before the demands of the Bonn government were met, since by its very *commitment* to participate in Western defense the Federal Republic had elevated its status from that of a military protectorate to that of an essentially equal and sovereign ally. Perhaps a similar phenomenon had already occurred in September, 1950, when the very raising of the German rearmament question by the leading power of the alliance meant that it had in some way to be answered. The

[38] Charles Wighton, *Adenauer—Democratic Dictator: A Critical Biography* (London: Muller, 1963), p. 16 and Chap. 2 *passim*. See also Gordon A. Craig, *From Bismarck to Adenauer: Aspects of German Statecraft* (Baltimore: The Johns Hopkins Press, 1958), p. 144.

[39] Otto Kirchheimer, "Notes on the Political Scene in Western Germany," *World Politics*, VI (April, 1954), p. 308; Hanreider, *West German Foreign Policy*, pp. 50–52; Adenauer, *Memoirs*, pp. 345, 311.

French took substantially the same view when they rejected the suggestion that Paris could rest on an outright refusal, although opinion in France was virtually unanimous that the remilitarization of the Federal Republic was highly undesirable.[40]

Long before the threat of an "agonizing reappraisal" of the U.S. commitment to underwrite European security, the French were aware that the American leadership looked to a Europe which, in the future, would be sufficiently autonomous economically and militarily that its dependence on the United States could cease. The French approach to the German rearmament question remained inseparable from the French approach to the creation of an integrated Europe generally, as was reflected in the Truman-Pleven communiqué's reference to "a European army based on European political institutions." That this institutional structure was to be within the framework of the North Atlantic Treaty Organization did not indicate any shift in French thinking, which continued to stress supranational controls as the means to dissipate the danger of war between France and Germany.[41] If the Schuman Plan used economic means toward the political goal of European unification, the Pleven Plan envisaged political means toward the objective of permanent military security for France.

On the eve of the Paris conference, the French position that no recruiting of German units could begin until the European army agreement had been signed was indirectly underwritten by the Eisenhower statement of February 1. Paris knew that American pressure for German rearmament would at least temporarily diminish, and that hasty steps were unlikely. It was realized, however, that Washington's patience with Europe's efforts was limited, and that if the Pleven Plan collapsed the Germans might be directly pressed into a military contribution, regardless of the delicate nature of the Franco-German relation-

---

[40] Jules Moch, *Histoire du rearmement allemand depuis 1950* (Paris: Laffont, 1965), pp. 131–33. The French army was the only exception. Paul-Marie de la Gorce, *The French Army: A Military-Political History* (New York: Braziller, 1963), pp. 365ff.

[41] Cf. Donald C. McKay, *The United States and France* (Cambridge: Harvard University Press, 1951), p. 251.

ship and notwithstanding the lack of a democratic tradition in the Federal Republic.

French opinion saw General Eisenhower's trip to Europe in January as especially important. France was gratified that the new Supreme Commander was encouraged by reports on the defense buildup, and appreciated his discretion concerning the rearmament of the Federal Republic. His statement in Bonn that he did not believe the German soldier as such had lost his honor was seen in France as little more than a politically appropriate gesture.[42] The French government went to unusual lengths to insure that Eisenhower's reception in Paris would not be overly marked by protest demonstrations.[43]

The general himself noticed the lack of enthusiasm among the people. This was not unusual, since in 1951 "neutralism" was a movement with a great appeal in France. It was based on the hope that if war came the French would somehow be allowed to remain out of it—but it reinforced American impressions of France as an ally of highly dubious reliability. Neutralism disturbed the French government to such an extent that several ministers, including Jules Moch, denounced it as treason. The Pleven cabinet in this sense did not reflect French opinion; the ministers were much more anxious to please the United States and to make a good impression on Washington than the people or the press were.[44] The reason for the government's behavior was above all to keep the American flow of arms and money coming in, and French officials went to great lengths to reassure those who were losing confidence in France.

At the same time, the Paris government was irritated by its de-

[42] Eisenhower distinguished between the regular German soldier and the criminal Hitler group. Onslow, "West German Rearmament," p. 482. This was important to the American diplomatic effort to make German rearmament palatable within the Federal Republic, and met the Chancellor's demand, noted above, that the "defamation" of the German soldier cease.

[43] For example, on January 24, more than 3,000 "suspects" were arrested in connection with a demonstration at the Hotel Astoria. *L'Annee Politique, 1951*, p. 24.

[44] Eisenhower in his first annual report as SACEUR noted the tendency toward neutralism in Europe generally. Clarence W. Baier and Richard P. Stebbins, eds., *Documents on American Foreign Relations, 1952*, Vol. XIV (New York: Harper, 1953), p. 143.

pendence on the United States, and looked to European integration for a greater voice in Atlantic affairs without either alienating the Americans or precluding negotiations with the Russians. France hoped for maximum EDC membership and sent invitations to the European army conference to all the European members of NATO in addition to the Federal Republic. But the reality of the situation did not permit genuine independence for Paris in this or other matters. There was speculation, even after Pleven's statement that there were "absolutely no" differences between the two countries, that Washington might nevertheless take more rapid action toward German rearmament. During his visit to the United States in January, the French Premier's references to the German rearmament question were ambiguous. He said that differences between allies were "completely natural," but the duty of statesmen was to maintain unity. "It is in this spirit that France accepted the compromise plan which looks to a German contribution to Western defense. It is in this spirit that we have proposed the creation of an integrated European army above national differences and frontiers." [45] Once more, there appeared to be agreement and disagreement at the same moment, with the approaches of France and the United States, respectively, to be explored at the French and German capitals.

THE BONN AND PARIS CONFERENCES

Chancellor Adenauer had met with the High Commissioners on December 21, 1950, and together they decided to set up a commission to explore the "scale and manner" which the defense contribution of the Federal Republic might assume.[46] The meetings held pursuant to this agreement began on January 9 and continued until July 8, 1951, producing late in June the "Petersberg Plan"

[45] The Premier's address at the National Press Club on January 30 is noteworthy for its obvious pro-American tone. Text in *L'Année Politique, 1951*, pp. 613–16.
[46] Richard P. Stebbins, *The United States in World Affairs, 1950* (New York: Harper, 1951), p. 432.

for the recruitment of German units. These months of diplomatic labor, although they did not ensure that there would be German rearmament in any form, were an important prelude to the U.S. shift toward the European army. No less important, for distinguishable but related reasons, was the Paris conference, which began on February 15 and produced an agreed interim report on the European army (together with the supranational paraphernalia which were to accompany it) in late July, 1951. The Petersberg Plan and the report of the Paris conference were no more compatible than the contradictions of the Brussels formula for German rearmament which led to them, but meanwhile American diplomacy was able to clarify its direction so that Washington thereafter could seek to reconcile the two approaches.

The series of meetings at the Petersberg, near Bonn, was to explore on the technical level the possibility of implementing the Brussels decisions. Representatives of the occupying powers' High Commissioners met with German experts, the latter including Theodor Blank, Chancellor Adenauer's adviser on defense matters, and two former Wehrmacht generals, Hans Speidel and Adolf Heusinger.[47] On February 15 at Paris, the European army conference began, with France, Germany, Italy, Belgium, and Luxembourg as full participants, and with observers from Canada, Britain, the United States, Denmark, Norway, Portugal, and the Netherlands.[48] The Bonn and Paris meetings were exploratory in the broadest diplomatic sense, and implied no political commitment to any particular aspect of German rearmament on the part of any of the parties, including the Federal Republic. They occurred at a time when many felt the German rearmament issue had lost its urgency, and was perhaps becoming merely academic.

The reason for the change was Eisenhower's February 1 statement to the effect that the time was not ripe for the appearance of German soldiers. At a stroke, this had the dual effect of taking

[47] Stebbins, *United States, 1950*, p. 435. See also *The Times* (London), February 15, 1951.
[48] Royal Institute of International Affairs, *Britain in Western Europe: WEU and the Atlantic Alliance* (London: Royal Institute of International Affairs, 1956), p. 29. The Netherlands became a full participant in October.

away the sense of American pressure in Europe for German rearmament, and also of damaging the French chance to press for a European army, since the principal *raison d'être* of the Pleven Plan thus disappeared. It can only be speculated upon whether this might have been an appropriate moment for the United States to drop the idea of German rearmament indefinitely. As it was, military requirements—even if they had to await diplomatic explorations and agreements—still dictated that the European balance would rest upon Western ground strength, as the atomic advantage diminished. In the long run, this implied that the Germans would somehow have to be brought into defense arrangements.[49] Even to begin the admittedly lengthy lead time for this, agreement first had to be reached between the occupying powers on the one hand and the Federal Republic on the other.

The foreign ministers of the three occupying powers had agreed at Brussels that German participation in defense would involve the establishment of contractual relationships, or treaties, with the Federal Republic.[50] Since German interest in defense participation was wholly subordinate to the concern with reunification and the recovery of sovereignty and equality, there was not the same emphasis in Bonn as elsewhere that speedy German rearmament was militarily essential. Adenauer tenaciously embraced the Korean analogy and continued to warn his people of a similar act, but was certainly aware that German political interests would be better served if the allies recalled the comparison as well. German policy followed a basically opportunistic approach as the cold war permitted an acceleration of earlier trends toward rehabilitation and convinced many Germans that "if the way back to political sovereignty had to be bought by sharing in Western defense, then this must be done." [51] The advantages of the international

[49] This was implicit, for example, in the conclusion of the second semi-annual report on the Mutual Defense Assistance Program, transmitted by the President to the Congress April 25, 1951. See *Department of State Bulletin*, May 7, 1951, p. 758.

[50] M. E. Bathurst and J. L.. Simpson, *Germany and the North Atlantic Community: A Legal Survey* (New York: Praeger, 1956), p. 114.

[51] Franz-Josef Strauss, *The Grand Design: A European Solution to German Reunification* (New York: Praeger, 1966), p. 94.

situation were supplemented by interallied disagreements, as uncoordinated handling of the rearmament issue enhanced Bonn's position.

The intrinsic contradiction between the attempt to make the Federal Republic an ally while still an enemy was demonstrated as the allies, particularly the United States, made one concession after another *without* believing that the Federal Republic was ready for full international equality. Eisenhower's belief that this had to be earned and could only come in time was shared by the U.S. High Commission. In basic terms, the desire for the utilization of German military potential was unaccompanied, even in Washington, by a willingness to allow immediate political rehabilitation. The representatives of the Federal Republic, led by the Chancellor, appreciated keenly their opportunity to capitalize on the inconsistency of allied policy, and were uninhibited by the fact that what they were promising in return was nonexistent. Adenauer was aware that the United States preferred a German contingent under NATO command to the French plan for a European army with German units, but probably realized that he did not have to choose between them other than as avenues to his political objectives of sovereignty and equality. He was also aware of American hesitation about a too quick restoration of German sovereignty. With only minor refinements, the original Acheson proposal was the one the United States still preferred.

It was revealed several times during the Petersberg negotiations that the Germans had not yet "earned" the equality Eisenhower had referred to as part of the political basis for German rearmament. Assistant High Commissioner Benjamin J. Buttenwieser stated an American viewpoint as follows: "It is obvious that after the diabolic occurrences of Germany's Nazi regime, equality in the society of nations is not a status to be automatically accorded to her. It is a standing which she must win in the forum of nations. . . . This can only be achieved if there has been a real and sincere inner purging of the convictions of the German people themselves. . . ." [52] He noted the recent failure of any official of

[52] *Department of State Bulletin*, March 26, 1951, p. 488.

the Bonn regime to support McCloy's decision not to commute the death sentence of seven Nazi mass-murderers as a sign that conditions were not reassuring. "This ominous silence of key figures," Buttenwieser said, "when they had this opportunity to disavow this black spot on German history, is causing wonder and disappointment abroad, especially in the United States."

There was no doubt that by such criteria Germany had not cleansed itself of past sins, and this American conviction was surely even more strongly felt among the more proximate victims of Nazi aggression.[53] High Commissioner McCloy in a radio broadcast at the end of April said that any revival of German militarism or an independent German army would be carefully guarded against. Indirectly referring to recent concessions to the Federal Republic, he added, "We believe that German participation in an integrated European force is a decision which the German Government and people must make for themselves. We are not attempting to buy or force such participation." [54] The reference to the United States not "buying" Bonn's consent to remilitarization is somewhat curious, since it was assumed that if German rearmament was to be gained at all, it would only be because it had been bought. The Petersberg negotiators were aware that rearmament remained highly unpopular among the Germans themselves.

The other side of the coin of unworthiness to become a trusted partner of the West was Germany's hesitation about doing so. Early in March, the United States suggested officially for the first time since German rearmament had been proposed that Germany itself might refuse rearmament.[55] The preliminary exploration of the question at the Petersberg, conducted on the part of the United States by Major General George P. Hays, Deputy High Commissioner, and Buttenwieser, showed from the outset that

[53] Even the British continued to share European hesitation in transforming yesterday's foe into today's friend, and many felt as the French did that "Germany was still *the* European enemy in a way that was not possible for Americans to comprehend." Leon D. Epstein, *Britain—Uneasy Ally* (Chicago: University of Chicago Press, 1954), p. 247.
[54] *Department of State Bulletin,* May 7, 1951, p. 737, and also June 11, 1951, pp. 941–42.
[55] *Ibid.,* March 26, 1951, p. 487.

the detailed discussions of the many military questions of how, what, and when the Federal Republic could contribute concerning men and supplies were only parts of the larger investigation of the political conditions whereunder Germany might reappear in the Western community on an equal basis. And just as the occupying powers did not, after all, feel Germany *should* be completely rehabilitated, the Germans felt little attachment toward the allies, even though their own wartime role in bringing about their status was not contested. Allied-German relations, independent of the German rearmament issue, were poor, and the infusion of the latter into an already complex political and psychological situation did little to ameliorate this—indeed, it afforded the Germans an opportunity to express accumulated grievances stemming from their status as an occupied country.[56]

One concurrent development was the agreement on a number of specific concessions to the Federal Republic. The earlier expressed readiness of the three occupying powers "to place their relationship with the German Federal Republic to an increasing degree upon a basis of equality" led to a significantly improved status for the Federal Republic in nonmilitary matters.[57] On March 6, 1951, pursuant to the September 19, 1950, communiqué, and after Acheson had pressed the French hard, it was announced that many new steps were about to be taken, as the Occupation Statute and the Charter of the Allied High Commission were revised and amended.[58] Henceforth, the Federal Republic was authorized to establish a ministry of foreign affairs and to enter diplomatic relations with friendly states; various powers which the allies had enjoyed under the Occupation Statute were relinquished or reduced; the Bonn government was to receive increased sovereignty in many internal sectors; legislation was no longer to be subject to prior High Commission approval; and

[56] Brookings Institution, *Major Problems*, p. 213.

[57] Raymond Dennett and Robert K. Turner, eds., *Documents on American Foreign Relations, 1950* (Princeton: Princeton University Press, 1951), p. 511.

[58] As noted in Chap. II, the foreign ministers' communiqué of September 19, 1950, looked merely to an amendment, not a replacement, of the Occupation Statute. See also Dennett and Durant, eds., *Documents, 1951*, pp. 527-32, for the texts of these instruments.

other steps were envisaged which were intended to normalize German-allied relations as much as possible without, however, changing the legal basis for the occupation itself, although provision was made for further revision.[59]

The Federal Republic, in return, agreed to assume responsibility for the prewar debt of the Reich; acknowledged its postwar debt to the occupying powers and gave repayment of this priority; and expressed a desire to repay other German debts including those of the 1938–45 period.[60] At the beginning of April, in the interest of the common defense effort, further concessions were announced concerning the relaxation of economic controls and industrial restrictions on the Federal Republic.[61] The importance of these several steps was that they were part of the indispensable preconditions for a German defense contribution: the trend seemed to be toward the political recovery of the Federal Republic without German rearmament, but there had been no change in basic U.S. policy.

After almost three months of discussions at Bonn on the technical details of German rearmament, which High Commissioner McCloy had been instructed to commence "as a matter of urgency" following the Brussels meeting, the military committee of representatives of the four states was moving toward agreement on the form of a German contribution. These accords, which emerged from highly secret meetings among general officers, emphasized the military approach embodied in the original U.S. proposal for German rearmament, not the political aspects of the Pleven Plan counterproposal. It was somewhat anomalous that the French representatives agreed to detailed plans for German rearmament, but perhaps not surprising if it is recalled that these technical conversations implied no political commitment, and were conducted by high officers of the French army, which had no objection to German rearmament—even national German rearmament

---

[59] *Department of State Bulletin,* March 19, 1951, pp. 443–46. On March 15 the Chancellor himself assumed the duties of foreign minister.

[60] See the summary in *International Organization,* Vol. V, 1951, pp. 412–13.

[61] Stebbins, *United States, 1951,* p. 67, and see *Department of State Bulletin,* April 16, 1951, for the Big Three statement.

—in the first place. In addition, High Commissioner André François-Poncet, who was at the Bonn talks responsible for the French position, was given no discretionary powers by his government and according to one American participant "couldn't change a comma without the approval of the Quai d'Orsay." Finally, even while agreeing to the Petersberg Plan for German rearmament, France permitted no implementation of any agreement: "the French negotiators were adamant in opposing any steps designed to initiate German defense planning or set up a training program for the new German troops." [62] Hence just as the American consent to the French conference to explore the European army idea was given long before the United States accepted EDC, the French tendency to go along with the trend toward technical agreements at the Petersberg may be seen as simply the other side of this diplomatic coin. Neither Paris nor Washington, in this period of rival conferences, had changed position by virtue of giving the public impression of wishing the success of an approach it disfavored.

The "Petersberg Plan," as agreed upon in June, 1951, went beyond even the original American proposal for ten German divisions: it suggested the creation of a German national army of twelve divisions, each with a peace strength of 15,000 and a war strength of 18,000, organized in four army corps consisting of nine infantry and three armored divisions, with a total force of 250,000 men.[63] The basic German military unit was to be the division because the military representatives of the Federal Republic insisted upon this. Apparently the Spofford Plan, which at Brussels was supposed to have formed the basis for the Bonn negotiations, was all but ignored in the Petersberg Plan's formulation. Not only was the Federal Republic being consulted, but its generals had persuaded their counterparts to go along with a German rearmament scheme which exceeded the September, 1950, package-plan demand and bore almost no relation to the

[62] Moore, *NATO,* p. 43. There were, of course, no "new German troops" at the time.

[63] Edinger, *West German Armament,* pp. 17–18; Stebbins, *United States, 1951,* p. 64.

earlier compromise proposal, particularly with reference to the size of the basic German unit. Following these agreements at Bonn, it was reported that General Speidel had submitted a forty-page memorandum on the German position which, in addition to an army of 250,000 (including six corps of two divisions each), called for a "German command," conscription and two years' military training, an independent war ministry under a civilian, a Luftwaffe with 2,000 fighters and bombers, and a small Federal navy for Baltic and North Sea coastal operations.[64]

As described above, the Petersberg Plan obviously did not meet all these German demands, but it represented at least one tack toward the marker of German rearmament. It took on additional meaning once the representatives of the High Commission agreed with the Federal Republic, in May, to begin discussions looking toward final termination of the occupation and the restoration of German sovereignty. The Petersberg Plan for German rearmament, however, was only an agreement on a technical level reached by experts. It remained to be seen whether it could be reconciled with the emerging results of the Paris meetings.

The German rearmament question, said Adrian S. Fisher, legal adviser of the Department of State, pointed up "the granddaddy of all European difficulties," the relationship between France and Germany. If military cooperation could be achieved between these old enemies, "we can do practically anything." [65] The basis for such cooperation for Bonn was equality and for Paris control of Germany: unlike the Petersberg talks, the European army conference was not limited to technical military matters but extended to the political framework essential to a solution to the over all Franco-German relationship.[66] American diplomats were aware that it would be impossible to please everyone fully in such a

[64] *The New York Times,* July 29, 1951. See also Edinger, *West German Armament,* p. 18.

[65] *Department of State Bulletin,* March 5, 1951, p. 377.

[66] See *L'Annee Politique, 1951,* pp. 625–28, for the comments of the French delegation covering the subject matter of the conference and the opening remarks of Foreign Minister Schuman.

situation, but proceeded on the assumption that a mutually acceptable solution was not impossible.

The Paris conference to explore the European army proposal convened in mid-February, and was attended by Ambassador David K. E. Bruce as the officially designated U.S. observer. German rearmament remained "a political and psychological rather than a purely military issue," [67] which may partially explain how one group of French spokesmen at Bonn could agree to one thing while another group in Paris was arguing for something quite different. On the governmental level, France never dropped the European army-cum-political framework approach, with its implicit insistence on the permanent preclusion of a German "national" military force.

When the Paris conference began on February 15, Foreign Minister Schuman stated at once that the plan as outlined by Pleven on October 24, 1950, had not changed, although it was to be regarded as a working paper and not stand in the path of other measures for the defense of the NATO area.[68] Committees were designated to examine the political, military, and financial aspects of the problem of a unified European army. Apart from innumerable details, the uncertainties were political; France asked herself whether *any* solution to the German rearmament problem could be trusted. The answer depended on Bonn, but even more on Washington. It also depended on whether an East-West detente was possible, and in this matter the French were much more optimistic than the United States.

The Big Four deputies meeting, which began in Paris on March 5, tended for the time to overshadow the European army conference. It was still hoped that if an easing of the cold-war confrontation could be begun, then the German rearmament question could be set aside, and with it of course the European army plan.

---

[67] Onslow, "West German Rearmament," p. 481. The German delegation to the Paris conference was "installed in a shabby four-room suite at the Hotel d'Orsay, where entrance to their offices was made through a toilet." Theodore H. White, *Fire in the Ashes: Europe in Mid-Century* (New York: Sloane, 1953), p. 269.

[68] *L'Annee Politique, 1951*, p. 56.

The impression was gained, however, that the Soviet Union, once it seemed that German rearmament was being postponed indefinitely, lost interest in the proposed foreign ministers' meeting, which the United States was never enthusiastic about in the first place.[69] Acheson told Pleven that a change in Russian policy which would make rearmament unnecessary would take "almost divine intervention," but the French government was still convinced that the public would not accept German remilitarization without further proof of Soviet obduracy.[70]

Little progress was made on the German question in March and April; by early May the proximity of the June elections dominated French political life, particularly since the Western allies would have to await the results of the vote before a French government could act with full authority. At the same time, the awareness that the United States was becoming impatient with the slow pace of allied rearmament made the French feel that the period of stagnation of the German rearmament question was ending. When High Commissioner McCloy brought the Petersberg Plan to Washington in June, American expectations were high. On June 26 McCloy announced he was sure that the Federal Republic would participate in defense, which implied that new concessions would be made to Bonn. The Quai d'Orsay issued a reminder that its views had not changed, and contradicted a report by an American news agency that the European army conference was deadlocked.[71] On June 29 Hervé Alphand repeated that there would be no German defense participation except in a European army framework. France also remained firm that there could be no German general staff or membership for the Federal Republic in NATO. As July began, a new French government had not been formed, and indeed was not for the rest of the month.[72]

The rival conferences of the first half of 1951 had reflected the basic interests of the parties. The Petersberg Plan emerged from a background of moves toward a restoration of political equality

[69] *Ibid.*, pp. 83ff., 115.
[70] Acheson, *Present at the Creation*, p. 553.
[71] *L'Annee Politique, 1951*, pp. 119–20, 144, 170–172.
[72] The Queuille caretaker regime resigned on July 10. *Ibid.*, pp. 179ff.

for the Federal Republic in addition to a military establishment which amounted to national rearmament. The Paris meetings proceeded in an atmosphere of mutual doubt about whether anything as complicated as a European army based on European political institutions could succeed, when it was apparent that its real origin was pressure for German rearmament from Washington and its real purpose control of—not equality for—the Federal Republic.

One issue at the Paris conference which illustrated the ambivalence of the situation was that of the size of the basic national unit for the European army. In a sense this was totally irrelevant, pending agreement on the supranational political framework which France insisted must accompany the army plan, but throughout the five months of meetings, haggling over the unit size gave this the impression of being a crucial issue.[73] To trace briefly this example: when the conferees assembled in February, France was said to be thinking in terms of units of about 5,000 to 6,000 men, the maximum size understood at the time of the Spofford Plan. The word "division" was a touchy subject, because of unpleasant connotations when used in reference to German troops, although Pleven himself had used it during his visit with President Truman. The term used in Paris was *groupements de combat*. France insisted on a modified version of the original Pleven proposal, calling for about twenty German *groupements,* integrated into supranational divisions of a European army, with no divisions under a German commander.[74] These units, called combat teams in the English-language press, were to be grouped into divisions on a basis of three in each, with no division to have more than two combat teams of the same nationality. Later, France agreed to consider 8,000 as the basic unit's size, and by June seemed ready to accept national divisions of 10,000 men, which was only 2,000 less than the figure suggested by the Germans in Paris, although still short of the figures being discussed at Bonn.[75] Perhaps the

[73] Again in contrast to the Petersberg meetings, where at German insistence the French readily gave in to the idea of divisions of substantial size.

[74] Edinger, *West German Armament,* p. 18.

[75] It was reported at this time that the German representatives were calling for about a dozen units from the Federal Republic, each of 11–13,000, a total German

whole question of the size of the unit was a case of putting the cart before the horse, but the issue is better understood as a manifestation of French confusion.[76] Even after Schuman, at Acheson's urging, had shown himself "wholly receptive to a militarily workable unit rather than a politically palatable one," it was clear that "France was not of one mind on policy toward Germany." [77] Schuman said from the outset that France would have preferred integration in spheres other than the military as a matter of the timing of Europe's unification, but the pressure of events had brought the Pleven Plan forth and now this was part and parcel of France's policy.[78]

Franco-American disagreement led to the parallel negotiations of the Petersberg and Paris talks, and shortly after General Eisenhower assumed his new duties as SACEUR he was faced with the difficult task of choosing between two radically different proposals for rearming Western Germany. In spite of Secretary Acheson's lukewarm endorsement of the French approach, American policy for the first half of 1951 was *not* clarified prior to Eisenhower's decision to push for European unification, which was the turning point of American policy on the German question.[79]

Until then, the Federal Republic no less than France blocked any chance of a German military contribution. The position of the Bonn government was quite firm on the demand for equal treatment. The Germans, prior to American endorsement of the European army, backed the Petersberg Plan, which they believed

contribution of 150,000, plus hundreds of fighter and light bomber aircraft. *The New York Times*, May 6, 1951. See also Stebbins, *United States, 1951*, pp. 65–66.

[76] *News from France*, March 15, 1951, referred to the December, 1950, acceptance of the Spofford compromise as no more than an agreement in principle by France. On the disagreements over unit size, see also *LeMonde*, February 15, 1951; Calvocoressi, *Survey, 1949–1950*, p. 108; Senate, *Assignment of Ground Forces*, p. 54.

[77] Acheson, *Present at the Creation*, p. 552.

[78] *The Times* (London), February 16, 1951. Interviews indicated that Jean Monnet shared this view.

[79] One comment was that "The United States Government has given its blessing to the conference as an effort at the further integration of Europe within the North Atlantic Treaty Organization, but not yet to the European army as a means of doing this." *The Times* (London), February 14, 1951. Another observer found American policy so muddled as to be "utterly schizophrenic." White, *Fire in the Ashes*, p. 273.

had the support of U.S. military leaders, and were encouraged by American opposition to the European army plan. It was not expected that the Federal Republic would develop much interest in the French plan as long as Washington gave clear indications that its preference for the approach of the Petersberg talks remained.[80] Nor was the unwillingness of such other NATO powers as Norway, Portugal, Denmark, the Netherlands, and especially Britain to join the European army conference as participants conducive to Germany regarding this as a project with a high probability of realization, particularly since the leaders of both British parties agreed that the United Kingdom could not join "an army forming part of a European federation." [81]

The Petersberg conference had produced agreement apart from the political platform which Eisenhower had told the Congress was indispensable to the inclusion of "units of Germans in any kind of army." It was this failure to provide a political basis for the technical agreements that made the Petersberg Plan, in this fundamental way, irrelevant. The Supreme Commander had said that not soldiers, but diplomats and statesmen, would have to find the proper answer to the German rearmament problem. It was only after he saw no other alternative to the approach being explored in Paris, however, that the latter received his genuine endorsement, and shortly thereafter, the endorsement of the U.S. government.

[80] Just the reverse occurred later on: the earlier U.S. focus on the military aspect encouraged Bonn to keep to the Petersberg instead of the Paris approach, but once the American shift in favor of EDC had occurred, this meant a wider integrative sector than simply the military was sought, which in turn gave Bonn even more bargaining power than had been enjoyed as a result of the rearmament question alone. Cf. Hanreider, *West German Foreign Policy*, p. 82.

[81] Sir Anthony Eden (Lord Avon), *Full Circle* (Boston: Houghton Mifflin, 1960), p. 35.

CHAPTER IV

The American Shift
toward EDC

W HEN President Vincent Auriol of France visited Washington in the spring of 1951, he told the U.S. Congress that his country was fully committed to the achievement of the ideal of a European federation, which would end the antagonisms of the past with Germany. France, he said, had put aside her legitimate resentment against her recent enemy. The Federal Republic must, however, bring to this new cause "the proof of its redemption through the repudiation of its old regime and the sincere attachment to the cause of democracy." [1]

This statement, not unlike those being made by spokesmen of the U.S. High Commission, echoed the dictum of General Eisenhower that equality for the Federal Republic would have to be eventually earned, not immediately bestowed. American spokesmen, however, did not specifically link this with the European integration movement prior to mid-1951. United States leaders were aware of the importance of the Franco-German relationship, and were committed to policies which in their view would end the cycle of wars between these traditionally rival states. But they were somewhat insensitive to the psychological and political aspects of

[1] *Department of State Bulletin,* April 9, 1951, p. 565.

such a reconciliation, and tended in their stress on its military aspects to denigrate the French approach.

Washington's reaction to the initialing of the draft of the Schuman Plan treaty on March 19 was instructive: unlike the extremely cordial welcome the original proposal had received almost a year earlier, Secretary Acheson now revealed hesitation about the supranational implications of the European Coal and Steel Community, saying "these revolutionary agreements and institutions deserve the most careful study." [2] It is noteworthy that this was virtually the same language used to "welcome" the Pleven Plan in October, 1950, when U.S. displeasure was hardly concealed at all. Acheson did give the Schuman Plan credit for attempting to solve the critical problem of Franco-German rivalry, but showed little enthusiasm for the aspects of the project which in his view represented "an experiment in new concepts of sovereignty and international organization." Such language indicated American unwillingness to see in the French approach a practical method of strengthening the free world.[3] Acheson had testified in February: "If Germany, instead of being a threat to world peace, is to be a constructive partner in Europe, it is necessary to build a European framework within which her skills and energies can be used for the benefit of all." [4] The European framework, however, was so far not a supranational one.

On July 3, 1951, in London, General Eisenhower made a strong plea for the unification of Europe—a statement which marked the first genuine American shift away from the attempt to achieve national German rearmament and toward the European army. Eisenhower did not specifically mention the European army plan or otherwise endorse a European Defense Community, but he stressed the positive benefits which unity would bring. While vague, this speech was the real beginning of the "mushroom" of American expectations, and contained elements which persisted

[2] *Ibid.*, April 2, 1951, p. 523.

[3] Cf. Dean Acheson, *Sketches from Life of Men I Have Known* (New York: Harper, 1961), p. 43.

[4] Quoted in McGeorge Bundy, ed., *The Pattern of Responsibility* (Boston: Houghton Mifflin, 1952), p. 55.

through the remainder of the Truman administration and into the next.[5]

The achievement of European unity, General Eisenhower said, would bring strength not otherwise available: were the free nations of the old continent "truly a unit" it would then be "difficult to overstate the benefits" this would bring. The difficulties of integration, however, were great—unity was hampered by history, custom, language, prejudice, customs barriers, and other economic obstacles. But maximum political or economic well-being could not be achieved as long as Europe remained divided by "patchwork territorial fences." For adequate security in the military sector, unity was no less essential. If achieved, it would produce "miracles for the common good" for Europeans themselves and permit them to become independent of American and other outside aid.

Because of all these factors, Eisenhower stated, the goal must be "a workable European federation"—and this problem "cannot be attacked successfully by slow infiltration, but only by direct and decisive assault, with all available means." This was the key passage in the general's address, and set the stage for what developed into steadily increasing American enthusiasm for EDC. The goal was, above all, the security of the NATO area: "a solid, healthy Europe would be the greatest possible boon to the functioning and objectives of the Atlantic Pact."[6] The military emphasis in the Eisenhower address was consistent with American policy generally, and in terms of the German problem may be seen as simply another approach toward the same goal: rapid German rearmament.[7] The framework for this could only come from European institutions, which ultimately would only work if supranational, hence the solution to the German rearmament

[5] The text of the Eisenhower address is in *Department of State Bulletin*, July 30, 1951, pp. 163–65. Quotations which follow are from this source.

[6] Eisenhower expressly excluded Britain, stating in effect that the United States and the United Kingdom should play the role of helpful outsiders.

[7] Until this point the United States had *avoided* facing the problem of European unification as a militarily desirable goal. Ben T. Moore, *NATO and the Future of Europe* (New York: Harper, 1958), p. 44. Cf. also Theodore H. White, *Fire in the Ashes: Europe in Mid-Century* (New York: Sloan, 1953), p. 273.

problem must be "a workable European federation." The enthusiastic but naïve plea that it must be achieved at once, with all available means employed for a direct and decisive assault, was typical of Eisenhower.

This concept of European unification achieved at one great stroke seems to have emerged after a sudden decision. Late in June, the general told his surprised luncheon companions at a Saint-Germain golf club that in his forthcoming speech in London he was going to press for European unity with maximum speed. "After all," he said, "when a person goes to a hospital for surgery the doctor doesn't operate 10 per cent each time. We should set a goal for unification within six months or a year and work hard for that immediately." It was later reported that the shift in Eisenhower's opinion of a European army away from seeing it as impractical and unworkable and toward approval of what became EDC was the result of an all-day meeting with Jean Monnet, which had been arranged by High Commissioner McCloy.[8]

The omission in the London address of any mention of EDC or a European army did not mean that Eisenhower considered European unification apart from the military arrangements.[9] A supranational European arrangement had been considered economically desirable by the United States for some time, but now it was also militarily indispensable. This was the basis for his new policy, even though "the most significant element in this decision went unmentioned . . . the hard fact that there was no other way to get a German contribution to defense save by supporting the French proposal for a European army." [10]

Eisenhower realized that "France had to be convinced that if Germany were rearmed she would never again use her power to

[8] C. L. Sulzberger, *The New York Times*, March 31, 1967; Joseph and Stewart Alsop, *Herald Tribune*, December 29, 1952. See also C. L. Sulzberger, *A Long Row of Candles: Memoirs and Diaries (1934–1954)* (New York: Macmillan, 1969), pp. 647–48.

[9] It was assumed at the time that the general meant the European army. Richard P. Stebbins, *The United States in World Affairs, 1951* (New York: Harper, 1952), p. 346.

[10] Lewis J. Edinger, *West German Armament*, Air University, Maxwell Air Force Base, Alabama, October, 1955, p. 19; Moore, *NATO*, p. 44; interviews.

turn on her Western neighbors." [11] He knew also that the Federal Republic would not accept "this legitimate objective" by any means which "would impose humiliating restrictions on a sovereign—even though lately defeated—nation." The device, the general became convinced, which could meet these dual objectives was the EDC. German rearmament was, because of French feelings especially, primarily a European political problem which had to be solved before the military question of where to get more manpower could be dealt with. The pressure for German rearmament which Eisenhower had eased with his address to Congress on February 1 was henceforth replaced by pressure for European unification.

American representatives in Germany agreed. High Commissioner McCloy, after some hesitation, accepted the Pleven Plan as a sincere attempt to deal with the delicate problems implicit in the reversal of allied policy of German disarmament.[12] He said on his return to Europe in July that the Petersberg Plan should be integrated with the European army proposals. McCloy perceived the German problem as an extremely complex part of a situation wherein the organization of Western Europe could only be achieved if Germany was included, but felt that the manner in which this was done must be such that when the United States sooner or later reduced its involvement, the other states should not again be faced with an "uncontrolled" German army. "The case of German rearmament leading to the European Defense Community," McCloy wrote, "is an illustration of a problem on which policy had to be evolved in such a manner as to take into account many limiting factors." [13]

---

[11] Dwight D. Eisenhower, *The White House Years: Mandate for Change, 1953–1956* (Garden City: Doubleday, 1963), p. 398, from which quotations are taken.

[12] See Laurence W. Martin, "The American Decision to Rearm Germany," in *American Civil-Military Decisions,* ed. Harold Stein (Birmingham: University of Alabama Press, 1963), p. 654, for an outline of earlier considerations within Hicom.

[13] John J. McCloy, *The Challenge to American Foreign Policy* (Cambridge: Harvard University Press, 1953), pp. 32–33. See also *The New York Times,* July 5, 1951; and cf. C. G. D. Onslow, "West German Rearmament," *World Politics,* III (July, 1951), p. 454.

This suggests that there could have been no "simple" solution to the German problem, that German rearmament grew into the mushroom of the EDC because of the very nature of the question, which in the long run involved the nature of the European balance. In this sense, McCloy's approach was comparable to the French—although he did not share their emotional resistance to the rehabilitation of the Federal Republic. The High Commissioner, said a U.S. official who worked closely with him, "had no special love for Germany" in the sense of attempting to assure unfairly advantageous terms for Bonn. His transcendent objective was to contribute to European stability by the building of a Franco-German relationship that would definitely "end the bloodbath" between these states.

The almost simultaneous U.S. endorsement of the "European" instead of the "Atlantic" approach to German rearmament was articulated in Paris by Eisenhower and in Bonn by McCloy more noticeably than it was in Washington by Truman, Acheson, or Marshall.[14] As with the original German rearmament decision and its presentation, President Truman does not seem to have had much to do with the shift in favor of EDC. He tended in such matters to listen to the advice of his closest consultants, who, pertaining to Germany, were Acheson and McCloy. One significant step the President took at this time was to request that the state of war with Germany be ended.[15] This was envisaged by the September, 1950, statement of the occupying powers, but that it came

[14] Moore, *NATO*, p. 44, noted that it was the American leadership in Europe which took the initiative in supporting a new approach to unification, and that Washington's support for the European army project was in response to their urging. It can only be speculated upon whether the United States would have shifted in favor of the European army, and in turn whether the EDC mushroom would have sprouted, if Truman and Acheson had not been prompted by Eisenhower and McCloy. As far as the immediate situation was concerned, it was Eisenhower who counted most in the decision to support European unification and—it was assumed—the European army. "Once his decision was made," Drew Middleton reported from Germany, "the issue was never in doubt." *The New York Times*, August 2, 1951. See also Edinger, *West German Armament*, p. 20.

[15] Britain and France did the same. See *Department of State Bulletin*, July 16, 1951, pp. 90–92.

at exactly the same moment as the shift in favor of the European army—which Bonn had little interest in so far—is noteworthy. Rights under the occupation were to be retained, with full sovereignty to be "eventually" restored.

The Secretary of State was hesitant about projected supranational institutions when he did not feel there was a logical and clear scheme which as a whole would amount to sovereignty, a feeling he experienced concerning the French approach to Europe.[16] Unlike Eisenhower and McCloy, Acheson made no direct statement enthusiastically endorsing the unification of Europe or the European army plan. The security emphasis remained, and when the secretary did mention European unity it was almost invariably in a context of its military benefits.[17] In an address which stressed warnings that the Western rearmament effort should not be distracted by any "Russian lullaby," Acheson said the United States was deeply concerned with the success of the Paris conference. He compared the European army with the Schuman Plan and said they were "of a piece"—similar steps toward greater unity and greater strength for Europe. He did not, though, affirm either the Eisenhower plea for a direct attempt to achieve a federation, or the McCloy warning of the need for a European organization to check a rearmed Germany's possible future unilateral action. European political integration for its own sake seems to have occupied a minor place in the secretary's mind, above all because he doubted it could work. Yet he decided that the European army approach should be backed by the efforts of American diplomacy.

Writing many years later, Acheson said that during the summer of 1951 he concluded that American support of EDC would be "the best way to an adequate German contribution to defense" based on two ideas which he developed.[18] First, the Paris negotiations were so complex and difficult to understand that the very obscurity of Schuman's incursions upon sovereignty might allow

---

[16] Acheson, *Sketches from Life*, pp. 43–44.

[17] See, for example, *Department of State Bulletin*, August 6, 1951, p. 211.

[18] Acheson, *Present at the Creation*, pp. 557–58, upon which this paragraph is based.

the European army plan to be adopted, much like the U.S. Constitution had been adopted under "the delusion of innocuousness created by its simplicity," only in reverse. Second, the secretary's doubts that the European army was militarily sensible were dispelled after studying the Eisenhower charts of the integrated NATO command, which showed how this army would be related to the Central European command under a European commander who in turn would be under the supreme authority of the SACEUR. This setup would allow what had been sought all along: German divisions but no German defense department or general staff. Acheson put these thoughts in a memorandum which became the basis for a mid-July meeting of State and Defense representatives, who reached unanimous agreement that the European army should be supported with emphasis on the military rather than the political, to seek progress on (in Acheson's words) "the interconnected problems of bringing Germany into European defense, ending the occupation of Germany, and moving into a constructive phase of the integration of Western Europe, all of which were now stalemated." The President approved the State-Defense paper on July 30, and U.S. policy was officially committed to the European army plan. The persuasiveness of Acheson's arguments will be mentioned, but there must have been some doubts in Washington all along, since the United States was henceforth to "go all out" for the European army as Acheson "deduced it to be, without stirring up trouble by asking for clarifications from Paris."

A State Department official, at about the same time Acheson was working out these ideas, said "the United States Government has constantly supported all practicable approaches to the achievement of closer European integration and will continue to do so. At the same time, it would be a mistake to believe that this problem can be easily solved or that European unity, even if achieved, would be a panacea for all ills." [19] The awareness that even if European unity could be achieved it would *not* be "a panacea for all ills"

[19] Director for International Security Affairs Thomas D. Cabot, *Department of State Bulletin*, August 13, 1951, pp. 272–76.

later disappeared as the EDC path to German rearmament mush-roomed into the one-shot solution to major problems on both sides of the Atlantic. What is not clear is why the United States, in July, 1951, should have looked to the European army scheme as "practicable" when the Pleven Plan had been dismissed as the reverse. Here again, it would seem—similar to the original American demand for German rearmament—that what the United States desired was to be sought by what was considered the only available means *apart* from its practicability.[20] It was the U.S. shift that cleared the way for the interim agreements reached at the Paris conference, which in turn made it possible for the European states involved to proceed with what became the EDC project.

INTERIM AGREEMENT AT PARIS

A year after the Korean attack had convinced U.S. military plan-ners that a German contribution was needed immediately, the basic disagreement between the French and German positions seemed without prospect for compromise. This was abruptly changed at the beginning of July, when the U.S. High Commis-sion made it clear "that technical desiderata in regard to German rearmament must be subordinated to the essentially political con-cept of a European army." In the Franco-German relationship, "technical desiderata" were of the greatest political significance, because the equality implicit in the Federal Republic's demands for an autonomous force under a German defense minister, and with a German high command, was exactly what the French would not accept.[21] At McCloy's suggestion, the Bonn government sent two special representatives to Paris to accelerate progress on the

[20] This tendency reappeared with the Multilateral Force (MLF) project of the early 1960's.

[21] Stebbins, *United States, 1951*, p. 346. It was reported that even the United States considered what the Germans were asking rather extravagant, although this was denied in Bonn. *The New York Times*, July 10 and 20, 1951.

European army plan, now that the Petersberg and Paris talks were considered parallel rather than rival conferences.[22]

In an address on July 16, McCloy stressed to a German audience the American concern with European economic strength and social stability as well as military security. He said "there is a widespread conviction in the United States that Europe cannot long play a decisive role as a mere series of independent states," and expressed his government's interests in both a European defense structure and a European federation. There persisted the fear, however, that the Federal Republic might "go off on a military venture of her own"—and for this reason, as well as to restore the East-West military balance, the inclusion of Western Germany in a larger European organization was essential.[23] This fear had finally led the United States to the same general conclusion France reached immediately upon presentation of the German rearmament demand. "Can the Germans be trusted with any arms at all?" he asked. The High Commissioner, rejecting criticisms that the U.S. attempt for German rearmament was "a shortsighted policy of expediency," assured his listeners that sufficient progress toward democracy already had been made "to warrant confidence in Western Germany as a partner in the defense of the West." There need be no fear the militarism of the past would recur, because allied policy would not allow a German general staff, a military caste, or a German national army. "The fundamental principle of all proposals made to date," McCloy said, was that "whatever German contribution to defense is made may only take the form of a force which is an integral part of a larger international organization."[24]

[22] *Christian Science Monitor*, July 16, 1951; *Herald Tribune*, July 9, 1951.

[23] *Department of State Bulletin*, August 13, 1951, pp. 252–54. Ambassador Bruce later testified to the same effect about EDC: "Now, the theory behind all of this was to make it impossible for any nationals, even if they wanted to do so, to embark on what you might call a national adventure of a military sort." U.S. Congress, Senate, *Hearings on Executives Q and R, A Convention on Relations with the Federal Republic and a Protocol to the North Atlantic Treaty and Related Documents*, 82nd Cong., 2nd Sess., 1952, p. 55.

[24] *Department of State Bulletin*, July 9, 1951, pp. 63–67.

This probably meant that had the Petersberg Plan, worked out under High Commission auspices, been retained, the German force would have been under SACEUR command and part of the integrated NATO force. But France, with reason, never considered the alliance an international organization which would meet the criterion of integration to a point where withdrawal would be difficult, if not impossible. Acheson himself later wrote that even under EDC "the power—and very possibly the right—to secede remains in the various states." [25] If EDC was questionable as an international organization composed of genuinely integral parts, NATO was obviously far short of this. Not until McCloy endorsed the European army as the institutional device to contain the Federal Republic could the French give credence to the U.S. pledge to prevent a new German danger. The immediate obstacles to interim agreement at Paris were removed by the endorsements of McCloy and Eisenhower, which gave a strong impetus to the negotiations. Thereafter it was clear that definite decisions would not be taken until the European army conference reported.

The participants in the Paris talks, deadlocked since early July, reached agreement on July 21. During the few weeks before this, accord was blocked mostly by the refusal of the Bonn representatives to accept repeated variations by the French which meant an unequal position for the Federal Republic. France, for example, took the position German officers could not play the same role as others in the European army, on the ground that their training and experience did not qualify them for its strictly defensive nature—that is, the Germans, whose experience was limited to aggressive military action, would have a minor role pending their adoption of defensive habits. This French behavior in turn reflected the unwillingness of Paris to accept even the European army approach to German rearmament unless it could control its composition and character. The French continued to fear equality in theory because they regarded it as a certain step toward German superiority in practice.[26]

[25] Acheson, *Sketches from Life*, p. 44.
[26] French apprehension involved the speed with which European army units

The Franco-German divergence was the object of a great deal of American diplomatic activity, with Eisenhower in Paris and McCloy in Bonn repeatedly saying that the European army framework could and should be adjusted in such a way as to satisfy both French demands for security against a new German danger and German demands for a role equal to others. This dilemma was partially solved by the element of timing: the Supreme Commander, by enthusiastically embracing European political unification, led Paris to the conclusion that there would be a period of delay while the institutional arrangements were worked out and then implemented, and also that once this had occurred there would be no more "Germany" but instead a Europe composed of integral parts. At the same time, the High Commissioner resolved the difficulties with Bonn by assuring the Germans that they would enjoy eventual equality, even if the Federal Republic at first accepted a somewhat constricted place in the European army.[27]

With the two principal antagonists at least partially satisfied after a mixture of American promises and pressure, the other three participating states created no difficulties. The Netherlands, which was expected to join the Paris conference as a participant in the near future, was still too doubtful that the project would be anything but a waste of time to change its status as an observer only.[28] On July 24, the five participants transmitted to their governments the "Alphand report" which, like the Spofford Plan and the Brussels compromise before it, was—insofar as it provided for German rearmament—an optimistic formula with only a tentative basis in political reality. The interim agreement recommended "that

would be created once agreed upon: even if all the members should begin at the same time, it was feared the Federal Republic would be the first to reach the military limit and then use its relatively superior position for greater advantages. *Christian Science Monitor*, July 25, 1951. French pessimism hence coincided with earlier American optimism in its refusal to accept the fact that the Germans themselves were *not* in any rush to rearm. Cf. *The Economist*, July 28, 1951, and *The New York Times*, July 22, 1951.

[27] *Christian Science Monitor*, July 12 and 16, 1951; *The New York Times*, July 22, 1951.

[28] Dirk U. Stikker, *Men of Responsibility: A Memoir* (New York: Harper and Row, 1966), p. 301.

the countries participating pool their military forces and resources under a European defense commissioner responsible to a supranational cabinet and parliament. The German Federal Republic was to have full equality with the other members; details remained to be worked out." [29]

The agreement covered both organizational principles and military targets. A European Defense Community would be established by a fifty-year treaty which would provide for the whole range of supranational institutions, such as a European executive authority, ministerial council, parliamentary assembly, and court of justice, to be supplied and financed through a single common system and fund. On the military side, twenty divisions comprising between 600,000 and 700,000 men, and a supporting tactical air force to be created by early 1953 and placed directly under SHAPE command, were envisaged. Among the details which had not been agreed to were the military questions of the size of the individual combat units or the level at which integration would occur. Nor had such problems as the makeup of the proposed European parliamentary assembly or the method of apportioning the financial contributions of the participating nations even been considered. These matters were of essential political significance, and would have been extremely delicate even if the states involved had trusted each other or desired German rearmament, neither of which condition obtained.

The reaction of the U.S. Department of State to the interim report emphasized its military rather than political aspects, proclaiming it "one of the most constructive steps taken in the common effort to build the defensive strength of the West." [30] French officials stressed the reverse, greeting the proposed institutions as a great step toward European federation.[31] The aspect of the agreement whereby the supranational European authority, which would control the European army, would have its armed force under an American officer, responsible to *no* European authority, was

[29] Edinger, *West German Armament*, p. 20.

[30] *The New York Times*, July 26, 1951.

[31] Statement of Hervé Alphand, Ambassade de France, Service de Presse et d'Information, August, 1951.

either unheeded or ignored. Most comment at the time tended to separate "military" and "political" aspects of the European army plan, but there was a general awareness that the complexity of the scheme was such that it might not work at all, and at best a long delay would ensue.[32]

By shifting in its favor at this time, the United States prepared the ground for German rearmament in the long run by permitting the European army approach to be tried.[33] Far-reaching institutional projects looking toward a supranational Europe could, however, not be explored without agreement on the details which gave them substance: American impatience, German ambitions, and French fears had not yet found a common denominator.

THE EUROPEAN ARMY QUESTION IN MID-1951

The French, throughout the EDC period, were quite aware that American interest in European unification was inseparable from Washington's preoccupation with military strength. Paris nonetheless was gratified that the European, rather than the Atlantic, approach had been given preference—even though the European army project as preliminarily agreed to in mid-1951 had already lost much of its resemblance to the original Pleven Plan.[34] Recent "provocative" statements by the Federal Chancellor made the French more sure than before that the only solution to the German problem was European political unity. France, moreover,

[32] Acheson said that by the summer of 1951 the Paris negotiations had become so complex only Ambassador Bruce and an aide understood them, and neither of them could explain the scheme to the others. Acheson, *Present at the Creation*, p. 557.

[33] American officials were aware that at the time no other approach was available anyway. Cf. William T. R. Fox and Annette B. Fox, *NATO and the Range of American Choice* (New York: Columbia University Press, 1967), p. 26.

[34] There was, in fact, no Paris government at the time of the July accords— which perhaps was what allowed the civil servants, headed by Monnet and Alphand, to make the switch in favor of the much larger unit size and hence a radical revision of the original Pleven Plan. Cf. White, *Fire in the Ashes*, p. 275, who said that in addition to U.S. pushing for the accords in the first place it was Americans who actually worked out the details once the switch occurred, Eisenhower's staff handling the military questions and Bruce's the political.

until this time had been asked to accept the U.S. view that the Petersberg Plan for a German force, under the command of Eisenhower and without its own general staff, had adequate safeguards, when the Germans themselves were rejecting it as discriminatory.[35]

Having already consented to German troops in some form, Paris could hardly turn the political clock back to the time when France might legally have flatly vetoed any German rearmament at all: implicit in the idea of rival solutions to the German problem being worked out in Bonn and Paris was that one of them would be selected. A merger or integration of the two plans would be impossible if it meant a too-great watering down of the institutional aspects of the European approach to make it closer to the Atlantic one. One reason to select the European army plan was American support for it. Ambassador Bruce, consistent with the Eisenhower emphasis on a rapid assault on the question of a European federation, pushed diplomatically for the preparation of a draft treaty as soon as possible. When Pleven was able to form a government on August 10, the outlook in Paris for the forthcoming conferences of the Big Three at Washington and the North Atlantic Council at Ottawa was uncertain.[36] Even though the European army seemed to be evolving further away from the Pleven Plan, it was still to be preferred to what had been worked out at the Petersberg.

The worried French were somewhat reassured in August, first by indications that Britain would participate more closely even though remaining outside the European army, and second, by continued American support for EDC from General Eisenhower and statements by U.S. leaders that German participation in Western defense did not mean there would be either a new German national army or general staff. Paris knew, however, that if Amer-

[35] Edgar S. Furniss, Jr., *France, Troubled Ally: DeGaulle's Heritage and Prospects* (New York: Praeger, 1960), p. 68. In July, Adenauer told the Bundestag that the Federal Republic would soon see the Saar question settled on German terms, a direct slap in the French face even if partially justified by the intransigent position Paris maintained. *The New York Times*, July 22, 1951.

[36] The new minister of defense was Georges Bidault; Schuman remained at the foreign ministry.

ican support was to continue there would have to be concrete progress toward a European army, particularly since the process of restoring sovereignty to the Federal Republic seemed to be going on apart from EDC.

Foreign Minister Schuman told the National Assembly on August 30, the eve of his departure for Washington to discuss the German question, that there had been no change in the determination of France to prevent the creation of a German army under the control of a German government. A genuinely integrated European army, which France demanded, could only *follow* approval by the respective parliaments of the states involved, that is, further delay was certain. In any case, Schuman noted, the European army could not be taken up by the NATO Council at Ottawa "for the good reason that the solution is not ripe." [37] If the United States had opted for the European army approach as the only way to obtain a German military contribution, and France had maintained it as the only way to control renewed German power, why did the Federal Republic go along when it promised to grant neither military nor political equality?

While Adenauer shared Schuman's desire to make war between France and Germany impossible once and for all, and while he thought the future European balance would require a Western European army to face the Russians, since "the time would certainly come when America would withdraw from Europe," the Chancellor's immediate objective was still to regain sovereignty. The optimal means in mid-1951 seemed to be institutional arrangements designed to merge sovereignties rather than restore or preserve them. For the Federal Republic, a pro-European policy was not so much a manifestation of idealism or altruism as "the only escape hatch we had, the only approach that made a comeback possible," as Strauss wrote.[38] The turning point for Bonn was the American shift: the endorsement of European unification

---

[37] *L'Annee Politique, 1951,* pp. 213–14, and for the text of Schuman's address, pp. 647–50.

[38] Konrad Adenauer, *Memoirs, 1949–1953* (Chicago: Regnery, 1966), pp. 407, 356; Franz-Josef Strauss, *The Grand Design: A European Solution to German Unification* (New York: Praeger, 1966), p. 104.

by Eisenhower, and of the European army by McCloy, led at once to a new interest in the success of the Paris conference. It was, however, not without U.S. "prodding, pushing and a lot of 'or else' " that the Germans accepted the European army rather than the Petersberg Plan—especially since the United States had for some time encouraged them to insist on the latter. High Commissioner McCloy was still saying that the analogy between Korea and Germany continued valid, "both geographically and politically," but it was not for security reasons that the Federal Republic reconsidered its position.[39] Above all, it was because the United States had made it clear that no German military contribution was expected in the absence of a restoration of German sovereignty, and if the United States was now to give its full support to the European army, then Bonn could be confident that whatever was worked out would be advantageous.

For example, while the European army-EDC plan did not admit the Federal Republic to NATO, Adenauer had no doubt that membership would follow as soon as the German defense contribution had begun to take concrete form. The European approach also happened to coincide with Adenauer's deep aversion to militarism in its historic form in Germany, and represented no particular setback to reunification, which the Chancellor downgraded in any case. Furthermore, the necessarily time-consuming European army scheme was not as risky in the security sense as it had seemed in 1950, since the feeling in Europe in mid-1951 was that the danger of war had sharply receded.[40] Finally, the Federal Republic had nothing to lose: membership in a scheme for European military integration for a German state both richer and more populous than any other participant held out the possibility

[39] *Department of State Bulletin,* July 9, 1951, p. 64. He repeated the analogy several weeks later. *Ibid.,* September 10, 1951, p. 412. See also *Christian Science Monitor,* July 12, 1951 (Volney D. Hurd); Hans Speier, *German Rearmament and Atomic War: The Views of German Military and Political Leaders* (Evanston: Row, Peterson, 1957), p. 9, and cf. Edinger, *West German Armament,* pp. 18–19.

[40] General Eisenhower was having difficulty setting up NATO defense forces because of the "considerable relaxation of the near panic of the year before." Walter Millis, Harvey C. Mansfield, and Harold Stein, *Arms and the State* (New York: Twentieth Century Fund, 1958), p. 352.

of not only equality but leadership, and in the interim concessions would be forthcoming at once: "[Adenauer] was prepared to sacrifice *potential* sovereign rights in return for the surrender of *actual* sovereign powers by other nations participating in the creation of a European defense community." [41] It was at this point that the policies and hopes of Bonn, Paris, and Washington began to coincide, with each looking to the European army as a means to further its interests, and perhaps the interests of the larger European or Atlantic community as well.

U.S. DIPLOMACY AND EUROPEAN UNIFICATION

While European unity had been repeatedly mentioned as one of the major concerns of U.S. policy since World War II, particularly as a matter of economic cooperation and recovery, General Eisenhower was the first prominent American spokesman to endorse the political federation of Europe as a goal to be achieved rapidly and by means of direct action.[42] His remarks in London foreshadowed the later tone of American diplomacy, and began the process whereby German rearmament as a practical and limited objective was inflated into the balloon of European unification, with the latter now sought by the same method the former had been—with emphasis on speedy, positive results. While the Pleven Plan had earlier been dismissed as a bar to, rather than a method of, German rearmament, once it came to be seen as the *only* way to obtain a German defense contribution the theretofore unnoticed virtues of the French approach were rapidly discovered.

The essential tie between the union of Europe and U.S. foreign

[41] Karl W. Deutsch and Lewis J. Edinger, "Foreign Policy of the German Federal Republic," in *Foreign Policy in World Politics,* ed. Roy C. Macridis (2nd ed.; New York: Prentice-Hall, 1962), p. 119.

[42] Eisenhower's role as Supreme Commander of NATO was as important politically as militarily, and much broader than that of a commanding officer in the traditional sense. It is appropriate to consider his statements as an integral part of American diplomacy. Cf. U.S. Senate, Hearings, *Assignment of Ground Forces of the United States to Duty in the European Area,* 82nd Cong., 1st Sess., 1951, pp. 9–10.

policy, under both Truman and Eisenhower, was the rearmament of the Federal Republic within the EDC. This central fact was partially obscured by the eloquence of American diplomacy's efforts to unify Europe in the next years, but again became obvious in the post-EDC tone of U.S. policy, when interest in European unification declined as soon as the German issue had been solved in the NATO framework. Washington's language did not clarify whether German rearmament was the way to achieve European unification, or vice versa.[43]

European unification promised to benefit the old and new worlds economically, militarily, and politically, the argument ran.[44] Not only would all these sectors enjoy rewards, but they were now proclaimed interdependent. Real military strength in Europe required both political unity and economic well-being. And in turn, successful political unification depended upon the achievement of security through military and economic self-sufficiency, as economic rehabilitation would, in the long run, remain viable only if accompanied by the strength of the permanent political and military institutions which were now envisaged as integral parts of the European army plan. The projected European army under NATO command would also satisfy rival American approaches to Europe: the "Europeans" would be satisfied both because of the strength which integration would bring to Europe for its own sake, and because this would permit the United States to reduce its burden of aid and support. The "Atlanticists" would at the same time be pleased that the new European army would be placed under the orders of an American Supreme Commander, which would insure that the United States would remain closely

[43] See, for example, the statement of Ambassador-at-Large Philip C. Jessup, *Department of State Bulletin,* August 6, 1951, pp. 220–25. See also F. S. C. Northrop, *European Union and United States Foreign Policy* (New York: Macmillan, 1954), p. 13.

[44] The following generalized resumé of American views on the benefits of European unification is drawn from a number of sources, including Stebbins, *United States, 1951,* pp. 214–16, 346; Martin in Stein, *Decisions,* p. 654; Robert R. Bowie, *Shaping the Future: Foreign Policy in an Age of Transition* (New York: Columbia University Press, 1964), pp. 13ff. See especially Theodore Geiger and H. van B. Cleveland, *Making Western Europe Defensible,* Planning Pamphlet No. 74 (Washington, D.C.: National Planning Association, August, 1951).

tied to Europe and would avoid having Germany emerge stronger than her neighbors.

Not only would the addition of a German contribution deter Soviet forces, but also EDC would eliminate the possibility of future wars among the West European states themselves—both of which would contribute enormously to American security. Economically, a united Europe would be a viable unit which would at once be strong enough to finance its own rearmament effort and dispense with outside assistance, as well as to achieve a level of prosperity and living standard which would destroy the social appeal of Communism. And politically, a united Europe would not only be an additional force for peace-through-strength in its own right, but also would be a "partner" for the United States which would facilitate Atlantic cooperation, enabling Washington to work with its allies as a group rather than dealing with each separately.[45] Finally, the German problem would be definitively solved by the merger of the Federal Republic into a larger entity.

Secretary Acheson's account of the U.S. shift does not suggest that the sudden American commitment to the political federation of Europe was the result of a policy decision based on careful study and perceived as an option which was relevant as well as desirable. Rather it was more a case of a particular policy objective (German rearmament) and a general policy goal (European unification) coming together in what was a policy means (EDC). Given the long-frustrated U.S. commitment to German rearmament and the endorsement of European unification by Eisenhower, it is not surprising that the European army project's support became official U.S. policy. What remains curious is the process whereby EDC's realization was elevated to a point in the American imagination which sometimes prompted intimations of catastrophe should it fail.[46] In any case, American diplomacy became wedded

---

[45] Moore, *NATO*, pp. 44–45. This assumption persisted, although it was not explained why one strong political unit would really be easier to deal with than a number of weak ones.

[46] Even McCloy shared this; he wrote, shortly after he resigned as High Commissioner, "If the European Defense Community does not stand, the effect will be alarming and perhaps disastrous." McCloy, *Challenge*, p. 32.

to the European army approach until the rejection of EDC just three years later by the French parliament.

In contrast to the stops and starts of the preceding period, U.S. policy was extremely constant once the basic commitment had been made. No alternative was prepared by either Acheson or Dulles, and no great heed was paid to whether the Europeans themselves wanted political federation or a common army other than as means toward strictly national—in contrast to "European" —policy goals. Schuman had told the opening session of the Paris conference: "It is not enough to place the insignia 'Europe' on the sleeves of our soldiers and their officers . . . a European spirit is necessary. . . . Without this, our undertaking will be vain and artificial." [47] It remained to be seen whether such a spirit could be drawn upon and whether the cloak of German rearmament could be hung upon the peg of European unification, however harmless German soldiers might seem wearing the escutcheon of the European army.

Once European unification became official U.S. policy, the task of American diplomacy was to induce the Europeans concerned to move forward toward the realization of the EDC. The first step was to create the conditions which would make it possible, legally no less than politically, to include the Federal Republic in the new setup, since otherwise EDC would lose its *raison d'être,* the containment of a rearmed Germany. Industrial controls were further relaxed on August 30 and the state of war was terminated by the Western occupying powers.[48] But if the basic contradiction between attempting to make Germany a military ally while retaining controls over the Federal Republic was to be sufficiently even if

[47] *L'Annee Politique, 1951,* p. 628.
[48] Britain and France did this on July 9, at which time President Truman requested the Congress to do the same; the United States completed the process on October 19, 1951, when the joint resolution was approved. The Truman letter is in *Public Papers of the Presidents of the United States. Harry S Truman, 1951* (Washington: Government Printing Office, 1965), pp. 378–81, and the resolution in Raymond Dennett and Katherine D. Durant, eds., *Documents on American Foreign Relations, 1951,* Vol. XIII (Princeton: Princeton University Press, 1953), p. 512.

not completely resolved, the Occupation Statute had to be replaced by a contractual agreement which more closely resembled a treaty between equally sovereign states. This, in turn, involved not only agreement between the occupying powers and Germany but among the allies themselves on a number of matters. Only thereafter could the states interested in participating in a European Defense Community contemplate the preparation of a draft treaty.

The next months were spent in multifaceted attempts to lay the groundwork in the political, legal, economic, and military sectors which would make possible an agreement on a European army and its institutional structure. In terms of the interests of the United States in European security based on the reconciliation of Germany and its neighbors, important progress was made toward the rehabilitation, if not the remilitarization, of the Federal Republic.

Not only had the likelihood of general war in the immediate future appeared to decline in the summer of 1951, and developments in atomic weaponry put a new face on war, but economic constraints in Europe were such that Britain and France could justifiably come to the United States with a tale of woe. This was so persuasive that Acheson was convinced "it made no sense to destroy them in the name of defending them." The foreign ministers of the occupying powers convened in Washington on September 10 to consider especially the German question, by which date, Acheson said, "it was pretty plain that the specifications of the soldiers for European defense were too grandiose." [49] This did not mean that NATO's planners had abandoned their view that a force approaching 100 divisions would be necessary to withstand a Soviet invasion—rather, by this time, it was already obvious that "only the fear of imminent invasion" could motivate

[49] Acheson, *Present at the Creation*, pp. 559–60. Acheson was joined by Herbert Morrison and Robert Schuman, Morrison having succeeded Bevin at the foreign office. Acheson considered him "a friend of many qualities and abilities, but none fitting him to deal with foreign affairs or foreigners." *Sketches from Life*, p. 45.

a massive, conventional military effort.[50] Nor had there been a change in Washington's belief that a proper division of labor required the European allies to provide the bulk of the troops while the United States furnished the air-atomic power. But since the allies themselves were not adequately doing this, the United States continued to see German rearmament as indispensable. This was the more urgent since for the allies the economic picture was determinative: "Not only was it impossible for them to do more, but they could not long continue the present rate of rearmament." [51]

The Franco-German relationship was more malleable now that it was realized both that the Federal Republic's cooperation had to be bought by political concessions and that European rearmament could not go forward without the consent of France.[52] If France had to accept American insistence on a German military contribution because she herself was unable to provide the troops to defend Western Europe, the United States seemed to have no choice about the French conception of how a German contribution must be handled.[53] It was with these elements in mind that the three foreign ministers, at Washington, considered allied policy toward Germany and agreed on negotiations with the Federal Republic, the effect of which would be to transform their relationship completely.

Since it had for some time been realized that willing German participation in Western security matters could not be expected

[50] Robert E. Osgood, *NATO: The Entangling Alliance* (Chicago: University of Chicago Press, 1962), pp. 80–81.

[51] Acheson, *Present at the Creation*, p. 560.

[52] Part of the reason for the American shift from the Petersberg to the Paris approach may also have been because the Germans demanded too much, and used bargaining tactics which some thought amounted to "blackmail." Cf. *The Economist*, July 28, 1951, p. 195.

[53] "France's geographical position made her cooperation absolutely necessary. If Europe could not be defended well without German power, it could not be defended at all without France. France was NATO's strategic rear; without its harbors, arms and munitions depots, and supply lines, NATO was defenseless. France's determination to create a European army was therefore decisive." John W. Spanier, *American Foreign Policy Since World War II* (2nd rev. ed., New York: Praeger, 1965), p. 67.

as long as Germany was officially occupied, the Allied High Commission had looked to first revision and then replacement of the Occupation Statute. German demands for this had grown increasingly bold, but political equality remained firmly linked with the rearmament question.[54] Even though Germany's participation in the common defense should "naturally" be attended by a new contractual relationship, the foreign ministers of the occupying powers declared, the High Commission was instructed to proceed with negotiations "which will, it is hoped, culminate in early agreements between the four Governments to enter into effect together with the Agreement for German participation in Western Defense through the proposed European Defense Community, whose forces would form part of the joint defense forces under the North Atlantic Supreme Command."[55] This was, in political practice, more than a hope—it was a necessity.

The American position was clear and simple: for a number of reasons, the United States was desirous of satisfying both Bonn and Paris, and would do whatever it could to further the realization of what in effect had become a Franco-German "package." France agreed that a revision of the international status of the Federal Republic was appropriate, but linked this tightly to the actual parliamentary ratification, not merely the diplomatic approval, of the other major European projects.[56] Paris considered the connection "very tight" here, and it was understood that the Schuman

[54] Cf. F. Roy Willis, *France, Germany and the New Europe, 1945–1963* (Stanford: Stanford University Press, 1965), p. 156.

[55] Communiqué of the three foreign ministers of September 14, 1951, in Dennett and Durant, *Documents, 1951*, pp. 506–7.

[56] This was only one among a number of interdependent or overlapping aspects of the European army approach, which was extremely difficult to implement "because it necessitated separate agreements on (1) the relationship between the new Defense Community and NATO; (2) the technical military aspects of integrating six national armies and on the political and financial administration of the Community; (3) the role of West Germany in the European army, settled by West Germany both with its future partners and with the occupying powers; finally (4) a series of Contractual Agreements between West Germany and the occupying powers to replace the Occupation Statute. Only when agreement had been reached on all these points could the even more difficult process of ratification by the national parliaments begin." Willis, *New Europe*, p. 133.

Plan, the Pleven Plan, and the contractual accords would all have to be ratified together.[57] Finally, the ministers agreed, Germany was to be integrated in the European community "on a basis of equality," but because of the division of the country and the security problem, certain special rights (concerning the stationing of troops and their security and questions affecting Germany as a whole) were to be retained "in the common interest." On the question of German units, it was understood that the French plan would generally be followed.[58]

While the French were relieved that the other occupying powers had finally accepted their views, the victory in principle would not be worth much unless transformed into realities. The question was whether the United States would have the patience to wait for the outcome. Acheson's proclamation of the goals of integrating Germany into Europe before the end of the year and of a peace treaty with Bonn (which France rejected) was seen by the French as "a new American diplomatic offensive to hasten German rearmament."[59] Reports that the foreign ministers had agreed at Washington to an American proposal that Germany be permitted to raise forces as soon as possible and that the United States train them at once for later inclusion in a European army were denied, but only after Premier Pleven had personally tele-

[57] *L'Annee Politique, 1951*, p. 243. Acheson recalled that as the United States and Britain showed increased sympathy for the European movement, Schuman became "more flexible and forthcoming" on the German question. Acheson, *Present at the Creation*, p. 559.

[58] This remained unclear, however; the French had made what they considered substantial concessions amounting to a prospect for military integration at a level closer to the classical division than the combat team of the original Pleven Plan. *L'Annee Politique, 1951*, p. 242; Alexander Werth, *France: 1940–1955* (London: Hale, 1956), p. 547. The issue was further placed in doubt because of General Bradley's conviction that if the European army were to be effective there could not be integration at any level below that of the division. Edinger, *West German Armament*, p. 19.

[59] *L'Annee Politique, 1951*, p. 242. Eisenhower had enthusiastically endorsed European unification, as noted, but not until the Rome conference, discussed below, did he embrace EDC with equal enthusiasm. He later wrote that he supported the EDC concept from its inception in 1951. Eisenhower, *White House Years*, p. 398. See also Janet Flanner (Genet), *Paris Journal 1944–1965* (New York: Atheneum, 1965), p. 161.

phoned to his foreign minister before assuring the National Assembly that no German rearmament could occur prior to an agreement on the European army.[60] *L'Annee Politique* later explained
that the "subtle compromise" Schuman had in fact made was to
the effect that he would permit—without accepting a national
German army even temporarily—contingents to be recruited in
the Federal Republic by SHAPE "between the time European
defense organisms were begun and the time when they would be
able actually to function." Schuman stated that this concession on
his part was made only in the interest of saving some time and did
not amount to any change in France's general policy, and indeed
it did not. The incident is noteworthy for its illustration of Franco-
American sparring on the German rearmament question even
after there was agreement on the EDC approach. At the time of
the Washington meeting, the Americans were attached to the
European army idea as the only way to achieve German rearmament, and the French were equally attached to it for precisely
the opposite reason.[61]

The September 15–20 Ottawa conference of the NATO Council
was the first time since the December, 1950, Brussels meeting that
the Atlantic allies met on the ministerial level. The session was
announced as a meeting preliminary to the already scheduled (for
November) Rome session of the North Atlantic Council, "to consider such problems as may be ready for discussion." [62] Although
the United States hoped for action on military questions, the meeting dealt mostly with economic matters, both because the divergence between what seemed to be militarily necessary and what
was economically possible was increasing and because other matters
were not ready for discussion.

The establishment of the temporary council committee and the
appointment of the "three wise men" was the result of a French

[60] *The New York Times,* September 14 and 15, 1951.

[61] Sir Ivone Kirkpatrick, *The Inner Circle: Memoirs of Ivone Kirkpatrick* (London:
Macmillan, 1959), p. 243; *L'Annee Politique, 1951,* p. 243.

[62] Dennett and Durant, *Documents, 1951,* p. 235. It was not specified what this
meant, but German rearmament was probably included.

suggestion to review military programs in light of European economic weaknesses. It was based on the U.S. view that the world situation would not allow a curtailment of the Western rearmament program, and the Europeans' insistence on economic and social stability. It was hoped that a report might be ready in time for the next meeting of the North Atlantic Council at Rome. The result at Ottawa was that nothing significant relating to German rearmament was decided or done, which was reflected in the communiqué issued by the council and in the remarks of Secretary Acheson which followed the meeting.[63]

The NATO Council, informed by the occupying powers about the talks concerning the establishment of a new relationship with the Federal Republic, did not endorse the European army plan. The language of the communiqué blandly said that the council was informed of the statement made by the three foreign ministers after their Washington meeting, at which time the occupying powers had "welcomed the plan for a European Defense Community of which Germany would form a part." For its part, the council as a whole did not welcome the plan.

Secretary Acheson, who now supported EDC both officially and as a matter of personal conviction, would have preferred as broad an allied endorsement of the European army as possible, which would have been helpful, if nothing else, as the tail on the kite of Washington's German rearmament policy.[64] But steps toward a military role for the Federal Republic were not possible, not only because Franco-German differences were far from being resolved, but also because of such factors as the position of the Netherlands, considered for political and geographical reasons an essential participant in a European army. The Dutch foreign minister, who apparently considered EDC from start to finish a French

---

[63] See Stebbins, *United States, 1951*, pp. 357–58; Dennett and Durant, *Documents, 1951*, pp. 229–30, 235–43; Acheson, *Sketches from Life*, pp. 45–46, and *Present at the Creation*, p. 570; Osgood, *NATO*, pp. 83–84; Lord Ismay, *NATO: The First Five Years, 1949–1954* (Paris: NATO, 1955), pp. 43–46.

[64] Acheson, *Sketches from Life*, p. 44. This is an example of the United States seeing one of NATO's roles as supportive of American policy objectives. For a full discussion of U.S. perspectives on the role of the alliance, see Fox and Fox, *NATO*, Chap. 3 *passim*, and especially pp. 34ff.

device to retain discrimination against Germany, was convinced that the European army project was wasting valuable time. In October the Netherlands became an EDC-conference participant, more because of Stikker's "desire to keep in step with our Benelux partners" than because he thought the European army had a real chance of success. The reason above all that EDC would not work, he wrote, was that the French wanted to contain and control the Germans at the same time they were trying to bring the Federal Republic into a European federation as an unequal partner: "such a policy was bound to stumble over its inherent contradictions, not the least being the deep-rooted anti-German popular sentiment. . . ." [65] The burden of the past could not be wished away. In these circumstances, American diplomacy might encourage agreement but was not in a position to impose it.

Part of the problem involved the negotiations which were then proceeding between the High Commissioners and the Federal Chancellor. These were enormously difficult, the British High Commissioner said, because Bonn "objected fundamentally to the conditions laid down by the Foreign Ministers for the grant of independence to Germany." On September 24, for example, Adenauer asked for an end to *all* controls by the allies. This provoked a sharply worded note from the American delegation to the effect that while the United States desired an early German defense contribution, it was not so anxious for this as to give in to such a sweeping demand. Relations were strained, particularly because the equality that Adenauer sought was not within the French program for the future of Western Europe. The Chancellor saw a note from Paris to Moscow of September 26, 1951, which said the inclusion of the Federal Republic in the Western defense community would mean nothing other than a demilitarization of Germany. This is an unusual case of what seems to be direct evidence that, even with an EDC, France somehow planned to

[65] Stikker, *Memoir*, pp. 299–301. See also *L'Annee Politique, 1951*, p. 250. General de Gaulle continued to ridicule the EDC idea as "alchemy" and asked, "How can one seriously conceive a European army when Europe does not exist?" *The New York Times*, September 13, 1951.

block German rearmament. Adenauer saw it as one more example of the two-faced nature of French policy.[66]

The discussions at Bonn took a peculiar course, remaining deadlocked on such matters as German refusal to accept the allies' intention to prevent the re-establishment of a German arms-industry, to agree to a projected doubling of the Federal Republic's financial contribution to defense, or to allow allied troops in Germany to keep extraterritorial status. But in spite of this it was possible, by October 10, to agree that the drafting of the contractual texts should proceed to the extent possible—that is, without returning to what had already been revealed as a matter of controversy. Even the tentative accords which were reached in the following weeks were not negligible, considering the divergent allied and German views on almost every issue.

On November 3, 1951, the U.S. High Commissioner told a German audience that the time had come for the Federal Republic to enjoy a status of equality, and occupational controls could now be ended; but an essential factor was "a defense contribution on a basis of equal partnership within the European Defense Force." [67] McCloy thus linked the contractual arrangements and the EDC as closely as the French government had done earlier; he added that the choice of whether to proceed on this basis was for Bonn to determine. Implicit in this was the probability that should the Federal Republic not elect to take the path of EDC, the ending of occupational controls might not ensue. He mentioned that concern persisted that antidemocratic elements had not yet been completely eliminated from the Federal Republic, but stressed that EDC membership would both aid the process of internal German democratization and also insure that a rearmed Germany could not contemplate any "military adventure." [68] Washington

[66] Adenauer, *Memoirs*, p. 378. Adenauer did not consider Schuman himself two-faced, but applied this more to the Quai d'Orsay, because of the latter's long tradition of ties with Russia. The Chancellor's thinking here is not especially precise, but this does not change the importance of the point. See also Kirkpatrick, *Inner Circle*, p. 244, and *International Organization*, Vol. V, 1951, pp. 826–27.

[67] Text is in *Department of State Bulletin*, December 10, 1951, pp. 942–45. The quotations in this and the next paragraph are from the same.

[68] Shortly before, Adenauer had admitted that 134 officials of his foreign ministry

and Paris hence seemed to agree that EDC would contain the Federal Republic, but this convergence of policies was not accompanied by a similar accord on the nature of the proposed European army.[69]

The Paris negotiations were difficult, especially in the French view, because of the related meetings at Bonn where the German government rejected every restriction which it considered inconsistent with the sovereignty of the Federal Republic, and where Adenauer's demands did not seem to diminish even as the number of allied concessions multiplied.[70] Perhaps because another Soviet atomic explosion had been announced earlier in October, or perhaps because Eisenhower kept warning that war might be close, it seemed easier to agree on military details than on other related matters, especially financial and budgetary.

What were still termed technical military arrangements—that is, agreements among the representatives at the Paris conference which did not necessarily commit their governments to back them up—emerged early in November with the assistance of expert advisers who had been furnished by General Eisenhower with Washington's approval.[71] It was reported that the six governments agreed that a European defense force should be created as soon as possible, to be composed of forty-three divisions, of which fourteen were to be French, twelve each from Germany and Italy, and five from the Benelux states.[72] The European army was initially to amount to about 500,000 men and reach an anticipated

---

had been members of the Nazi party. Cf. Richard C. Snyder and Edgar S. Furniss, Jr., *American Foreign Policy* (New York: Rhinehart, 1954), p. 702.

[69] It was widely noted that the American shift toward EDC coincided with the evolution of the project away from the original Pleven Plan. General de Gaulle remarked, "If our allies now want the European army, it is because its whole character has changed since last year." Werth, *France,* p. 548.

[70] *L'Annee Politique, 1951,* pp. 275–77.

[71] *The New York Times,* November 28, 1951.

[72] The label on the basic national contingent was still a matter of Franco-German controversy, but it appeared the size of the unit was approaching that of a division. *International Organization,* Vol. VI, 1952, p. 144. This source said that each basic national contingent would be 30,000, with a ratio of 2:3 of combat-support troops. This explains the apparent difference between the total expected at the end of 1953 and the smaller combat unit.

total by the end of 1953 of something more than a million and a quarter. The basic combat unit was to consist of national groupings of 12,000 to 13,000 men; logistical services were to be commonly supplied, which was to create the technical barrier to what otherwise would be national German rearmament.[73] France—and only France—was to be allowed six extra divisions as a national force. It was expected that German rearmament could begin in mid-1952 and the dozen German divisions be complete by the late spring of 1954. International command of the force was to be introduced only at the corps and army level, which seemed to indicate a clear victory for the German negotiators, who had firmly resisted the attempt to limit the size and autonomy of the national units. French diplomacy never dealt with this point again, and this marked the definitive turning away from the most controversial part of the Pleven Plan.

The November agreement was well short of the equality that the Federal Republic insisted on, however, particularly since France was so obviously excepted from the purely European limitations on the number of national contingents; but it was another case of the Germans accepting half-a-loaf in the expectation of more.[74] The agreement, moreover, was only a small island in an ocean of confusion and discord, even on the so-called technical military level. There were, for example, problems of how to achieve command and liaison with four languages in one army; who would court martial whom for what offenses; what staff system might be worked out; whether equipment could be standardized; whether grossly different pay scales could be reconciled, and so forth. But these military details were insignificant compared to the political. The agreement for the forty-three–

[73] *Herald Tribune*, November 8, 1951; Stebbins, *United States, 1951*, p. 365; *L'Annee Politique, 1951*, p. 314. The French were extremely attached to common logistical services as a control device. *Christian Science Monitor*, August 29, 1951.

[74] Nor was there to be equal German status in the formation of command and staff. Dennett and Durant, *Documents, 1951*, p. 523. An editorial in *Christ und Welt* on November 1, 1951, said German rearmament was not "for sale" for political concessions; nevertheless, real equality was not to be expected until *after* remilitarization, since "we are realistic enough to know that in this imperfect world those who are defenseless are without rights."

division army did not provide for one of the basic EDC ingredients, a common budget which could be controlled by a common political authority. "This revealed a fundamental problem: that of the creation of a supranational political authority to which could be delegated the sovereignty necessary to genuinely 'integrate' the military forces, rather than limiting them to only a coalition." [75]

Other sharp political differences concerned the Benelux states. The Netherlands' Foreign Minister Stikker said that as the Paris conference dragged on and went into almost every problem of European politics which concerned Germany and the unity of Western Europe, he was led to wonder "should we proceed gradually or start with the final phase?" As France insisted on the supranational character of EDC, which Italy apparently welcomed, the Benelux states were hesitant; they preferred, for example, a council of defense ministers which was closer to a coalition than a common European authority. Above all, questions of finance (which were really political) were bitterly disputed, including such issues as how national contributions to the common defense fund would be fixed and by whom, and whether the national governments of the EDC members would retain their budgetary prerogatives (as the Dutch insisted) or lose them to a "European" parliament. The major difficulties were not only political and financial, but "more fundamentally, the method of getting the nations concerned to put the project actually in execution." [76] Here, the EDC problem involved not only the Benelux countries, but the two states most intimately concerned.

The fact remained that—except on the governmental level and even then only with extensive qualifications—neither the French nor the Germans were ready for the remilitarization of the Federal Republic. SPD-leader Schumacher's prediction that in a European army "orders to attack will be given in German but orders to retreat in another language" might have prompted second

[75] *L'Annee Politique, 1951,* p. 275. French leaders feared just this, and vigorously continued to stress the supranational character of the project.

[76] Stebbins, *United States, 1951,* p. 365; Stikker, *Memoir,* pp. 301–2; *L'Annee Politique, 1951,* p. 314.

thoughts in France no less than in Germany.[77] In contrast to the situation in July when there had been broad (if vague) agreement on the principle of a supranational European army, but no accord on such matters as the size of basic units or the level at which integration would occur, there was now general agreement on the latter points and a fundamental divergence on the principle of supranationality itself. The German rearmament issue at this point was placed back in the laps of the protagonists. Whether or not the Six agreed was irrelevant unless the Federal Republic and the occupying powers could come to terms.

On November 22, in Paris, Adenauer reviewed the status of the discussions on the contractual agreements with the foreign ministers of the occupying powers. Acheson recalled that differences among the Big Three at this time were due, "as might be expected, to the American desire to move farther and faster than the French were willing to go, with the British in between us." [78] For example, Schuman's desire to prepare a list of armaments Germany should be prohibited from making impressed Acheson as evidence of inability to decide whether Germany was an ally or an enemy, when "to take an ambivalent attitude would be fatal." The four ministers were unable to agree on such matters as the amount of support which Bonn should pay for allied troops in the Federal Republic, or on Federal forces themselves, and it was impossible likewise "to determine the cost of German forces still not agreed upon." The secretary found the discussions helpful, particularly since they had for the first time met with Adenauer on a basis of equality and had reassured him that the allies would not, at German expense, make a deal with the Soviets on German unification. On German rearmament, however, Acheson regretted that there had been no movement "beyond bare fundamentals." The occasion seemed, once again, more beneficial to Bonn than to Washington, Paris, or London.

[77] *The Times* (London), November 27, 1951.
[78] Acheson, *Present at the Creation*, pp. 583ff., upon which this paragraph is based.

Acheson, Schuman, and Eden joined with Adenauer in a statement concerning sovereignty for the West German state.[79] The meeting itself, they said, marked "a notable advance in the progressive association of the German Federal Republic with the West on a basis of equal partnership," but once again affirmed the tight link between this and German rearmament. In approving a draft reached at Bonn with the Allied High Commission, it was stated that this could "only enter into force together with . . . the treaty establishing a European defense community." The "common aim" of the four powers was "to integrate the Federal Republic on a basis of equality in a European community itself included in a developing Atlantic community," but it was clear that this would not occur unless the whole interdependent bundle of considerations could be managed.

While this meeting marked a high point on the road to sovereignty for Bonn, it was only part of the way. The rest depended on a military contribution, about which American impatience was becoming increasingly evident. The French were afraid that the time might not be distant when the insistence of American diplomats would result in a "new Wehrmacht." The possibility of the latter was really the essential ingredient of what political leverage the United States possessed on the German rearmament question, but it was applicable only upon Paris, not upon Bonn. Acheson hoped for endorsement of EDC by the NATO Council as the next step in the attempt to make the European army acceptable to its prospective members, although he had found the Paris negotiations "stuck in subministerial bickering." [80]

No important results were expected from the Rome meeting of the NAC from November 24 to 28, and none were forth-

[79] Eden had replaced Morrison at the foreign office after the Conservative victory in the October 25 election. Dennett and Durant, *Documents, 1951*, pp. 532–33. The quotations are from this source.

[80] André Fontaine, "Vers la Nouvelle Wehrmacht," *LeMonde*, November 22, 1951. Jules Moch at the same time denied the paternity of the child which was emerging in Paris, calling EDC simply the camouflage for a new Wehrmacht, and deGaulle said the same. *L'Annee Politique, 1951*, p. 316; Acheson, *Present at the Creation*, p. 589.

coming. The report of the "three wise men" was not yet ready, and Acheson's suggestion that the council go on record in favor of the immediate establishment of the European army was not accepted, primarily because of strong opposition on the part of the Netherlands and Belgium. The final communiqué noted that the council "hoped that the Paris conference would conclude its activities at the earliest possible moment" and that "a definitive report" would be made.[81]

Away from the formal meetings, Acheson and Eden had told Schuman that "he must aim for some conclusion of his efforts by the end of the year. Otherwise we would be threatened by a permanent deadlock and would have to drop the European Defense Community." Exertion of this kind of pressure was consistent with Acheson's decision henceforth to "take a very active part, particularly with the French to help them make their own plan and initiative a success. . . ."[82] He thought that the deadline of December 31 was the only alternative to stalemate, and so cabled to the President.

In his public remarks, the secretary said the Rome meetings had helped to get matters "into a state where negotiations can go forward." As to the European army, the Paris conference, he said, had passed

the phase where you could make broad agreements dealing in generalizations. We are down to the point where you are wrestling with the toughest kind of questions which have to do with men and goods and money and organization.

The military aspects of this matter, I think, have been pretty satisfactorily resolved. The Ministers and their experts are now wrestling with the great problems of finance and the organization of supply, and that is a very tough and difficult thing to do with the forces of six nations being put together in one force.[83]

[81] Dennett and Durant, *Documents, 1951,* pp. 242–43. The opposition was due to both political and strategic considerations—a political preference for the Atlantic over the EDC viewpoint, and a military apprehension that a European army under French command might not give sufficient emphasis to the Benelux position.

[82] Acheson, *Present at the Creation,* pp. 589–90, 758.

[83] Dennett and Durant, *Documents, 1951,* p. 244.

In spite of the enormous difficulties, the secretary expressed optimism. Rejecting criticism that Europeans had not done enough, he countered that "they have done more in four years than they have done in five hundred to bring this about."

General Eisenhower, who had admittedly been "horrified" when he first encountered the complex European army scheme, but had changed his mind when it seemed to be the only solution to the German rearmament dilemma, expressed a mixture of optimism and caution at Rome. He stressed, as he had in London in July, that there could be no genuine security for Europe unless there was unity; but in addition he warmly endorsed the EDC as the way to the unity and the security which would not be attained without a German military contribution. At the same time, the Supreme Commander's doubts were implicit in his statement that "we have to attempt the impossible, and the European defense force is part of the impossible." [84] The general's complete support of EDC was probably more the result of the lack of an alternative method of German rearmament than an absent-minded, military pep-talk. He remained convinced that Germany simply could not be defended without the Germans, and while at Rome categorically placed himself in favor of a defense on the eastern border of the Federal Republic. "Western defense could never be anything but a stalemate established on the Rhine," he said, "unless something were done to consolidate the European army."

In contrast to Eisenhower's optimism, there were several matters which, for Acheson, together created the "depressing attitude" of the Rome meetings. The military report of General Gruenther, "a hair-raising description" of Soviet power, backfired and actually discouraged the Europeans from believing a successful defense effort was even possible. The deep split among the prospective members of EDC could not be papered over. The Benelux states were especially reluctant to risk intimate economic

---

[84] *The Times* (London), November 27, 1951. Interviews indicated that only General Gruenther's enthusiasm persuaded Eisenhower to reconsider his doubts about the practicability of EDC as a military scheme.

and military ventures with the larger states, both because such projects might not work and even if they did the smaller powers would be "submerged and powerless." There was also a general feeling among the ministers that the EDC project was not "going well, that the French chairmanship of the discussions is weak and confused, and that the people making plans for the establishment of the force are approaching the problem without regard to the political and parliamentary realities in Europe." Finally, Acheson recalled, Eisenhower himself offended the allies with his vigorous proclamation of the necessity of European unification. The general, unaware that integration was a deeply divisive subject, gave the impression of using his military position to bring pressure for a political result, and the allies believed Eisenhower had been so directed by the U.S. government.[85]

Acheson's cautious endorsement of EDC was grounded on the reality of the situation at the time. Even though the Benelux states rejected as too drastic the supranational aspects of the European army project, there seemed to be a better chance that these allies might be persuaded to accept EDC than that France would be willing to permit German rearmament without it.[86] The persistently difficult economic situation only underscored the apparently unavoidable disappointment with the scope of the defense effort, and the attempt at Rome to find a compromise between the Belgian, or "coalition," concept and the French concept of a European army responsible to and controlled by a supranational defense ministry was without success. Nevertheless, there was no alternative to EDC which would not have created as many new problems as it would have solved. For example, plans under consideration in Washington for German entry into NATO were feasible only with unanimous consent of all the allies and a new contractual agreement with the Germans; an agreement among

---

[85] Acheson, for his part, was "bewildered between the tone and the content of the speech. The tone was inspirational and vigorous; the content was the meagerest intellectual fare." *Sketches from Life*, p. 46. See also *Present at the Creation*, pp. 590–91, 757–58.

[86] See *L'Annee Politique, 1951*, p. 344. The objections of the Benelux states were directed toward EDC, not German rearmament as such.

the occupying powers on German rearmament without NATO membership for the Federal Republic might trigger the fall of the Paris government or be wholly unacceptable to the French parliament even if Bonn agreed. The United States was thus forced to continue the diplomatic attempt for a European army, at least for the time being. Others were less certain the EDC should be attempted at all; the Dutch Foreign Minister said his "main fear was that we were trying to do the impossible, and foreign policy is still *l'art du possible.*" [87]

Secretary Acheson's retrospective look at how EDC came to be formulated and agreed upon distinguished between the apparent lack of progress and what was happening in spite of appearances, as attitudes were adjusted as time went on. Whether the same adjustments would have occurred without U.S. pressure for agreement on EDC cannot be known. What was clear as the Paris conference resumed its work early in December was that the German rearmament tangle was not yet close to resolution.

Articles in the American press on delayed German rearmament showed increasing impatience; [88] the Germans were so insistent in their various demands that High Commissioner McCloy made reference to their behavior; the relationship of the United States and Britain to the EDC remained in doubt; economic conditions preventing further defense efforts persisted as the "wise men" failed to find a politically realistic solution to the problem of how to finance rearmament; the French continued to fear a German danger while in disagreement about whether this would be greater or less if the Federal Republic were included in European projects; and France produced only three of the ten fully equipped divisions which had been promised by the end of 1951. An EDC would remain problematical, even if politically arranged, because of the German need for a transition period of

---

[87] Stikker, *Memoir*, p. 306. See also *The New York Times*, December 5, 1951 (C. L. Sulzberger).

[88] For example, an article in *The New York Times* of December 4, 1951, by Hanson W. Baldwin called for national German rearmament if EDC did not materialize by early 1952, and on December 10 the *Times* referred editorially to France as "the worst straggler."

"psychological preparation," as Eisenhower said. Perhaps worse, France was said to be characterized by a state of depression and demoralization which could not be cured "by the recruiting sergeants of the European army." [89] In addition, by the latter half of 1951 the psychological impact of the Korean attack had almost disappeared.

While American officials would have preferred to continue to give the European allies instructions on their defense budgets, the impression that the United States had become preoccupied with military matters to the point of ignoring their economic and social impact was widespread.[90] Under these conditions, the bargaining power of the United States was constrained by the very devices available to it: one of the most persuasive sanctions for allied noncompliance with American wishes was the threat of reducing or terminating financial aid for rearmament, yet the same conditions which made the allies vulnerable to this also rendered them unable to increase their efforts.[91]

The British position was another factor in the EDC logjam of late 1951. The Attlee government would not participate in any European federation project, and the return of Winston Churchill to the prime ministry did not alter this. No British adhesion to "Europe" could be expected which would involve the surrender of sovereignty. In this respect London did not differ from Washington, but because of certain emotional as well as political factors the British position was considered highly relevant to the prospects of the European army. On the one hand, France wanted Britain as both a political counterweight to the Federal Republic and as an additional military guarantor

[89] Werth, *France,* p. 554, quoting *Esprit,* November, 1951. French failure to deliver on their promises was seen in Washington as additional evidence of their unreliability.

[90] Cf. Fox and Fox, *NATO,* p. 60. In October, the French were amazed when an American general stated the amount of the French defense contribution for the coming year when the Paris government had not yet fixed its military budget. *L'Annee Politique, 1951,* p. 274.

[91] During 1951, NATO ground strength in Germany rose to about fourteen divisions, but this total was seen as extremely modest, and "hardly commensurate with the dignity or dangers of SHAPE." Peter Calvocoressi, *Survey of International Affairs, 1951* (London: Oxford University Press, 1954), p. 25.

against possible future German misbehavior, while on the other the Benelux states hoped for British membership in EDC to avoid being dominated by a Franco-German combination.[92] In addition, the Federal Republic preferred British participation as insurance that its territory would be included in the area NATO was pledged to defend, and the United States looked to London's association with the Continent both for the long-term objective of European unification and for the immediate benefit British adherence to EDC would bring in the attempt for German rearmament. Foreign Minister Anthony Eden reported to Churchill on December 1 that the European army plan was "in political trouble over fundamental questions of sovereignty," adding that Britain was unfairly being made "the whipping boy" as EDC experienced difficulty in the states directly involved.[93]

American diplomacy in this situation seemed pragmatically flexible: the United States favored British membership in EDC to the degree this would enhance its prospects, and using this criterion shifted as circumstances changed. From mid-year to the fall of 1951, Washington urged London's membership, since this had been announced as desirable by the prospective members of the European army; but toward the end of the year, as agreements were reached among the Six without Britain, this was altered. In November, Eisenhower told Eden at Rome that an offer of British participation in EDC would be a mistake at that time, because this would complicate further the budgetary and other technical arrangements and cause delay, not haste.

The U.S. and British positions thereafter seemed to coincide; each would assume the role of a benevolent spectator. A British embassy statement in mid-December announced that Britain was "wholeheartedly in favor of a European army and supports the

---

[92] F. S. Northedge, *British Foreign Policy: The Process of Readjustment, 1945–1961* (London: Allen and Unwin, 1962), pp. 132–40; Stebbins, *United States, 1951,* pp. 366–68; *L'Annee Politique, 1951,* p. 343; Furniss, *France, Troubled Ally,* pp. 82–83; *The New York Times,* November 30, December 6, 1951.

[93] Sir Anthony Eden, *Full Circle* (Boston: Houghton Mifflin, 1960), pp. 36–37. Adenauer expressed regret that Britain refused to join EDC. *Herald Tribune,* December 8, 1951.

project with no less vigor than the U.S." The reasons for this were that German rearmament was essential, an independent army was not desirable, and "the only feasible way therefore to ensure effective German participation is through the inclusion of a German force within a European army." This was exactly why the United States favored EDC, although there was no British equivalent of American enthusiasm and no great wish in London that the Continent be unified. Eden favored a closer union between the continental states through EDC, but—like Stikker—thought the scheme overly imaginative and likely to fail because it attempted too much.[94]

It was reported that American officials at SHAPE were making great efforts to persuade the British to give the fullest public support to the project. In September, London had pledged, without further explanation, "the closest possible association with the European continental community at all stages in its development." After strong French and American pressure, Britain went much further during the December visit of Churchill and Eden to Paris. A joint Anglo-French communiqué repeated the earlier pledge of close association, but added that British armed forces would be kept on the European Continent "as long as will be necessary to fulfill their obligations toward the common powers." These forces would be "linked to the forces of the European Defense Community," which constituted "the true means of integrating democratic Germany in a purely defensive organization for European security." [95]

When the foreign ministers of the Six convened in Paris on December 27 to discuss the status of the European army, Eisenhower appeared before them to urge agreement on a federated Europe, saying he was "delighted by the progress" which had been made. But during the preceding weeks informal discussions which extended agreement on many details had left untouched

---

[94] "Britain and a European Army," background note, December 17, 1951, British Embassy, Washington, D.C.; Eden, *Full Circle*, p. 35; Northedge, *British Foreign Policy*, p. 155.

[95] Tripartite Declaration of September 14, 1951, Dennett and Durant, *Documents, 1951*, p. 524; *The New York Times*, December 6 and 19, 1951.

the basic problem raised by the proposed creation of the European army *prior* to the authority which would eventually control it. On December 30 it was announced at Paris that while no definitive institutional setup had yet been selected, there was agreement that EDC would have an executive, a council of ministers, a court of justice, and an assembly, the latter to study the institutional framework in its preparatory phase. For example, national parliaments were to keep financial control for the time being rather than attempt to agree on a common budget at once. Schuman eased his position somewhat by proposing a three-year probationary period of institutional adaptation, hoping to reduce the still-rigid resistance of the Benelux states. The question of the budget necessarily raised the problem of whether the interested states would be willing—with or without a transition period—to renounce their national sovereignty to the extent of yielding to a supranational body the right to set the figure for the military outlays in their national budgets.[96] And even if they should so agree, a constantly elevated level of political coordination would be essential in other sectors, since the military was inseparable from the economic situation in each member state, and conditions in any one part would be of direct concern to the others.

The budgetary issue was only one among many, but underlying all the difficulties of European unification was the political and psychological fact that it might all be backwards. Instead of rearming a still-distrusted Germany as part of a European army without a political counterpart, perhaps it would be better to create first the conditions of mutual trust among prospective members of Europe and thereafter look to the highly sensitive possibility of a denationalized military force. Even so devoted an enthusiast of unification as Italian Premier Alcide de Gasperi considered the European army a revolutionary step whose realization would require a complete reversal of preconceived ideas and sacrifices of sovereignty never before made between states. In the end, Euro-

[96] *International Organization*, Vol. V, 1951, p. 816; *The Times* (London), December 28 and 29, 1951; *L'Annee Politique, 1951*, pp. 348–49.

peans themselves were saying, it was impossible to separate military policy from foreign policy, and a minister of defense is automatically an official of the political authority that commands the army. If an army is an instrument of foreign policy, could there be a European army without a European state? [97] And if not, how could a European army under the command of an American general be a step toward a united Europe?

U.S. POLICY AND EUROPEAN UNITY

By early 1952, the American demand for a German military contribution had progressed well beyond the original ideas of even those who had earlier perceived a European army as one aspect of unifying Europe. The German rearmament commitment had evolved into the commitment of the United States to the political federation of the continent. The EDC was simultaneously to contain the Federal Republic and to create a new European state. "The German problem is the problem of Europe," Schuman had told the United Nations' General Assembly, "one cannot be solved without the other." [98] The United States finally seemed to agree.

Secretary Acheson looked back at 1951 as the year when the decisions were taken which, if acted upon, would solve the problem of Europe, as the restoration of Germany and the EDC went hand in hand to provide the security of German defense participation without reviving the menace of German militarism. If the currently active projects succeeded, he said, "Western Europe can realize its whole, rich potential for defense and for peaceful progress. . . . And 1952 can be a year of historic decision for Europe—a year in which Europe can enter into a new era." President Truman in his State of the Union message confirmed American hopes in these matters, and on the same day stated in a

[97] *Monde Nouveau* (Paris), December, 1951, summarizing a statement of Altiero Spinelli; *The New York Times*, December 19, 1951.
[98] Address of November 16, 1951, in *L'Annee Politique, 1951*, p. 674.

joint declaration with Prime Minister Churchill that the United States was in full accord with the Anglo-French communiqué of December 18, mentioned above.[99] Both governments would give full support to the effort to establish a European Defense Community, which was "the best means of bringing a democratic Germany as a full and equal partner into a purely defensive organization for European security." The emphasis was less on European political federation than on the military benefits. Perhaps even here London and Washington had simply smoothed over Churchill's strong belief that EDC could only lead to utter military confusion.

Optimistic assertions notwithstanding, U.S. officials were not at all sure that the new year would bring the EDC to fruition. Rather, as preparations were made for the forthcoming NATO conference at Lisbon, Acheson said "we seemed to have made no progress toward a defense of Europe or toward European unification." [100] The Lisbon meeting might be "the last clear chance" to launch the European army—otherwise, he thought, the EDC approach might not survive. And if it did not, American policy might be subjected to what his successor was to call an "agonizing reappraisal." According to High Commissioner McCloy, "The continued interest and support of the people of the United States cannot be taken for granted," unless Europeans—including the Federal Republic—took positive steps toward integration. Realization of the EDC, McCloy announced, would bring peace and security to Europe while solving the German problem, adding— as both carrot and stick—"it is the only way to ensure the continuing interest of the United States." [101]

Onto this concern for the military security of the NATO area was added the appeal of why the unification of Europe would

[99] Eisenhower had at the time written to urge the President to persuade Churchill to make "a ringing statement" for the European army. Harry S Truman, *Memoirs: Years of Trial and Hope*, Vol. II (Garden City: Doubleday, 1956), p. 259; *Department of State Bulletin*, January 7, 1952, p. 4; *Public Papers of the Presidents of the United States. Harry S Truman, 1952–53* (Washington: Government Printing Office, 1965), pp. 12–13.

[100] Acheson, *Sketches from Life*, p. 47.

[101] *Department of State Bulletin*, December 13, 1951, pp. 1051–53.

bring countless advantages to the West, with the American press and officials seemingly rivaling each other in a chorus of praise for EDC.[102] No longer a clever French delaying tactic or an unappetizing recipe for military smorgasbord, the European army was "an important step on the road to greater European unity," which would produce "a powerful new democratic state, capable of sustaining itself politically, economically and militarily, and able to contribute greatly to the achievement of world peace." [103] Unity was the only solution when no single European state could stand alone either against the foreign military threat or the domestic social and economic pressures which would be generated by a failure to raise standards of living. It was added, probably as a courtesy to Adenauer, that European unification would also bring German reunification, since "No division through the middle of Germany can persist in the face of the strength and moral pressure such an integration would present." [104] Both world peace and peace within the Western European family itself would ensue, since the political fragmentation of Europe was clearly part of the underlying causes of the many European wars of the past, and the democratic development of the Federal Republic would be enhanced through "continued contact and nourishment from the democratic instincts of the entire community."

Another factor, not often publicly mentioned but surely present in U.S. calculations, was that a European army containing a re-

[102] The press tended to sway back and forth between finger-shaking at the "straggler," France, and a kind of mindless optimism which often approached nonsense: "Maybe creating a European army without a political framework is putting the cart before the horse, but if the hardest step is taken first it is fairly certain that the rest will follow." (A. McCormick, *The New York Times*, January 28, 1952). The European press was much less sanguine. Cf. *The Times* (London), January 30, 1952; *Manchester Guardian* and *LeMonde*, January 3, 1952; *The Contemporary Review*, January 1952.

[103] President's Fourth Report on the Mutual Defense Assistance Program, *Department of State Bulletin*, February 25, 1952, p. 316. This language is from a resolution introduced in the Senate in late January, 1952, which President Truman said he hoped would receive that body's wholehearted approval. *Department of State Bulletin*, February 18, 1952, pp. 275–76.

[104] As noted, Adenauer took the same line (*Memoirs*, p. 298) and echoed the American view that the creation of a European army would be "an act of peace." *The New York Times*, December 26, 1951. See also McCloy's remarks in *Department of State Bulletin*, December 13, 1951, and March 3, 1952, p. 324.

armed Germany would allow American forces in Europe to be brought home in the future.[105] As President Truman said in his 1952 State of the Union address, "we want to see Europe freed from any dependence on our aid." Bringing U.S. troops back was implicitly part of the American goal of bringing nearer "the day when Europe will be able to maintain her forces without further assistance from us." [106] If all this was done, another potential super-power would be created. American advocates of just such a result stressed the political benefits which would come from a restoration of "Europe's role in the world," but some British observers found it curious that "the Americans encourage most vigorously a European integration which some of its Continental advocates regard as a counterpoise to the United States." [107]

Either way, the mushroom of European unification had sprung from the spawn of Germany rearmament. It was being presented in a sauce which Washington proclaimed delicious but Europeans were not sure they could digest. American policy retained its cloak of progressive language, but in practice was almost wholly subordinated to the practical exigencies of the rearmament program as 1952 began. The parties to the interdependent tangle of German rearmament through EDC now looked to the Lisbon meeting of the North Atlantic Council, when the United States hoped NATO might once more serve American interests, especially by formal endorsement of EDC, through whose powers of transformation German soldiers would become European soldiers.

[105] Cf. Stikker, *Memoir*, pp. 303–4.

[106] *Department of State Bulletin*, February 4, 1952, p. 180.

[107] Bowie, *Shaping the Future*, p. 13; R.I.I.A., *Atlantic Alliance*, p. 40. This "role" is rarely defined in such statements, and is at least partially incompatible with the American notion that one of the major roles of Europe in the world was to stumble into world wars; but this was the distinction between disunity and unity, presumably.

CHAPTER V

The Success and Suspension of American Diplomacy

THE record of the American diplomatic quest for German rearmament in 1952 to the close of the Truman-Acheson period was mixed. The enormous effort which produced the May treaties of Bonn and Paris was followed by a period of inactivity as marked as the activity of the preceding months. The long struggle to produce agreement culminated in an apparent mountain of international harmony which Secretary Acheson described as "a stack of documents about eight inches high," signifying "the birth of a new Germany, a new Europe, and a new period in history." [1]

This diplomatic masterpiece, however, was more dream than reality. Almost immediately after the signing of the Bonn treaty which was to restore the Federal Republic's sovereignty, and the Paris treaty which was to establish the European Defense Community, reaction against them began to set in. At the end of the Truman period the European Defense Community treaty had not been ratified by a single signatory, and in France neither this nor the peace contract with Germany had even been submitted to the National Assembly.

[1] *Department of State Bulletin*, June 16, 1952, p. 931. See also Richard P. Stebbins, *The United States in World Affairs, 1952* (New York: Harper, 1953), p. 150.

The brilliant culmination of the diplomatic effort of more than a year and a half was followed by more than two years during which the American demand for German rearmament within EDC remained frustrated. Agreement on the intergovernmental level meant that the next phase of activity would occur in the domestic political arenas of the states concerned. It was here that the fundamental ingredients for concocting "Europe" were either missing or unmixable, as it appeared increasingly less feasible to attempt to build a supranational relationship upon a foundation of international suspicion, mistrust, and animosities. Also, and of great importance, the American election year and the departure of key U.S. leaders reduced European willingness to proceed with the May treaties, as the future direction of U.S. policy became less certain and American leadership of NATO was all but lost.[2]

Many observers continued to wonder whether the EDC plan for a denationalized army under a supranational authority would amount to commencing the house with the roof, but even this might have been a tactical error rather than a strategic blunder had the inclination to construct the edifice been sufficiently strong. EDC as the way to European unity was questionable not because the military avenue toward cooperation was intrinsically inappropriate, but because the states of Europe had been impelled prematurely by American pressure to reach tentative agreement on highly sensitive political matters which would otherwise have come much later, if at all. The reality of late 1952 which replaced the dream of the earlier months was simply the normal result of the complex and aggravated European situation.

It was thought as 1952 began that the forthcoming Lisbon conference would be a crucial landmark for NATO, and, no less important, the future of the Federal Republic. For Acheson, it was "to be the supreme gamble, upon which we would stake our whole prestige, skill and power."[3] The long-hoped-for endorsement of

---

[2] These factors were relevant to nonratification of the EDC treaty, not to whether its provisions could have been implemented.

[3] The fear already existed that if Germany were not included quickly the con-

EDC by the North Atlantic Council was gained at the same time the allies agreed on various other matters, especially military-force goals, which seemed (to U.S. officials) to indicate that NATO was about to enjoy both a renewed defense effort and a direct contribution from the Federal Republic. The several prerequisites for meaningful agreement on a European army—a political settlement between Germany and the occupying powers; progress toward an accord on the Saar between the Federal Republic and France; clarification of the future role of the United States and Britain in continental security affairs; reconciliation of the conflicting goals of Bonn and Paris, respectively, of achieving political equality and maintaining control; acceptance of EDC's supranational characteristics by the Benelux states—appeared to be closer to realization.

At the same time, however, the external stimulus of the cold war sharply declined. Europeans felt increasingly unconvinced that military dangers were such that undertaking large-scale rearmament was worth the risk of provoking greater economic and political instability, or of raising the possibility of another military disaster should German rearmament rebound against its originators.[4] These factors impeded both ratification of the May treaties and achievement of the Lisbon force goals: the military and political answer to the German rearmament question, which EDC was to have provided, passed from the conference rooms of the protagonists' capitals into their legislative chambers, where diplomacy could reach only indirectly.

The accomplishment reflected in the international agreements of the first half of the year faded by the end of the Truman-Acheson period. Participants and observers alike agree that EDC's chances of realization declined as time passed, and the longer the attempt to achieve ratification was delayed the less likely was a

sequences would be enormous. NATO's vital interests included "bringing Germany into the Western camp and holding it there." Royal Institute of International Affairs, *Atlantic Alliance: NATO's Role in the Free World* (London: Royal Institute of International Affairs, 1952), pp. 110–11. Dean Acheson, *Present at the Creation: My Years in the State Department* (New York: Norton, 1969), p. 609.

[4] Peter Calvocoressi, *Survey of International Affairs, 1952* (London: Oxford University Press, 1955), p. 55.

favorable outcome. From the moment of signature to the moment of final defeat the Paris governments postponed submission of the treaty to the deputies for a vote as upon a question of confidence for the simple reason that they knew it would lose.[5] Similarly, there were no substantive changes in American diplomacy once the unqualified commitment to EDC had been made. While the tone and style of U.S. efforts evolved from gentle blandishment to somewhat heavy-handed pressure, no alternative to the European army was either embraced or articulated by American policymakers. The United States became more enamoured of European unification than it had been of even the remilitarization of the Federal Republic.[6]

The American preoccupation with military security had not changed. Its focus was simply enlarged as more and more items were added to the lists of benefits European unity would bring, and less and less attention was paid to the fact that implementation of the EDC treaty would in effect have placed the army that was to have served as the amalgam of continental unification under the command of an American general.[7] This implicit contradiction remained as long as the United States did not clarify whether it was pursuing "Atlantic" or "European" integration as its primary goal. To the extent that the EDC would—with its political aspect of European unity and its military aspect of NATO command and control—have emerged neither fish nor fowl, it is

[5] The initiative began to be lost "from the moment the treaty was signed." Alexander Werth, *France: 1940–1955* (London: Hale, 1956), p. 646; Edgar S. Furniss, Jr., *France, Troubled Ally: DeGaulle's Heritage and Prospects* (New York: Praeger, 1960), pp. 78–100.

[6] American disinclination against even mentioning alternatives to EDC was extremely strong. Later on, it was actually forbidden publicly to discuss the matter, or to mention it outside the government. Secretary Dulles was said to have complained after EDC fell that he did not like the new arrangements of September, 1954, because the Brussels Pact "had no supranational features" and would not lead to "real integration in Europe." Sir Anthony Eden (Lord Avon), *Full Circle* (Boston: Houghton Mifflin, 1960), pp. 182, 184.

[7] For a brief resume of the ambiguity of the framework—European or American—which unity was to have, see Max Beloff, *The United States and the Unity of Europe* (Washington: The Brookings Institution, 1963), pp. 63–75. Interviews indicated that U.S. officials supposed that the European army would eventually have a European commander, but the contradiction between the interim commander and the political authority remained.

hardly surprising that there was hesitation about it in every capital but Washington.

THE SITUATION PRIOR TO EDC AGREEMENT

While there had been little change in the respective national goals of the principal actors in the German rearmament situation, there was a general easing of previously rigid positions. There was a continuation of the tendency begun with the Spofford compromise and continued with the Brussels formula, the mid-1951 Paris accords, and the November European army agreements, to paper over fundamental disagreements with announcements of allied accord. U.S. leaders used every means available to induce formal agreement among the Europeans, but in the period before Lisbon "the crisis had only increased." [8]

American spokesmen, however, continued to express confidence in their public statements. High Commissioner McCloy found that "we have witnessed a modern fairy tale in terms of the reconstruction of Germany and the good will of Germany's former enemies." [9] Secretary Acheson, perhaps somewhat embarrassed by the Federal Republic's demand for full NATO membership even before agreement could be reached on a European army pact, said he was sure the German rearmament question could be worked out without prejudice to future steps concerning the role of Germany. General Eisenhower continued to give full support to EDC, and was reported to have staked his prestige, for political reasons, on the success of the European army. Leaders in the U.S. Congress on both ends of the political spectrum urged that a European federation be created as soon as possible.[10]

But alongside the optimism there was said to be "acute impa-

[8] Acheson, *Present at the Creation*, p. 608.
[9] *Department of State Bulletin*, December 13, 1951, p. 1053.
[10] *The New York Times*, January 31, 1952. See also Clarence W. Baier and Richard P. Stebbins, eds., *Documents on American Foreign Relations, 1952* (New York: Harper, 1953), pp. 6, 118; *The New York Times*, January 23 and February 10, *The Economist*, December 22, 1951; *Department of State Bulletin*, February 18, 1952, pp. 275–76.

tience" in Washington because Paris and Bonn had raised what U.S. officials considered "unrelated" questions, the effect of which was to complicate the possibility of reaching agreement on the European army project. The degree to which the German rearmament question affected the future European balance was still imperfectly appreciated.[11] For example, the French impression of American haste in fostering German resurgence was such that Schuman sent a personal letter to Acheson recalling his government's hostility to the Federal Republic's admission to NATO. Acheson found the idea of precluding German membership "dangerous and destructive." [12]

American policymakers believed that a definite move had to be made on the EDC, once the European army had been debated in the Bundestag and the National Assembly. Failure at Lisbon to agree on the German role in Western defense could end NATO as an effective alliance, they thought, particularly if there was an increasing divergence between France and the Federal Republic. At the same time President Truman stressed that the threat of world war remained "very real," Foreign Minister Schuman declared that he was "sure that war is not now imminent or inevitable." [13] The basic French view that war was not probable was shared by Bonn. France and Germany continued to perceive the cold war as, respectively, a regrettable and welcome stimulus to the rehabilitation of the Federal Republic, and neither shared U.S. apprehension that the international situation might rapidly deteriorate.

France looked to the only possible manner in which the former enemy could be contained satisfactorily: the virtual disappearance

[11] *The New York Times,* February 2, 1952; *The Times* (London), February 8, 1952. Some American officials who feared Germany would dominate whatever arrangements were made wanted the United States to plan accordingly and refrain from assuming it would be safe to leave Europe even if EDC materialized.
[12] Acheson, *Present at the Creation,* p. 609. See also *L'Annee Politique, 1952,* p. 305. The French suspected that Washington was feeding German ambitions and that Bonn would not have dared to demand NATO membership without at least tacit U.S. approval.
[13] Quoted in Stebbins, *United States, 1952,* p. 25. See also *Department of State Bulletin,* January 21, 1952, pp. 79–80.

of Germany into "Europe." French interest in European federation by means of a common army, and the hesitant behavior of successive Paris governments, revealed EDC as an emotional, ideological, and moral question, not—as some critics have argued it should have been—an organizational problem in continental defense. The questions being asked as American haste for German rearmament persisted involved the role France would play in an emerging Europe still under U.S. protection, and how the European equilibrium could be maintained if there was to be a rearmed Germany facing an economically inferior France.[14] For France, equilibrium required German inferiority, since there was still no method whereby equality for the Federal Republic could be checked short of becoming superiority.[15] Even if EDC were agreed to in place of national German rearmament, this would still bring the danger of the Federal Republic's later withdrawal from the organization, which the British did not consider an adequate check on German strength and whose integrity the United States firmly refused to guarantee.[16] In a situation still linked emotionally and ideologically with the recent past, French opinion simply could not accept the consequences of transforming her former enemy into an ally. Nor was French fear of future instability (or worse) allayed by the optimistic tone of U.S. diplomacy; "all the assurances by all the American diplomats and proconsuls cannot remove entirely the gnawing fear that German power means European trouble." [17]

[14] Cf. Daniel Lerner, "Reflections on France in the World Arena," in *France Defeats EDC*, eds. Daniel Lerner and Raymond Aron (New York: Praeger, 1957), p. 217. *L'Annee Politique, 1952*, p. 297. It was the assumption of inferiority rather than its actuality that was so disturbing. Once the French inferiority complex was cured in the mid-1950s, France had little further difficulty in accepting Germany as a competitor. These points are perceptively explored in Stanley Hoffmann, *et al.*, *In Search of France* (Cambridge: Harvard University Press, 1963), *passim.*

[15] The only exception remained the supranational solution, although as is mentioned below Schuman himself was convinced that the Federal Republic would soon be involved in European defense whether or not the federal umbrella opened.

[16] Leon D. Epstein, *Britain—Uneasy Ally* (Chicago: University of Chicago Press, 1954), p. 247.

[17] *The New York Times*, February 3, 1952 (Drew Middleton).

Persistent French suspicions were exacerbated by increasingly bold expressions of the ambitions of the Federal Republic. Earlier allied fears that the price would rise the longer rearmament was delayed proved well founded, and the more often German troops were proclaimed indispensable to Western defense, the more certain the Federal Republic became that it could insist on full equality.[18] In January, 1952, State Secretary for Foreign Affairs Walter Hallstein said in a press conference that equality required either that Germany be admitted to NATO or that the other prospective EDC members quit the alliance. Since the latter was unlikely, this presented at last the danger which France had originally feared at the time the National Assembly debated whether to accept the North Atlantic Treaty.[19] The Chancellor modified somewhat the rigidity of this demand a few weeks later, but left no doubt about his expectations: on February 7 he told the Bundestag that it was obvious NATO and EDC would be linked and German soldiers in the European army would be under NATO command. This in turn meant, Adenauer said, that "If we enter the European Defense Community, we shall become one day members of the Atlantic Pact as well, quite naturally." [20]

Secretary Acheson took no immediate public position on this question, but McCloy said on January 6 that although the Federal Republic was not yet a member of NATO the only question which remained was the form and extent of her participation in the Western defense system. Thereafter, Hallstein said Germany could not accept EDC if this involved permanent exclusion from the Atlantic Alliance. Meanwhile, he said, the Federal Republic would be agreeable if NATO decisions affecting Europe would be

---

[18] Adenauer of course realized that it was in his interest to retain Washington's good will by going along with the rearmament demand. Hans Speier, *German Rearmament and Atomic War: The Views of German Military and Political Leaders* (Evanston: Row, Peterson, 1957), p. 238.

[19] *LeMonde*, February 9, 1952, recalled Schuman's assurance to the deputies in 1949 that Germany would never be a member of the alliance and American statements that there would be no German rearmament.

[20] Quoted in F. Roy Willis, *France, Germany and the New Europe, 1945–1963* (Stanford: Stanford University Press, 1965), p. 155.

submitted to the unanimous approval of the EDC Council.[21] This softer German diplomatic voice reflected not an easing of the demands of the Federal Republic but an awareness of its superior bargaining position.

In addition to NATO membership, German spokesmen demanded the right to revive the arms industry and manufacture weapons on a basis of equality with other EDC states. They stated that the Federal Republic was prepared to provide twenty divisions (eight more than envisioned under the agreements already reached), and an air force of up to 1,500 planes plus naval units for coastal operations.[22] Federal officials also said that as soon as the EDC treaty was signed and approved, Bonn would call for 60,000 volunteers from the former Wehrmacht, making an effort to exclude Nazi fanatics. Important unofficial evidence of German military ambitions, or at least hesitation, had been already revealed in a book published in Germany containing the views on the European army of former high Wehrmacht officers. Their comments made it clear that EDC was unacceptable for political, military, and strategic reasons.[23] In addition, wide domestic opposition to the Chancellor's rearmament policy persisted, but—with U.S. support—Adenauer went ahead with the remilitarization plans, even though it was obvious that this would entail certain disadvantages.[24]

On February 8, the Bundestag voted in favor of the government

[21] *The New York Times*, January 28, 1952; *L'Annee Politique, 1952*, p. 302; and see *International Organization*, Vol. VI, 1952, p. 330, for a summary of the January 26–27 meeting of the EDC conference.

[22] *Christian Science Monitor*, January 21, 1952; *The New York Times*, January 17, 1952, reported that the United States was going to give full backing to a large German air force.

[23] This book is discussed in *The Economist*, February 2, 1952. The work, *Armee ohne Pathos*, is extensively referred to and quoted from concerning then-current military demands in Germany by Julian Lider, *West Germany in NATO* (Warsaw: Western Press Agency, 1965), Chap. 5, *passim*.

[24] Cf. Stebbins, *United States, 1952*, pp. 110–11; Calvocoressi, *Survey, 1952*, pp. 61–72. *The New York Times*, January 15, 1952, reported that German fears of the financial burden of rearmament were especially acute, although High Commissioner McCloy's report covering this period stated that "the Federal Republic's participation in the defense effort of the West was likely to insure a steadily rising standard of living in Western Germany, notwithstanding defense expenditures." *Department of State Bulletin*, July 28, 1952, p. 135.

continuing negotiations for German participation in EDC, but the vote laid down conditions. These were that there must be: a Saar settlement; membership in NATO; release of war criminals; an equal voice for Bonn in seeking German reunification; the removal of all restrictions on German industry; equal financial treatment in the sharing of defense costs; and an end to the occupation regime with full recognition of German sovereignty.[25] A German official was quoted as saying at the time, "You must choose between trusting Germans and doing without German contingents."[26] Once again, France faced the problem of how to reconcile her lack of trust with the fact that the United States had already opted for German contingents.

The French National Assembly debate on the European army coincided with the "high-water mark of sixteen months of trading by the Bonn Government on the basis of a contribution of non-existent German troops to a nonexistent European Army."[27] The foreign minister opened with an endorsement of EDC hardly different from the assurances offered in October, 1950, when the Pleven Plan was presented. The distinction was that on this occasion the parliament was told that if the European army plan did not succeed, it was Schuman's understanding that the United States would insist on German rearmament in another form. Earlier doubt that Washington would risk an open break with Paris faded as apprehension grew that a national German army would follow a failure of EDC. A French government memorandum to the deputies had already argued that *only* a European army would avoid the risk of "a German military renaissance" and ease recurrent U.S. pressure for national remilitarization of the Federal Republic.[28] Paris had little confidence in its veto power.

[25] *The New York Times*, February 9, 1952; *The Economist*, February 16, 1952; *L'Annee Politique, 1952*, p. 306; *International Organization*, Vol. VI, 1952, pp. 323-24.

[26] *Manchester Guardian*, February 7, 1952.

[27] James P. Warburg, quoted in Wolfram F. Hanreider, *West German Foreign Policy 1949-1963: International Pressure and Domestic Response* (Stanford: Stanford University Press, 1967), p. 47.

[28] *L'Annee Politique, 1952*, p. 308. The memorandum also stressed that inequality would remain, with no German general staff or defense ministry, and that there would be supranational organs and reciprocal guarantees with NATO.

Schuman recommended the EDC to the National Assembly on the following grounds: (1) France could not persist in a completely negative attitude toward German rearmament without seriously damaging Franco-American relations; (2) the European army would be the safest way to handle German forces, since the system would be difficult to withdraw from; (3) it would—as General Eisenhower had assured, and contrary to charges that it could not work—provide an effective military force; (4) EDC was necessary to improve Franco-German relations. It need hardly be pointed out that these arguments were of small comfort to the deputies, although Schuman again stressed that while the Federal Republic would enjoy equality *within* the European army, there was no reason for German membership in NATO, and that there would be a European political authority from the very beginning of EDC.[29]

After lengthy and often emotional articulation of literally dozens of distinct viewpoints on EDC—pro, con, and often mixed —the deputies voted a resolution expressing their wishes and, a few days afterward, permitted the Faure ministry to survive a confidence vote by 326 to 276. The resolution called for guarantees to EDC by Britain and the United States; asked for allowances to France in the sharing of defense expenses for the costs of the Indo-China war; stipulated that French forces in Europe should at all times be equal to those of any other member of EDC; [30] said that integration of national units should be at the "lowest possible level" and that there could be no recruiting of Germans until after the treaty had been fully ratified; requested that a special attempt be made to induce British participation; and declared that NATO, a purely defensive organization, "must not include

The Pleven ministry fell on January 8, and was succeeded on January 18 by a new government under Edgar Faure. Schuman remained foreign minister.

[29] A majority of NATO allies shared the French view that no state with territorial ambitions was eligible to join the alliance. Calvocoressi, *Survey, 1952*, p. 76. *L'Annee Politique, 1952*, pp. 307–12, has a resume of the debate, and the texts of the statements of Schuman and Bidault appear in the Annexes. See also Furniss, *France, Troubled Ally*, pp. 74–75.

[30] Bonn had earlier said that the creation of the twelve German divisions need not await the fourteen from France once EDC was approved.

states with any territorial claims." The vote sustaining the government was hardly a belated acceptance of German rearmament on the part of the deputies, but instead was a grudging and limited approval given because no one had anything else to suggest. Behind the immediate debate on the European army, *LeMonde* observed, was the impression that the National Assembly was engaged in a condemnation of U.S. policy, the meeting ground of French suspicions and German ambitions.[31]

In the aftermath of the recently frustrated U.S. attempt to gain either NATO endorsement of the European army or to foster agreement between EDC's prospective members themselves, the outlook was mixed.[32] Deep differences remained on the political level, as between Germany and the Western allies and among the allies themselves, while militarily NATO's modest progress was an ambiguous achievement in light of the apparent discrepancy between Soviet capabilities and Moscow's disinclination to seek forceful confrontations.

As American diplomacy elevated the EDC plan from a means toward German rearmament into an end in itself, several separate but interrelated geopolitical considerations emerged. The solution of the German problem through the integration of a re-armed Federal Republic into Western Europe would, at a single stroke, solve the problem of providing for the Western European balance by eliminating war between France and Germany, and that of the East-West balance by creating an effective counter-weight to the Soviet Union on the Continent. EDC would contain, internally and externally, both the Germans and the Russians while restoring Germany as a member of the international community and avoiding the error of the interwar period.[33]

[31] "Only the critics of the scheme showed any real enthusiasm." *The Times* (London), February 13, 1952. The EDC "victory" in the assembly was illusory, one analyst added, the majority having been obtained only by an anti-German appeal. Furniss, *France, Troubled Ally*, p. 75; *The New York Times*, February 19, 1952; *LeMonde*, February 14, 1952.

[32] Cf. Dean Acheson, *Sketches from Life of Men I Have Known* (New York: Harper, 1961), pp. 47, 119.

[33] High Commissioner McCloy constantly stressed the appropriateness of ending the occupation status, on the ground that, no matter how benevolent, this was not

Now, however, the path presumably would be a safer one since the additional simultaneous step of providing a European framework could be taken. In effect, occupied and demilitarized Germany would, with no dangerous interval as an independent and rearmed state, be included as an equal member of an international military organization responsible to a supranational political authority. As perceived by American officials, there was everything to be gained and nothing to be lost if EDC could somehow be made to work. There was little evidence that it would, but many indications that it would not.[34] Yet, as before, U.S. diplomacy proceeded on the assumption that there was no alternative available in any case, and in this limited sense Paris and Washington were in accord.

The major American figure pressing for EDC was General Eisenhower, who saw the goals of the United States and NATO as a whole as inseparable. Once committed to political unification, Eisenhower embraced wholeheartedly the European army project and thereafter declined to reconsider his decision. Concerning EDC as a military device, his full support rested on the beliefs both that it would work and that there was no other way to realize NATO progress.[35]

Some reports implied Eisenhower was so concerned with the European army that he would remain in Europe indefinitely for the express purpose of guiding the project to a successful conclusion, but more sophisticated observers noted that the Supreme

---

conducive to democratization and reducing the risk of a revival of totalitarianism. See, for example, *Department of State Bulletin,* July 28, 1952, p. 136.

[34] The American press was, by this time, so optimistic that this may have been one more factor which aided the growth of the mushroom. See *The New York Times,* January 1, 1952; New York *Herald Tribune,* January 2, 1952.

[35] The overriding factor in all U.S. considerations of whether the European army would work was the conviction of Eisenhower that it would. General Gruenther shared this, and had in fact been the key military figure to convince the SACEUR that EDC should be supported. Once Eisenhower "got religion" on the European army question, whether the scheme would be militarily workable seemed settled. When a military colleague of long standing later said that EDC was no more than a "gimmick," Eisenhower became upset and summoned General Gruenther to argue in its behalf. Interviews and Dwight D. Eisenhower, *The White House Years: Mandate for Change, 1953–1956* (Garden City: Doubleday, 1963), pp. 15, 398–99.

Commander had already given positive indications of a desire to be President.[36] The significance of this was that some Europeans saw in it exactly what they did not want, the withdrawal of American troops from Europe as a consequence of the formation of a European army containing a rearmed Germany.

While the United States had to make it officially clear to recalcitrant Europeans that this would not be the case, Eisenhower himself apparently hoped that in the not too distant future this might indeed be possible. As mentioned, Dirk Stikker had been convinced for some time by early 1952 that "in the back of Eisenhower's mind was the idea that the creation of the EDC would allow him to send American boys home." [37] In any event, without EDC there would be little possibility of a U.S. military withdrawal. Eisenhower himself believed that the signing of the EDC treaty was sufficient to allow him in good conscience to leave the NATO command.[38] While the impact of the Supreme Commander's impending departure on European fears of a U.S. withdrawal from the Continent cannot be measured, it did begin what later became an extensive change of American leadership in Europe, which observers agree was detrimental to the development of the sense of confidence which would have been necessary for the European army experiment.[39]

[36] One report said Eisenhower might sacrifice his political hopes in America to remain as commander-in-chief of the European army and "as the political co-ordinator of any supranational directorship and as Europe's spokesman in its relations with the United States." Raymond Daniell, *The New York Times*, December 18, 1951. This is an exaggerated example, but not wholly atypical of the nonsense which frequently appeared in the American press. Cf. Acheson, *Sketches from Life*, p. 46, who wrote that as early as November, 1951, Foreign Minister Joseph Bech of Luxembourg told him "the signs are unmistakable" that NATO would soon lose its commander.

[37] Dirk U. Stikker, *Men of Responsibility: A Memoir* (New York: Harper and Row, 1966), p. 303. It was reported that American officials took special care to assure the Dutch that this was not the case. James Reston, *The New York Times*, January 22, 1952. Cf. also Eden, *Full Circle*, p. 39; Beloff, *United States*, p. 78.

[38] Eisenhower, *White House Years*, pp. 22–24, 398–99. Montgomery had earlier urged him to return, saying Eisenhower could do more for EDC in the White House than at SHAPE. Bernard L. Montgomery, *The Memoirs of Field-Marshal The Viscount Montgomery of Alamein* (New York: New American Library, 1958), p. 462.

[39] The 1952 exodus of American officials had not yet begun, but there was wide apprehension this would occur. Bech's certainty that Eisenhower would leave ac-

European fears were also increased by the apprehension that Germany would emerge in a dominant position. As American officials openly declined to support French positions, the impression was inevitably given that the Federal Republic was more than ever in Washington's favor. McCloy's testimony in Washington to the effect that "German youth is patriotic, but not nationalistic," was probably of little comfort to Europeans who recalled the recent disappearance of the distinction. France, widely thought to be permanently inferior in population and industrial potential and chronically deficient in political cohesion, had only one advantage left over her old rival—the military one.[40]

Officials of the United States paid lip service to the legitimacy of French concern for the future European balance and the fundamental necessity of precluding another German threat. They assured Paris that EDC was a "safe" means to German rearmament, but did not offer a guarantee that would make it impossible for the Federal Republic to withdraw from the European army.[41] As France was pressed to agree to larger and larger units in the European army plans, and as the level of integration went higher and higher, there began what was to become—with the EDC treaty's signature—the process whereby France was presented with the Hobson's choice of German divisions in a European army *not* incapable of fragmentation and a revived American inclination to rearm the Federal Republic *without* a supranational framework. As it appeared that Bonn was going to recover its sovereignty anyway, the dilemma facing Paris prior to the Lisbon meet-

---

tually preceded the general's decision to do so. See Eisenhower, *White House Years*, pp. 14–23, concerning his decision to run for the Presidency.

[40] U.S. Senate, Committee on Foreign Relations, Hearings, *Relations with the Federal Republic of Germany*, 82nd Cong., 2nd Sess., 1952, p. 70. Steel production in the Federal Republic alone had just broken the German record of 1938, at the peak of Hitler's armament drive. *The New York Times*, February 3, 1952. At the same time, the other Western European states were beginning to experience their first overall annual decline in industrial production since 1947. Stebbins, *United States, 1952*, pp. 404–5.

[41] Even apart from the Constitutional difficulty which would have prevented such a U.S. guarantee, there was no practical way to do this, particularly in an election year. Acheson was very firm with Schuman in refusing even to consider the matter. Acheson, *Present at the Creation*, p. 612.

ing was that "No treaty at all might increase immeasurably the danger to France of a rearmed Germany, but a weak treaty might only plaster over that danger temporarily or, worse, handicap France more than Germany." [42]

The absence in the United States of a fear of Germany even remotely comparable to that felt in Europe allowed American policy to proceed free of the restraints felt in allied capitals. This, in turn, permitted the EDC to mushroom into an imagined panacea without second thoughts that the cure might be worse than the illness. With nothing to check this process, EDC became the cornerstone of U.S. policy: "It was as if highly complicated problems like the structure and strength of NATO, the problem of European unity, the German problem, the relation of European unity to the Atlantic Alliance, the basic relation of the United States toward Europe and NATO, were all reduced to one single problem—the fate of the European army project." The fact that European unity was an addition to, not a substitute for, German rearmament in American eyes, was apparent.[43] As the European army increasingly assumed the character of an American project, it also appeared to imply an "anti-French" solution to the German rearmament tangle. The one-sided nature of Washington's policy leading toward satisfaction in Bonn and frustration in Paris was so patent that—on the eve of the London meeting of the occupying powers' foreign ministers with the Federal Chancellor —*The New York Times* was moved to recall that "It was Germany against whom we had to fight for survival in two World Wars; it was the Nazi Germans who perpetrated deeds as cruel and vicious as any in recorded history. It is German militarism, German nationalism, German irredentism, German super-discipline and super-efficiency that must be feared in the years to come—

[42] Furniss, *France, Troubled Ally*, p. 72.
[43] Ernst van der Beugel, *From Marshall Aid to Atlantic Partnership: European Integration as a Concern of American Foreign Policy* (Amsterdam: Elsevier, 1966), p. 281. Cf. the language of the Truman-Churchill joint statement of January 9, 1952, in *Public Papers of the Presidents of the United States. Harry S Truman. 1952–53* (Washington: Government Printing Office, 1966), p. 18. See also the President's language in the Fourth Report on the Mutual Defense Assistance Program, *Department of State Bulletin*, February 25, 1952, p. 316.

not France, not anything French." What would follow French acceptance or rejection was still another question, but prior to this was the need for a NATO decision: "A lead—perhaps a push, too—had to come from the United States." [44]

THE LONDON AND LISBON CONFERENCES

Acheson arrived in London on February 13. At various times in the next few days he met with British and French representatives with the objective of pressing on them the need for immediate agreement. Convinced that it was "now or never," the secretary told Churchill that European defense could wait no longer: the choice was between EDC and "a national German army, general staff, and all the rest." Relations between the United States and the other occupying powers were not good, and those between France and Germany were positively bad.[45] American diplomacy at this point sought to foster an all-round accord on the European army, but the threat was apparent that Washington's drive to gain a German military contribution as well as to restore Bonn's international status would be directed elsewhere should EDC now falter.

The foreign ministers of the occupying powers, after conferring among themselves, met with the Federal Chancellor on February 18–19 to consider a number of questions, upon which depended the outcome of both the European army and the contractual agreements. These included the relationship between NATO and EDC; American and British policies toward EDC and whether security guarantees would be given; German membership in NATO; the amounts of defense contributions by individual states; the treatment of war criminals in the Federal Republic; the Saar question; the nature of armaments industries in Germany; limitations on sovereignty within the peace contract, and other

[44] Acheson, *Present at the Creation,* p. 608. Editorial, *The New York Times,* February 18, 1952.
[45] Acheson, *Present at the Creation,* p. 611; Konrad Adenauer, *Memoirs, 1945–1953* (Chicago: Regnery, 1966), pp. 403–5.

matters. The London conference was particularly important because of the opportunity it afforded the Western Big Three's representatives to meet with Adenauer.[46] Without this, the Lisbon conference might have repeated the error of producing agreement among the occupying powers which was unacceptable to the Germans.

Acheson later said that during the meetings, "More often than not, I found myself agreeing with positions taken by Adenauer; and Eden, with Schuman." The secretary, of course, did not want the impression of a split along these lines to be given, and added that "one of the tasks at Lisbon would be to work out a united allied position which the Germans could find reasonable." More than ever, the task of American diplomacy was to guide the less powerful allies of the United States toward a conclusion acceptable to all parties when—had pressure from the super-power protector not been present—it is highly unlikely any steps would have been taken to remilitarize the Federal Republic. For the time being, it would suffice if the parties could maintain the appearance of movement toward German rearmament, which they had probably realized was the minimum Washington expected.[47]

The London communiqués, one tripartite and the other joined

---

[46] The representatives were in London for the funeral of King George VI. The meetings between Acheson and Eden, then with Schuman, preliminary to their being joined by Adenauer, were extremely difficult. In particular, they involved the future of Germany (but in fact many more issues), and the split followed earlier tendencies as Acheson wanted to move quickly, Eden slowly, and Schuman hardly at all. The sessions are vividly recalled in Acheson, *Present at the Creation,* pp. 610–12, 615–17.

[47] Acheson, *Sketches From Life,* pp. 47, 70–71. Acheson's account of the London meetings makes clear his impatience with French hesitation. He considered Schuman's desire for a guarantee against German secession from EDC a "neurotic obsession"; dismissed his plea not to rebuild the Krupp arms-production facilities; found "pointless" the French minister's words about the adverse psychological effects of rebuilding German war factories; and thought the arguments with the French about German war material limitations an experience in "dreary repetition." Acheson, *Present at the Creation,* pp. 615–20. The secretary was correct in his view that it did not make sense to treat Bonn simultaneously as an ally and an enemy, but once again American logic and French emotions diverged. Acheson's description of Adenauer's readiness to close his eyes to restrictions amounting to discrimination against Bonn suggests that it was the Chancellor's flexibility which was indispensable to what accords did emerge.

in by Adenauer, affirmed that the numerous issues mentioned above had been reviewed and discussed, with the exception of the question of NATO membership for Germany.[48] This matter, which Adenauer explicitly raised with Acheson, Eden, and Schuman, was probably omitted from the communiqué because of the National Assembly's indirect but emphatically negative reference to it just two days before. The NATO question was temporarily shelved when the Chancellor agreed not to request membership for the time being, although this apparent concession had really been set up in advance by Bonn spokesmen demanding NATO entry when it was obvious Paris could not agree.

The Anglo-Saxon powers were aware that Schuman's position before the French Assembly was delicate and that a formal treaty of guarantees between them and EDC covering "secession or misbehavior" by an EDC member (which Schuman had repeatedly asked) was considered inappropriate in Bonn. They decided to express their countries' commitment to EDC as a unit, that is, to meet the French fear of unilateral misbehavior without offending the Germans. This was expressed in the tripartite communiqué, as the United States and Britain "declared their abiding interest in the establishment and integrity of the European defense community" and "recalled the decision of their governments to maintain armed forces in Europe which, in association with the European defense forces, will contribute their fair share in the joint defense of the North Atlantic area." On the same day, February 19, the four-power statement welcomed the progress which had been made toward agreement on EDC. All interested governments, it recited, will have as their concern "to ensure [its] preservation." [49]

The London meetings both committed the Anglo-Saxon powers to EDC and reminded Germany that without German rearmament in the European army framework the contractual agreements could not be expected. But it was still questionable whether they

[48] *Department of State Bulletin*, March 3, 1952. Quotes are from these texts. Adenauer, *Memoirs*, p. 409.

[49] *Department of State Bulletin*, March 3, 1952, p. 325; Eden, *Full Circle*, pp. 44–45.

removed the obstacles which delayed the negotiations sufficiently to make the result satisfactory in a broader political context. In France, the next few days seemed to confirm the suspicion that Bonn and Washington were working hand in hand. Moreover, the Anglo-American pledge to leave their troops in Europe, intended to assure the French that they would not be left alone with re-armed Germans, instead "seemed to underline the impression that Germany was France's problem within EDC, while Britain stood aloof and fancied herself on the same level of world power as the United States." [50]

Finally, the London meeting did little to render EDC acceptable on other than the governmental level. The *Manchester Guardian* said the statement of the four ministers "reads as if they had stuffed their ears with cotton wool" and ignored all the expressions in Bonn and Paris which made it clear that even if these govern-mental leaders agreed on German rearmament, they "cannot carry the confidence of their parliaments and peoples." [51] But these were considerations for the future. For the moment, the U.S. conviction was that apparent agreement on EDC by the ministers would allow this solution to the German rearmament problem to go forward, and if nothing else this was the lubricant which the London meeting gave to the Lisbon conference.

The North Atlantic Council's February 20 to 25 meeting at Lisbon, which adopted military-force goals so ambitious that questions were raised about everything from the necessity for their adoption to the sincerity of those who did so, was considered a high point in the American quest for German rearmament.[52] Secretary Acheson, accompanied by virtually every important U.S. official connected with the effort to rearm Germany, went to the Portuguese capital convinced that "if the tide did not turn at

---

[50] F. S. Northedge, *British Foreign Policy: The Process of Readjustment, 1945–1961* (London: Allen and Unwin, 1962), p. 156; see also *L'Annee Politique, 1952*, pp. 313–14.

[51] *Manchester Guardian*, February 21, 1952. See *The Spectator*, February 22, 1952, for a report on domestic opposition to rearmament in the Federal Republic.

[52] Roger Hilsman, "NATO: The Developing Strategic Context," in *NATO and American Security*, ed. Klaus Knorr (Princeton: Princeton University Press, 1959), p. 21.

Lisbon, it would turn, if at all, too late for the aims toward which Schuman and I were working." These aims were, presumably, European defense and European unification, but not national German rearmament: this meant EDC, the single catchall device available. Schuman himself proclaimed that "we are now certain that the work which we have for the last year prepared at Paris is militarily valid and politically acceptable." [53]

The NATO Council, after hearing reports on the status of the European army negotiations and the contractual agreements with Germany, agreed:

> The Council found that the principles underlying the treaty to establish the European Defense Community conformed to the interests of the parties to the North Atlantic Treaty. It also agreed on the principles which should govern the relationship between the proposed community and the North Atlantic Treaty Organization. The North Atlantic Council agreed to propose to its members and to the European Defense Community reciprocal security undertakings between the members of the two organizations. . . .[54]

The finding that the underlying principles of EDC conformed to the interests of the members of NATO was especially ambiguous. These principles, as defined by Schuman's report to the NATO Council, based on the agreements reached at the Paris conference, were largely a matter of military details.[55] For example, it was stated that the European army would be composed of forty-three national groups, each roughly the equivalent of a division (13,000 men); the lowest integrated unit would be the army corps of about 80,000 men, with three or four national divisions; the staff and tactical and logistical support units of the army corps would be integrated; air units would be integrated

---

[53] Acheson, *Sketches from Life*, p. 47; *L'Annee Politique, 1952*, p. 315.

[54] Baier and Stebbins, *Documents, 1952*, pp. 170–71.

[55] For a summary of Schuman's report, see Royal Institute of International Affairs, *Britain in Western Europe: WEU and the Atlantic Alliance* (London: Royal Institute of International Affairs, 1956), pp. 32–33. For the EDC provisions, see Calvocoressi, *Survey, 1952*, pp. 84ff.

only at division level and naval forces not at all; integrated European army forces would be under the control of a board of commissioners, whose activities would be harmonized by a council of ministers to conform to the policies of the six governments; there would be a common budget and armaments program; voting in the council would be weighted; there would be an assembly which could censure the board and cause it to resign; and other similar details. In short, the report whose provisions were approved stressed the military, not the political, aspects of the European army. The NATO Council, it seems clear, agreed because the project would be of military value. Schuman's list of items was a far cry from the Pleven Plan—but for the moment this was played down on the official level.

Failure to pay even lip service to what France had always considered the underlying principle of a European army—political unification within which the German danger would dissolve—was repeated in the council's "declaration of aims." Reference was again to EDC as consistent with a furthering of NATO's aims, primary among which was "the defense of the North Atlantic Treaty area." No mention was made in the declaration even remotely construable as an endorsement of genuine European political unification. The council limited itself to an approval of "the closer association of the Western European countries" which the establishment of EDC "will help to promote." [56]

Acheson himself suggested the qualified nature of the allies' acceptance of EDC a short time later when he commented that what the council did was "give its blessing" to the principles which the Six had worked out. The distinction may seem slender, but the whole story of the German rearmament issue had been characterized by such nuances, and once again there may have been an important difference between lack of approval of EDC as a political project and simply accepting the military principles upon which it was based. The secretary, nevertheless, considered

[56] Baier and Stebbins, *Documents, 1952*, p. 173.

the council's endorsement the most important single achievement of the Lisbon meeting.[57]

Among other matters disposed of at the conference the setting of NATO force goals was outstanding, in terms of the reaction produced if nothing else. The NATO Council, after considering the report of the temporary council committee, proclaimed that the allies would "provide approximately 50 divisions in appropriate conditions of combat readiness" during 1952.[58] While the plan specifically noted that it assumed a German military contribution would be made through EDC "in subsequent years" rather than at once, there is no doubt that the force goals of seventy-five divisions by 1953 and ninety-six by 1954 were targets which would not have been fixed apart from an expectation that the Federal Republic would furnish a substantial number of troops. On the one hand, this expectation was what allowed the goals to be set, and on the other, the goals could not be met without Germany's rearmament.[59] Just as there had been a chicken-or-egg relationship between the adoption of a forward strategy and German defense participation, there was now an interdependent relationship between officially announced NATO plans and German rearmament. One military adviser on the U.S. delegation at Lisbon said everyone knew the targets would never be reached without German divisions, and even then the force goals were "fantastic—but they *were* figures."

The endorsement of EDC by the NATO Council and the setting of higher military strength levels were clearly successes for the American diplomatic effort. For the United States, the accomplishments at Lisbon, which involved many NATO matters,

[57] *Department of State Bulletin*, March 10, 1952, p. 365; Acheson, *Present at the Creation*, p. 624.

[58] *Department of State Bulletin*, March 10, 1952, p. 369. About half the fifty divisions, it was later explained, were to consist of "ready reserves" which would not be mobilized until hostilities had already begun. Stebbins, *United States, 1952*, p. 127.

[59] Robert E. Osgood, *NATO: The Entangling Alliance* (Chicago: University of Chicago Press, 1962), p. 87. A few weeks later General Gruenther testified that in his judgment the Lisbon goals were "high, but attainable." See U.S. Senate, Committee on Foreign Relations, Hearings, *Mutual Security Act of 1952*, 82nd Cong., 2nd Sess., 1952, pp. 204–6. Cf. Hanreider, *West German Foreign Policy*, p. 71.

were crowned by the accord on Germany.[60] One of the great tasks of statesmanship, Acheson said, was to bring Germany back into the international family. A forward defense line was necessary for strategic reasons, and other Europeans understood that it was proper that Germans should participate in the defense of the area which included their own country. "But the problem that worried the people of Europe, including the Germans themselves, was: How to do this without raising again the danger of unbridled German militarism? And how to restore Germany to a position of dignity and equality in this effort so that it would willingly and enthusiastically participate?" The answer, of course, was EDC.

The achievement of this great unifying step, Acheson announced, was of vital importance to the United States. The common control of the European army forces would make sure that "none of these countries would constitute a threat to any other," and ratification of EDC would mean the appearance of German units and the close association of the Federal Republic with the whole European defense plan of NATO. Germany would be restored to a responsible and equal place among nations, and with EDC providing the necessary safeguards against aggressive militarism, the unification of Europe itself could proceed. The secretary said that it was inspiring and thrilling to see the progress made "against these ancient national rivalries which have caused so much mischief for so long." He felt certain that the agreements at Lisbon had "brought us to the dawn of a new day in Europe." [61]

In contrast to the enthusiastic American response, *L'Annee Politique* observed that the result of the occasion was indifference. The attempt of the three foreign ministers to act as if the EDC

[60] Among other matters important to the German rearmament issue, it was agreed that reciprocal commitments would be worked out between NATO and EDC, since the Federal Republic was the single EDC state not in NATO. Twin protocols between the organizations as such rather than specification of Germany alone in mutual defense pledges would solve the double problem of satisfying the French wish to keep Germany out of NATO and the German wish to avoid at least the appearance of discrimination. Acheson considered French financial and German arms-production questions the most difficult part of the Lisbon meeting; these were satisfactorily worked out after exhausting sessions. Acheson, *Present at the Creation*, pp. 623–26.

[61] *Department of State Bulletin*, March 10, 1952, p. 365.

agreement was a solemn, historic moment, it was said, fell flat. The subject was already old, the treaty had not yet been signed anyway, and it would still have to face the problems of ratification. The force goals, this French review observed, were at best naïve, an imaginary total based upon an unreal promise. As to the reciprocal guarantees anticipated between NATO and EDC, these seemed acceptable. The Federal Republic was not to be formally admitted to membership in the alliance—"but in fact?"

These sharply divergent expressions marked a high point in the transformation of EDC from a European to an American goal. Averell Harriman, at this time mutual security administrator, said: "For centuries, the rivalry of these two countries has soaked the soil of Europe in blood. Yet in a split second of history we are seeing these ancient enemies being brought together by the common need for security from a greater danger." Recognizing that it was an external threat—not an internal process of development— which was bringing these old enemies together, Harriman noted that EDC would be closely associated with NATO, using language which indicated the transformation of the European army from a European to an American policy objective: "In fact, the European Defense Community could not have been contemplated except within the context of the North Atlantic Community. The six-nation European army will be a part of the total NATO force— the Eisenhower Army, as they call it in Europe." [62] The same conclusion was reached later by a British study group: "American support gave the EDC reality as nothing else could." Without U.S. diplomatic efforts the project would have collapsed long before, and only heavy American pressure preserved it now.[63] The EDC force was still envisioned by American officials less as the amalgam

[62] *Department of State Bulletin,* March 17, 1952, pp. 411, 412. The general himself was a bit more modest in his memoirs, calling the anticipated EDC force "a NATO army." Eisenhower, *White House Years,* p. 399.

[63] R.I.I.A., *Britain in Western Europe,* p. 32. The U.S. government was not unanimous in its pro-EDC stand, and there were people in the Departments of both State and Defense who saw the European army as a highly dubious project if not an outright mistake. Nevertheless, there was no single figure of high official rank in Washington under either Truman or Eisenhower who dissented publicly from the pro-EDC policy.

of a European federation than as a military bonus for "the Eisenhower Army." NATO had accepted EDC, but could the reverse have occurred?

If the project lacked reality, due above all to the fact that the participating states were themselves dissatisfied with it, the power of the United States to bring it to realization was limited. At this point it is also possible that the concurrence of Schuman and Adenauer in the Lisbon results was misleading. Neither on the governmental nor the popular level was there support for the EDC which could have justified the U.S. conviction that NATO approval of the European army was what would really allow German rearmament to be achieved, although the American press shared Washington's sanguine prognosis.[64] And even on the NATO level, the allies had agreed to the scheme as the only feasible compromise between the original United States demand for German troops and the objections raised by the French, rather than due to a genuine conversion to faith in the European army. Acheson's impression that "the world that lay before us shone with hope," was simply not supported by the realities of the moment.[65]

If the Lisbon conference marked the zenith of the EDC's fortunes, it also marked the high point of American optimism. Acheson said on his return that "the unity of Europe has been brought closer to realization than ever before in history." [66] On the same day, the French government of Premier Faure was overthrown following his request for a substantial tax increase to meet French obligations under the Lisbon program. This phenomenon of American dreams and French realities, which characterized the

---

[64] *The New York Times*, February 23 and 24, 1952; *LeMonde*, February 21, 1952. Nor was the contradiction between the command of the European army by SACEUR and the control of the force by the EDC's board of commissioners resolved. The confusion this would have brought would have been militarily debilitating as well as politically counterproductive of cooperation, but General Eisenhower's assurances that the scheme was workable tended to calm such apprehensions.

[65] Lewis J. Edinger, *West German Armament*, Documentary Research Division, Air University, Maxwell Air Force Base, Maxwell, Alabama, October, 1955, p. 21; Acheson, *Present at the Creation*, p. 656.

[66] *Department of State Bulletin*, March 10, 1952, p. 366.

period after the Lisbon agreements on EDC, was a preview of a similar pattern of optimism in Washington and pessimism in Paris which followed the May treaties. The months in between were spent in "working out the innumerable details of ending the occupation, amending the North Atlantic Treaty to permit German association, and bringing the EDC to finality and signature." [67] But they were not indicative of French willingness to follow the American lead.

One important development, coming only two weeks after the Lisbon approval of the "principles" of the EDC, was the Soviet note of March 10, 1952, to the three Western powers, calling for a peace settlement for all Germany. This démarche, perhaps intended to check implementation of the NATO program generally as well as to impede German rearmament through EDC, was met in France as elsewhere in Europe with public relief that a new opportunity for a conciliatory settlement of the German problem had been presented.[68] The Russian note called for a reunified, neutral Germany which would be permitted to have its own national military forces, a proposal that met with a mixed reaction on its merits. France was interested in exploring the possibilities of settlement, at least to test the sincerity of the offer. Much was made of the Russian suggestion, especially in the popular press, but the fact that German rearmament remained unacceptable to France even in the Western framework of EDC made the plan irrelevant, since a remilitarized Federal Republic to which the GDR would be added was too dangerous to risk. Schuman told Acheson that the military part of the Soviet proposal had embarrassed even the French Communists.

Apart from its impact as a gesture whose meaning might have

---

[67] Acheson, *Sketches from Life*, p. 51, and *Present at the Creation*, pp. 640–42; *L'Annee Politique, 1952*, p. 317.

[68] Acheson and Adenauer lacked apparent interest in the Soviet proposal because they did not want to risk losing the momentum of the drive toward finalization of the Bonn and Paris accords. Cf. Acheson's statement, *Department of State Bulletin*, April 7, 1952, p. 530, which included his view that the United States will "not be deflected" from its goal of seeing the Federal Republic in the EDC. See also Coral Bell, *Negotiation from Strength: A Study in the Politics of Power* (London: Chatto and Windus, 1962), pp. 97ff.

been other than the allies assumed, the Russian note and its aftermath did not impede progress toward agreement on EDC or the political return of the Federal Republic.[69] The Big Three were in general accord that while the timing of the Soviet note was suspect, and its purpose probably to split the West rather than investigate a German settlement in good faith, it could not be rejected out of hand. Acheson, Schuman, and Eden (with Adenauer's concurrence) hence prepared identical notes to Moscow, which argued, *inter alia*, that the suggestion for the formation of German national forces was a step in the wrong direction, inimical to the common desire of all the parties to preclude permanently the possibility of another danger of German nationalism, militarism, or aggression. Exchanges of notes began, during which the Big Three half-heartedly explored the Soviet proposals. These led nowhere, and were virtually ignored when the May accords were signed. Acheson was so skeptical that he would have hesitated even if the Soviets had been "sincere." He later wrote that had Moscow been willing to pay the price of a genuine non-Communist government for all Germany to keep it from an association with the West, even this would have been dangerous since it might have produced "the same stalemate as in Austria." [70] The peoples of Europe might have been encouraged by then-current hopes of an East-West agreement on the German problem, but the Western leaders by this time perceived the problem differently: it was no longer possible (if it had ever been) to contemplate a Germany which would *not* be tightly tied to the West.

Other factors influencing French and European thoughts during this period included the steadily declining sense of military threat and the continuing relationship between economic and political factors stemming from the costly rearmament effort. Lord Ismay,

[69] Cf. John Lukacs, *A History of the Cold War* (Garden City: Doubleday, 1962), pp. 104–5. Schuman would have preferred to open talks with the Russians *before* going further with the EDC treaty or the contractual agreements, but Acheson took exactly the opposite view, and Adenauer apparently agreed. Cf. Furniss, *France, Troubled Ally*, p. 86, and Adenauer, *Memoirs*, p. 419.

[70] Acheson, *Present at the Creation*, p. 631; Baier and Stebbins, *Documents, 1952*, pp. 248–61.

NATO's new secretary-general, discovered that "to induce a country to increase its contribution was as difficult as getting blood out of a stone." [71] Voices in the U.S. Congress warned France that American aid might not continue unless the financial mess in Paris was cleaned up. In addition, the one figure whose commitment to EDC was the decisive element in the U.S. shift in its favor was shortly expected to depart. General Eisenhower's expression of his availability after winning the New Hampshire primary on March 11 made it certain he would leave NATO, and the American election campaign began to produce its impact.

Among other sources of insecurity and frustration, France was still unsatisfied with the Anglo-American position concerning a guarantee that a rearmed Germany not be able to withdraw from EDC. The assurances which Acheson and Eden had given at Lisbon to the effect that their governments fully supported the integrity of EDC, Schuman told the British representative at the Paris conference in March, were no longer enough to ensure ratification by the National Assembly. Schuman had told Eden in mid-February that "if France could be assured of the political presence of the United Kingdom in a way which would not leave his country face to face with Germany, he thought that French opinion would be satisfied." This is one example where Schuman might have been out of touch with French political reality, since there is no convincing evidence Britain's position would have been determinative at this time, any more than it was at any point.

France was not the only hesitant party to the EDC project. By early March, the Paris conference generally was in disarray. The Dutch refused to accede to the German demand that EDC forces be committed under the treaty to resist automatically an attack on any member of the EDC, because NATO had no such provision and because without a British guarantee "they feared they might find themselves fighting for a German interest without

[71] Hastings L. Ismay, *The Memoirs of General Lord Ismay* (New York: The Viking Press, 1960), p. 460; *L'Annee Politique, 1952*, pp. 317–18. See also the testimony of David Bruce at the hearings on the *Mutual Security Act of 1952*, 82nd Cong., 2nd Sess., 1952, pp. 250ff.

United Kingdom forces by their side." This matter, Eden wrote, "brought negotiations to a standstill." [72] In addition, there were disagreements about the location of European army headquarters, military forces outside the organization, and the duration of the treaty. That the latter should have been a sharply contested issue, when the framework for building Europe was to have been permanent, reflected the depth of divergence in national viewpoints. Difficulties in the form of domestic opposition also arose in Bonn, and here as elsewhere they persisted until the very eve the treaty was initialed. Altogether, the difficulties of the weeks preceding the May meetings were so filled with complications (in Germany hardly less than in France) that Acheson found them "nightmarish." [73]

Notwithstanding obvious problems among the Europeans, the U.S. diplomatic effort remained confident. The secretary of state went beyond his usual military emphasis before the Senate Foreign Relations and House Foreign Affairs Committees, painting his conception of the European tableau with broad strokes.[74] The present time was a moment in European history, he said, when "things are fluid" and enduring achievements possible. American policy since the war has understood this, "working with the vast new forces which are developing in Europe—forces of unity and cohesion." These considerations, the secretary did not add, were hardly present a year-and-a-half before when German rearmament was first demanded. But the Schuman Plan, EDC, and the return of Germany to the European community, Acheson said, could change the historic rivalries which had brought recurrent war. "These things can be brought to fulfillment now. If we lose this momentum—if they are not accomplished now—they might not be accomplished for a long time to come." The military emphasis was not lost, but it had been wrapped in the dictum that only an integrated community could serve as a basis for an

[72] Eden, *Full Circle*, pp. 45–47; see also Stikker, *Memoir*, pp. 312–13.
[73] Acheson, *Present at the Creation*, p. 642; Adenauer, *Memoirs*, pp. 410–12.
[74] *Department of State Bulletin*, March 24, 1952, pp. 463–64, from which the following quotations are drawn.

effective defense force.[75] The emphasis in Washington was, as earlier, on formal agreement.

The Supreme Commander agreed. Eisenhower had already told his aides at SHAPE that first priority on his military docket was initialing the EDC treaty. Shortly thereafter, on April 2, 1952, the first annual report of the Supreme Commander was presented to the NATO Standing Group. The significance of this for the German rearmament question was apparent at once; its importance as a manifestation of the American propensity to underplay the obstacles to the surrender of national sovereignties was not appreciated for some time. Political realities were still obscured by what were considered military necessities. There was no real military security yet achieved in Europe, Eisenhower reported, but a beginning had been made, and the key lay with the Federal Republic: "Even with the maximum potential realized through the collective efforts of member nations, there is little hope for the economical long-term attainment of security and stability in Europe unless Western Germany can be counted on the side of the free nations. . . . With Western Germany in our orbit, NATO forces would form a strong and unbroken line in central Europe from the Baltic to the Alps." [76] There could be no question that the military rationale for German rearmament was no less cogent than in mid-1950. But the political problem intervened.

"At first glance," General Eisenhower observed, "a military alliance between Germany and the European nations of NATO would seem to lose sight of history. Too recently has Germany been the destroyer of peace in the Western world." But the arrangements of the EDC, he said, would preclude any single member from embarking on an aggressive course. "If the free nations of this region were really a unit, tremendous benefits would accrue to them individually and to NATO. . . . Yet progress toward full cooperation has been limited by the intricate and

[75] Cf. Ben T. Moore, *NATO and the Future of Europe* (New York: Harper, 1958), p. 47.

[76] *Department of State Bulletin,* April 14, 1952, pp. 575–76. The text of the report is in Baier and Stebbins, *Documents, 1952,* pp. 139–66.

artificial maze of national obstacles erected by man himself." [77]

This statement is noteworthy not only for its assumption that what is militarily desirable should somehow be politically possible, but also because Eisenhower's words revealed one of the basic errors in the American approach to European unification. The general's impression that national obstacles were artificial rather than real, and that these barriers to unification could be swept away since they were, after all, only man-made, failed to appreciate that the obstacles were not susceptible to a cavalier dismissal. They were real, of course, because they were political and involved power relationships among major states and involved sovereignty itself, the latter possessed of striking tenacity as a value apart from its alleged obsolescence. The linking of German rearmament and European unification, begun almost a year before with Eisenhower's acceptance of EDC, had culminated in the conviction that these were inseparable. "American military thinking had drawn the conclusion," a British study group observed, "not only that German soldiers were indispensable but that the Continent would fight shoulder to shoulder or would not fight at all." [78] Such a conclusion did not exhaust the alternatives.

In spite of Anglo-Saxon reassurances, the French were still convinced that a resurgent Germany could only be a dangerous Germany. The impression was reinforced with shocking impact late in April when Chancellor Adenauer proclaimed that once German reunification was achieved the treaties between the Federal Republic and the allies which were about to be signed would no longer be binding. What France really wanted, and what could not be had, was an unequivocal American guarantee that Germany could never withdraw from EDC. Acheson said that the withdrawal of German troops from EDC would cause the United

[77] *Department of State Bulletin*, April 14, 1952, p. 576. Eisenhower said the integration would only be at the army corps level; the basic military unit of the EDC force would remain the *groupement*, or division. "At this level," the general said, "troops would not be mixed as to nationality, thus preserving the language, customs and esprit of the home peoples." This was just what the French were afraid of! Cf. Acheson, *Present at the Creation*, pp. 598–99.

[78] R.I.I.A., *Britain in Western Europe*, p. 34.

States to be "seriously concerned," but did not specify what might be done.[79] If there was a single step whereby American diplomacy, looking toward ratification by France, might have brought EDC success, perhaps this was it—but it is more probable that the opportunity never existed at all. This probability is underscored by the fact that even when the United Kingdom in mid-April offered France the military guarantee of automatic aid Paris had long pleaded for, the French balked; "the question now turns more on human emotions than on hard reasoning." [80] This was true from the outset, but "rational" answers had to be exhausted before this became clear.

THE SUCCESS OF U.S. DIPLOMACY, MAY, 1952

Only twenty months after the American demand for the raising of German troops, treaties intended to meet the desires of France and Germany, which amounted to preconditions to the rearmament of the Federal Republic, were ready to be signed. This striking shift in state policies if not national attitudes was a singular triumph for U.S. diplomacy, whose efforts were in the broad sense responsible for both the EDC treaty and the German peace contract.

When the draft treaty for a European Defense Community was initialed on May 9, *The New York Times* hailed the event as the greatest step so far toward a United States of Europe. But even at this late moment there were many last-minute crises. The interdependent nature of the multiple aspects of the European army accords, the contractual agreements, the NATO protocols, and so forth, both threatened the proposed across-the-

[79] *L'Annee Politique, 1952*, pp. 327–29. The treaty question was settled on the day before the Peace Contract was signed through the device of reciting that a reunified Germany could claim the rights in the treaties provided it accepted the obligations. Adenauer, *Memoirs*, p. 423; *International Organization*, Vol. VI, 1952, pp. 474–75.

[80] The official text of the British offer is in Document T.26, April 18, 1952, Information Office, British Embassy, Washington, D.C. Quote from *Manchester Guardian Weekly*, April 17, 1952.

board settlement because one disagreement threatened all, and aided progress because it was becoming almost unthinkable that after so much laborious endeavor the whole lot might be lost.

The bargaining in Bonn, agreement having been reached for the most part in Paris, was especially sharp during the first weeks of May, but concessions were made by all sides as one question after another was solved or placed under the rug. On the most basic issue of all, that of full equality for the Federal Republic, it was still not the wish of the members that Germany be admitted to NATO. Arrangements which everyone knew were aimed at Germany were made with reference to EDC as a whole. Perhaps it could not be expected that more be done, but *ipso facto* this was a kind of discrimination. For their part, the French were convinced that U.S. pressure was such that postponement would not be in their interest. The meetings between the High Commissioners and Adenauer were lasting as long as seventeen hours a day, and once the foreign ministers of the occupying powers arrived in Bonn, the activity became "feverous" and the atmosphere "strained and anxious." [81]

During the days just before the May treaties it was remarked in France how very far from the original Pleven Plan the military provisions of EDC were, especially since integration of national contingents was to be at the level of *groupements* of 12,000 to 13,000 men, "in other words, divisions." The military disappointments were compounded by the departure from the political spirit and substance of the earlier plan:

As to institutions, the difference was great between the starting point and the result. The Commission, essentially the executive organ, is far from possessing the powers of a supranational high authority. . . . The essential organ is the Council. The whole matter of supranational organization finds itself sent to the Assembly, by article 38, for

---

[81] Cf. R.I.I.A., *Britain in Western Europe*, p. 37; Speier, *German Rearmament*, p. 161. It was difficult for Adenauer to induce his own coalition to go along. See Calvocoressi, *Survey, 1952*, pp. 95–101; *L'Annee Politique, 1952*, p. 333; Acheson, *Sketches from Life*, p. 52; *Present at the Creation*, pp. 643–46; Adenauer, *Memoirs*, pp. 413–15; and Eden, *Full Circle*, p. 51.

study. If this provisional structure as thus put together does not genuinely amount to a supranational solution, the denationalization of the armed forces is, however, extensive. Altogether, it has the somewhat disconcerting character of a hybrid.[82]

This French observation of the nature of the EDC edifice is extremely important. If the original Pleven Plan had been scrapped; if there was to be German rearmament on the level of divisions; if there was no genuine provision for the supranationality which would have precluded secession; but if nevertheless France was to lose aspects of her own military sovereignty as well as control over her budget in the bargain, then from the very moment of signature France had good reason to pause. Neither fish nor fowl, the EDC as thus envisaged was both too supranational and not supranational enough. In the French judgment, it denationalized the army without affording the framework of an integral institution whose components were inseparable.

If this appears unduly pessimistic, it serves again to show the depth of emotional resistance to any German rearmament at this point in time.[83] French disenchantment with EDC preceded May 27, and was not simply a reaction thereafter. Nor, in light of the transformation of the Pleven Plan, is it correct to say that France proposed and then rejected the European army.[84] It is appropriate,

---

[82] *L'Annee Politique, 1952,* pp. 336–37.

[83] When Schuman arrived in Bonn, Acheson felt that he was not only unsure of his control of French foreign policy but not even in control of his own ministry—Schuman was "obviously tired, nervous, and depressed." Acheson, *Present at the Creation,* p. 644.

[84] Moore, *NATO,* p. 46, for example, said that "The EDC treaty was based closely on the original Pleven Plan," and many others took a similar view that in not later approving EDC "France had torpedoed her own proposals." Prince Hubertus zu Lowenstein and Volkmar von Zuhlsdorff, *NATO and the Defense of the West* (New York: Praeger, 1962), p. 80. Jules Moch, one of the original sponsors of the European army suggestion in 1950, has written a comparative analysis of the two projects. See Jules Moch, *Alerte! Le probleme crucial de la Communaute Europeenne de Defense* (Paris: Laffont, 1954), pp. 132–42. Moch stressed especially that EDC would—in contrast to the Pleven Plan—bring German divisions instead of small combat teams; result, in effect, in a German minister of defense and a general staff; have integration on a level never contemplated in the original proposal; have only weak political institutions and substitute a collegial technocracy for a political minister of defense; and be composed of only a few

however, to regard the over all process as having given the chief antagonist to German rearmament the opportunity to find another solution.

The last important barrier to agreement was seemingly swept away on the eve of the signing of the treaties; France had decided to impose new conditions, focusing on wide-ranging Anglo-American guarantees. On May 23 the Paris government notified Schuman, who was then in Bonn with Acheson, Eden, and Adenauer, that he should demand a precise commitment against the secession of any member from EDC; a guarantee by Britain and the United States against the restoration of an autonomous German Wehrmacht; and a general declaration that the allies would not allow Germany to become stronger in Europe because of France's overseas responsibilities. The British and American ministers said they could not give any guarantee directed solely against Germany, but solved the issue by a rewording of the Anglo-American declaration of intent. The United States and Britain would regard as a threat to their own security any action, from whatever quarter, which threatened the unity or integrity of EDC, and in such case would act in accordance with Article 4 of the North Atlantic Treaty, which provided for consultation.[85]

This episode manifested sound diplomatic sensibility on the part of London and Washington to French fears of a German withdrawal from EDC, but it also showed again that what Paris really wanted was not external reassurance, however worded, but no troops at all from the Federal Republic. Nothing else was left, though, and the moment had come to sign the Bonn and Paris treaties. American diplomacy was—for this instant—irresistible. The British High Commissioner said he "had never known so punishing an ordeal. Everything was against us. Neither the

---

of the democracies intended by Pleven to be members, with especially Britain and the Nordic countries now to be omitted.

[85] Acheson considered the French demand for a guarantee against German secession from EDC "the accumulation of all the French Government's neuroses," which could hardly be considered by what was now a "dying administration." Acheson, *Present at the Creation*, pp. 640–45; Baier and Stebbins, *Documents, 1952*, pp. 246–48; Calvocoressi, *Survey, 1952*, p. 103.

Germans nor the French nor indeed the British liked the idea of German rearmament." [86]

The May treaties amounted to a vast number of accords which together comprised a web of agreements emerging from discussions among the EDC Six; the EDC states and Britain; the Six and NATO; and the occupying powers and the Federal Republic. They included the contractual agreements between Germany and the Big Three; the EDC treaty and related protocols; reciprocal guarantees between NATO and EDC; the guarantee treaty between Britain and EDC; and the joint declaration of the United States, the United Kingdom, and France, with the one condition for entry into force of all the others the ratification of EDC.[87] The basic goal of U.S. diplomacy relating to the German rearmament question was now at a stage of realization very close to the limits of American statesmanship: the May treaties established the legal basis for the restoration of sovereignty to the Federal Republic and for its direct participation in NATO defense through the European army.

While the entire set of accords was considered interdependent and was so proclaimed, the foreign ministers of the occupying powers, at Adenauer's request, published a letter stating that if there was any undue delay in the ratification of the EDC treaty, a conference would be called to consider interim restoration of sovereignty to the Federal Republic. With this key concession gained, "Adenauer demonstrated his pragmatism and restraint by the degree to which, though insisting on the principle of equal-

[86] Sir Ivone Kirkpatrick, *The Inner Circle: Memoirs of Ivone Kirkpatrick* (London: Macmillan, 1959), p. 245.

[87] The European demand for a special pledge of British support for EDC was met by a separate treaty between Britain and the Six which, using the 1948 Brussels Treaty language, militarily bound Britain and the Six to come to each other's assistance in case of attack. Stebbins, *United States, 1952*, pp. 165–66. The tripartite declaration included the Anglo-American pledge to leave their troops in Europe, although the language of the pledge was not without a certain ambiguity which clearly preserved their freedom of action. Summaries of the principal accords are in Baier and Stebbins, *Documents, 1952*, pp. 211–48; texts are in U.S. Department of State, *American Foreign Policy 1950–1955; Basic Documents* (Washington: Government Printing Office, 1957), pp. 486–610, concerning the Federal Republic, and pp. 1107–98, concerning EDC and related documents.

ity, he tacitly accepted a number of inequalities." These included acceptance of France's right to maintain national forces outside EDC; not insisting upon a German general staff; a renunciation of the Federal Republic's right to produce atomic, biological, or chemical weapons; and a dropping of the demand for immediate NATO membership. In addition, although under a different name, the occupation was to be continued. One analyst judged that these restrictions on German military sovereignty were such as to give Germany second-rate status. But even though there were checks, the Federal Republic could rearm.[88]

The German contribution to the European army, as already described in Schuman's report on the EDC to the NATO Council and as anticipated under the EDC treaty, was to be a dozen national divisions, still called *groupements* (plus air and naval forces). This force was to be provided only after all parties had ratified the agreements. Thereafter, it would be a part of a community which would eventually have the supranational characteristics of a common institutional defense framework, a common defense budget, an executive authority, a common court and parliamentary assembly, and other "European" aspects. Militarily, the one control device which was to insure against independent action was the provision that none of the national divisions would be self-sufficient in either logistics or supporting units; over all command was to rest with the SACEUR.

Politically, EDC did not of itself create the broad edifice envisaged under the early European army scheme, but there was no question that the political unification of Europe was implied in its institutions, and this was accordingly proclaimed. Unity in

[88] Quote from James L. Richardson, *Germany and the Atlantic Alliance: The Interaction of Strategy and Politics* (Cambridge: Harvard University Press, 1966), pp. 22–23. See also Baier and Stebbins, *Documents, 1952,* p. 231; Adenauer, *Memoirs,* p. 414. "In order that the Germans shall be treated as equals, they are not forbidden to produce certain weapons; instead it is agreed that these weapons must not be produced in 'strategically exposed areas,' one of which is east of the Rhine and Neckar rivers." R.I.I.A., *Atlantic Alliance,* pp. 116–17. The prohibition also included long-range missiles, heavy warships, and military aircraft. Essentially the same formula was followed in the 1954 settlement. See also Alfred Vagts, *Defense and Diplomacy: The Soldier and the Conduct of Foreign Relations* (New York: King's Crown Press, 1956), p. 161.

defense matters necessarily implied unity in the political sector as well. The key to this crucial point lay in the integration of Germany into Europe, first as an independent state, then as part of the community. The Occupation Statute was to be repealed and the High Commission abolished, with ambassadors henceforth to conduct relations with the Federal Republic. Troops of other nations in Germany were to be defense forces, not occupation forces, remaining there "for obvious geographical and political reasons," since the Federal Republic "is regarded as a forward, exposed, strategic area." The immediate objective of the Bonn accords was "to integrate the Federal Republic, on a basis of equality, in the European community now being shaped." Germany, it was added, "freely undertakes to participate in the European Defense Community." [89]

The British foreign secretary, who found the occasion of the Bonn and Paris treaties a strange experience after the two world wars which had filled his life, observed that "all was signed and sealed, but far from delivered." The reversal of alliances seemed complete: U.S. diplomacy had succeeded in providing for "containment of the new threat with the cooperation of our former enemy." [90]

At the very moment that American diplomacy tasted success in the form of the May treaties, the dream of European unity was marred by the fragmentation of the parties who were to join in the new union. Basic to the situation was the divergence between France and Germany, neither of which was satisfied with the accords. The divergence had been masked, but not eradicated, in drafting the treaties and their accompanying materials. The Federal Republic still did not have equality, nor did France have the protection she wanted against a new German menace.

---

[89] *Department of State Bulletin,* June 9, 1952, pp. 888–91. This seemingly gratuitous assertion was perhaps meant to preclude forever any charge that the *diktat* of Versailles was being repeated.

See Speier, *German Rearmament,* pp. 158–59, for some views in the German government on EDC as symbolic of Germany's return to a place of prestige in the international community.

[90] Eden, *Full Circle,* pp. 51, 52; Acheson, *Present at the Creation,* p. 647.

Acheson, who was told personally "with considerable passion" by French President Vincent Auriol that the entire thrust of U.S. policy toward Germany was a great mistake, chose to de-emphasize indications that a unified Europe might be largely in the American imagination.[91] "We are standing," he said, "on the threshold of a new Europe and a new world." He reported to the nation on June 2 that "the striking thing about these two meetings in the capital cities of the two countries who have fought each other so bitterly in the past—France and Germany—was the free agreement of all upon measures that looked toward the future, and not toward the past. . . ." [92]

But in Paris, Edouard Herriot, Speaker of the National Assembly, was saying that "guarantees on paper are not enough." German independence and power were being restored under U.S. pressure too rapidly, at a moment when France was certain Germany desired to regain her former grandeur but was not so sure the Federal Republic would respect her signed obligations. A British editorial said that the replacement of the Pleven Plan scheme for a European army with the EDC was tantamount to replacing "a pile of dry kindling" with a "bundle of tough faggots." [93] It added that because of this, however, the French might ask what would prevent the twelve new German *groupements* from becoming a new Wehrmacht. Prior to their dream of European unity being interrupted by the reality of French resistance, American leaders had achieved as much as the circumstances of the moment allowed.

[91] The secretary actually had such an indication the very morning after the EDC treaty was signed, when he met with a large group of French leaders and observed their apprehensions about Germany and "pent-up resentment" against U.S. policy generally. Acheson, *Present at the Creation*, pp. 647–48; *Sketches from Life*, p. 53.

[92] Department of State press release, May 28, 1952; *Department of State Bulletin*, June 16, 1952, p. 931.

[93] *Manchester Guardian Weekly*, May 29, 1952.

THE SUSPENSION OF U.S. DIPLOMACY

The months following the zenith of the American diplomatic endeavor for German rearmament, which began at the Lisbon conference of NATO and culminated with the May treaties, brought in rapid succession a European reaction against EDC, the loss of American leadership, and the beginning of a period of inaction in Europe even more frustrating than the earlier search for agreement. This process of the decline of the fortunes of the EDC was not so much a European reaction against U.S. leadership as a reflection of the power of that leadership in the first place. For what American diplomacy was now seeking, the political unification of Europe, was infinitely more complex than the attempt to remilitarize the Federal Republic had ever been. This was no surprise to sophisticated Europeans, but it took some time for Washington to see.

Just as Secretary Acheson was reporting to the American people that "there will not be a national German army," it was being asked in France whether the case might be just the reverse.[94] French critics who looked to the Indo-China war feared that Germany would have a preponderance in European economic and military matters. Others wondered whether there was among the EDC participants the requisite political will to make the new common structure function. In France there were fears of German offensive ambitions; of German intentions to press claims in the East; and of being drawn into adventures by the Federal Republic as the result of a resurgent German dynamism which EDC was supposed to channel. These fears served to show that in French eyes the basic purpose of EDC was to contain, not rearm, Germany. Once the supranational safeguards of the early Pleven Plan were discarded, there was lacking for France a meaningful connection

[94] *Department of State Bulletin,* June 16, 1952, p. 932; *L'Annee Politique, 1952,* p. 337.

between the common army and European unification. Observers noted that even if ratified, the problems were enormous: the language of the treaty was ambiguous and new questions were bound to arise; there were many problems of a technical-political nature (for example, the common pay-scale did not explain how this was to be reached, in whose currency, how different values could be reconciled, or who would pay the bill when there was a deficiency); and above all, the German military role was not clear.[95]

Others also questioned the new scenario. A Royal Institute of International Affairs study group, examining the subject in mid-1952, said that EDC as a device to federate Europe involved "momentous changes," such as loss of foreign-policy autonomy, loss of the national defense establishment, a significant loss of control of national financial policy, and additional sacrifices. There had been other attempts at federation, it was observed, "But no consciously created federation of states so dissimilar in language, history, and tradition as the European States has ever been attempted." [96] Even as a solution to the German rearmament problem, this group found, the basic divergence between the German demand for equality and the French refusal to grant this persisted, exemplified by the question of NATO membership for the Federal Republic. One proposal was developed that when questions of interest to Germany were to be discussed in NATO, the two organizations, NATO and EDC, could meet jointly and Germans attend; when matters affecting the Federal Republic had been handled, the Germans would leave. "The strategem is patently absurd and no one realizes this better than the French and German officials who worked it out together. . . ." [97]

The reaction against EDC in France was, in the most fundamental sense, a reaction against the restoration of German power.

[95] Hanson W. Baldwin, *The New York Times,* June 1, 1952.
[96] R.I.I.A., *Atlantic Alliance,* pp. 102–3. See Calvocoressi, *Survey, 1952,* pp. 114–17, for the situation in the Netherlands, Belgium, and Italy, all of whose leaders felt hesitation about the EDC gamble.
[97] R.I.I.A., *Atlantic Alliance,* p. 113.

French fears were seemingly justified, as Bonn officials manifested what the French considered a dangerous willingness to assert their new independence.[98] Convinced that EDC ratification had to be delayed for some time, Paris could find no escape from the dilemma implicit in the German problem, even in the European army. The feeling in Paris was that EDC had given Germany "not only the right to equality but a chance for mastery." [99]

For its part, the United States (as did Britain) promptly ratified the Bonn convention and the EDC protocol to the North Atlantic Treaty. In Washington, the hearings in the Senate on these agreements evoked repetitions of earlier American pronouncements, particularly by Secretary Acheson. High Commissioner McCloy repeated the views that Germany must be restored to a respectable international position and the occupation ended, but added that he could not deny that people were "apprehensive about the possible domination of the Germans in this situation." The Senate overwhelmingly voted for ratification of the Bonn convention and the EDC-NATO protocol on July 1, and Washington now looked to Europe for swift action.[100] But at this very point in time American leadership was lost—physically, with the departure of Eisenhower and McCloy; militarily, as the strategy and weaponry of the alliance looked to new atomic possibilities; psychologically, as cold-war tensions eased and anti-American feeling increased; and politically, as the U.S. election contest caused Europeans to hesitate as they waited for the outcome of the campaign.

Since early 1951, Eisenhower's activities in Europe had been inseparable from the U.S. commitment to European defense. In a personal sense, the general's presence at SHAPE was closely related to the presence of American forces on the Continent, and was a source of confidence for the allies.[101] The general's depar-

[98] The Chancellor's defense adviser, Theodor Blank, announced plans for a German army of sixty divisions by 1960. Werth, *France*, p. 592; *The Times* (London), June 14, 1952.

[99] *The New Republic* (Percy Winner), June 16, 1952.

[100] The votes were 77 to 5 and 72 to 5 respectively. Senate, *Relations with the Federal Republic*, pp. 8, 15, 21, 74, 110.

[101] See Wesley B. Truitt, "The Troops to Europe Decision: The Process, Politics, and Diplomacy of a Strategic Commitment" (unpublished Ph.D. disserta-

ture cannot be measured in terms of its impact on European attitudes, but there is no doubt that it compounded the already growing psychological uncertainty connected with the U.S. election campaign.[102] High Commissioner McCloy, while less symbolic an American figure than the retiring NATO Commander, was nevertheless an official whose role in the evolution of the German rearmament question toward the European army project was outstanding.[103] The same was true of Secretary Acheson, whose authority to speak for future American policy was necessarily limited by the certainty that President Truman would not seek re-election. In addition to these leaders, a number of other high officials had either gone or were shortly to leave, including David K. E. Bruce, Robert R. Bowie, Charles M. Spofford, and others closely associated with the U.S. effort to sponsor agreement on EDC. There resulted a "vacuum of leadership" concerning American policy in Europe, and this was not filled for the remainder of the period of EDC's consideration.[104]

The loss of these individuals was detrimental, but it was minor compared to the impact of the U.S. presidential campaign. The uncertainties generated by this began in the spring of 1952, and lasted into 1953. Prior to the election there was the problem of the general direction of American policy, but even after Eisenhower's victory "it would be difficult to imagine a European army without knowing what position the new administration would

tion, Columbia University, 1968), Chap. 3. Truitt pointed out that Eisenhower's stature was such that he actually made up for the lack of greater numbers of U.S. troops in Europe.

[102] Eisenhower's resignation from SHAPE probably damaged the confidence of EDC's European advocates. His successor, General Ridgway, did not make up for this, as perhaps no one could have, since Eisenhower's wartime role somewhat uniquely qualified him to be the commander of a mixed military force. Eisenhower himself was fully confident that General Gruenther, who stayed on as Ridgway's chief of staff, would see to it that the European army was workable. Interviews.

[103] McCloy left Bonn in June; he was succeeded by Walter J. Donnelly. Donnelly resigned effective December 31, 1952, and was succeeded by James B. Conant. *The New York Times*, September 3, 1952; *Department of State Bulletin*, December 15, 1952, p. 967.

[104] Interviews. See also Stebbins, *United States, 1952*, pp. 388–89. Stebbins said "no successors could wholly fill the gaps" left by the departure of Eisenhower and McCloy, and no one did.

take, especially without knowing to what extent it would accept it or collaborate with it. . . ." [105] There was in Europe simultaneously a desire—particularly in France—to exploit this doubt to further delay already unpopular steps, including the rearmament effort and the ratification of the EDC treaty.[106] American leaders were aware that the approaching election was a cause of anxiety and uncertainty in allied capitals. "While Europeans' fears regarding Presidential elections have so far proved groundless," one study observed, "their estimate that a new President means new policies of great significance for NATO has been repeatedly confirmed." [107] In 1952, although somewhat reassured by Eisenhower's nomination, Europeans were highly upset by the general's proclamation of a "great crusade" for freedom and the possibility that this might take the form of "liberation" policy advocated by John Foster Dulles, the leading Republican foreign-affairs expert.

Acheson looked back at the "accident of the calendar," that the American election came in 1952 rather than in 1953, and found it highly unfortunate that this coincided with the translation of the Lisbon decisions into the May treaties. He felt that these agreements had generated great momentum toward European institutions. Had the administration lasted longer, the United States "would have had a good chance of helping Schuman get the European Defense Community through the French National Assembly. . . ." [108]

[But] as the conventions made their nominations, Europe became aware that whatever the result of the election no one who had been speaking and deciding for the United States would be doing either after January 1953. So governments waited to see with whom they would deal. The puzzlement grew, as Mr. Stevenson said what Europe

[105] *L'Annee Politique, 1952*, p. xv.
[106] Cf. Werth, *France*, p. 595.
[107] William T. R. Fox and Annette B. Fox, *NATO and the Range of American Choice* (New York: Columbia University Press, 1967), p. 191. See also Harry S Truman, *Memoirs: Years of Trial and Hope* (Garden City: Doubleday, 1956), p. 260. The period from Truman's announcement that he would not run again until the new administration gained effectiveness was a "virtual interregnum." Acheson, *Present at the Creation*, pp. 632–33.
[108] *Ibid.*, p. 633.

had expected to hear from its late Supreme Commander, and heard from him what it had expected to hear from Senator Taft.

The momentum of the spring and early summer died. Europe still waited. Nothing visible happened; but decay and disintegration set in. Second thoughts took the place of earlier thoughts. . . .[109]

What Acheson considered "second thoughts" were more deeply rooted than this language would suggest. But even if it could be shown that the election's impact was less, it remained true that "the momentum and movement of the first half of 1952 were not recovered again, or American leadership re-established." [110]

Another factor was the divergence of views on the rearmament effort generally. Militarily, the United States pointed to the shortage of troops which German rearmament was supposed to have made up for; General Matthew B. Ridgway, the new Supreme Commander, stated that the threat of Soviet aggression had not in any way abated.[111] Europeans, however, replied that their economic difficulties persisted; that the Russians in fact had not committed military aggression; and that the increases in American air-atomic power rendered a further conventional buildup unnecessary. Although NATO's inability to check a major assault remained, the uncertainty about the direction of U.S. policy, combined with the military-economic factor, placed the allies' policies beyond the power of American persuasion.[112]

Finally, American leadership suffered from a phenomenon of psychological resistance to U.S. pressure and satisfaction in the frustration of Washington's desires. Europe had, since the begin-

---

[109] Acheson, *Sketches from Life,* pp. 53–54.

[110] *Ibid.,* p. 54. While analysts agree that the loss of U.S. leadership was important and the American election campaign a source of uncertainty, there is no convincing evidence that EDC would have fared better had the circumstances been otherwise.

[111] *The New York Times,* August 12, 1952.

[112] James E. King, Jr., "NATO: Genesis, Progress, Problems," in *National Security in the Nuclear Age,* eds. Gordon B. Turner and Richard D. Challener (New York: Praeger, 1960), p. 156. By 1952 not even the former German military felt much sense of threat. Hans Speier, "German Rearmament and the Old Military Elite," *World Politics* (January, 1954), p. 160. See also Ismay, *NATO,* p. 103; Osgood, *NATO,* p. 88.

ning of the NATO alliance and especially since the outbreak of hostilities in Korea, been compelled to accept American leadership simply because there was no other available source of financial aid or nuclear protection. During this period of "enforced collaboration" there was an ambivalent allied attitude of gratitude for protection, but resentment against the heavy hand which accompanied the charity. Having been dragged into the German rearmament tangle in the first place, and pressured to reach formal accord on the European army as the road to unity, it was a relief—and perhaps a pleasure—to deny the United States its hope for swift EDC ratification.[113] The matter had left the shelter of intergovernmental bargaining and entered the arena of parliamentary politics, where the evidence that Europe was ready for political unification was scanty.

Proponents and critics, politicians and scholars, are generally in accord that the EDC treaty was the victim of time.[114] This judgment refers to ratification by France rather than the broader question of whether the European army in practice could have functioned either as a military organization or a political instrument. The reasons for French inaction on the treaty are commingled with the impact of the delay.[115] While it was the National As-

[113] Cf. Raymond Aron, *France Steadfast and Changing* (Cambridge: Harvard University Press, 1960), p. 151.

[114] Cf. Acheson, *Sketches from Life*, p. 55. In a way, time and France are synonymous in the period after May, 1952, but however persuasive the hypotheses of those who lament the failure of swift ratification, they remain speculative: the National Assembly did *not* ratify EDC, and the better question might be why *should* the deputies have done so rather than why they did not.

[115] The sequence of events in the French National Assembly concerning EDC was as follows: the May accords were not submitted by the Pinay government throughout 1952. The discussion which did take place was hence necessarily informal, for example Herriot's warning against the European army in October. The Mayer government, formed early in 1953, did submit the treaties to the Assembly in late January, but only with the simultaneous announcement that France would seek additional protocols, that is, no vote would be requested pending the outcome of the new initiatives. Even after the other five prospective EDC members had completed arrangements for extra protocols, in the first months of 1953, and after France had been granted additional special privileges, the Paris government still did not call for action. Further meetings among representatives of the Six were held, and France held out for such demands as a settlement of the Saar question. By November, 1953, Premier Laniel said he would not ask the Assembly to ratify until several matters were resolved, and the United States and Britain

sembly which eventually rejected EDC, even French analysts have written that the failure of the Paris government to deposit it for ratification was "the ultimate cause of the failure of the treaty." Once the delay had occurred, domestic political realities prevailed: "The EDC was conceived in the fear of Germany and in the hope of Europe. It was, from the moment it appeared on the Parliamentary scene, doomed to failure." [116] This evaluation, shared by many observers, is relevant to the ability of American diplomacy to achieve the goal of German rearmament through a European army. If French domestic political factors *were* determinative, then U.S. leadership, even if hobbled by the departure of key figures and the election campaign, did not fail. If indeed the National Assembly would have ratified the treaty in 1952, or even 1953, there can be no question it was the victim of time. Whether this was the case, however, is extremely questionable, since there is no reliable evidence that there was at any time a majority for the treaty among the deputies.

The basic political factors which made the EDC attempt to unite Europe premature, having been apparent to many beforehand, were manifested shortly. A phenomenon began, whereby the American attempt to make German rearmament palatable by stressing its linkage with European unification provoked a European reaction against unification itself. In a way, EDC was

---

gave further assurances that their troops would be left in Europe, at least during the first years of EDC.

In June, 1954, Mendes-France took office with the pledge that he would both call for new agreements among the Six on EDC, and also that France would finally face up to the "cruel prospect" of German participation in Western defense, that is, an answer would finally be given by the National Assembly. By August total disagreement between France and the other EDC states was obvious. The French Premier decided to take no stand on the treaty as the assembly prepared to debate EDC. At the end of August the government asked the deputies to vote on the treaty but made no recommendation how, that is, no question of confidence was involved. But even this vote did not occur, since early in what would have been a very long debate a procedural motion was used to force the issue. The EDC treaty was thereby indirectly rejected, although it was of course fully clear that thereafter there could be no vote on the merits.

[116] Jacques Fauvet, "Birth and Death of a Treaty," in *France Defeats EDC*, eds. Daniel Lerner and Raymond Aron (New York: Praeger, 1957), pp. 133, 128. See also Guy de Carmoy, *The Foreign Policies of France 1944–1968* (Chicago: University of Chicago Press, 1970), pp. 36–41.

"the gravest error" on the part of those who did seek to make German rearmament acceptable, since once it evolved to the point where the Federal Republic *would* enjoy equality, then there was no intrinsic way to limit German rearmament: "this inevitable development turned all the hostility aroused by German rearmament against the European Army." [117] American spokesmen no less than European suggested that, even if the EDC were to be created, it alone would not be enough to contain Germany, and that if it was to guard against nationalist—that is, German—aggression, the European army would have to remain under NATO, that is, American, control.[118] This was hardly an inducement to France to consent to a surrender of sovereignty and a loss of her national army, particularly when there was widespread doubt about post-election American policy.

It should be stressed that France, and indeed the United States, repeatedly confused the question of whether or not there would be national control of the armed forces of the European army members. France, concluding partially on the basis of her fears that German units *would* be capable of independent military action, also believed that EDC meant a surrender of French sovereignty in terms of her own army. The latter was actually true, in part, because of the nature of the EDC framework, outlined above; although neither fish nor fowl, its limited supranational authority would still mean a surrender of some French sovereignty.[119] The United States, for its part, compounded the confusion. For example, on an occasion when Churchill was criticizing the projected European army as "a polyglot mob," Acheson convinced him that "the formations of the EDC would not be polyglot, since through the divisional unit they would be on a

---

[117] Paul-Marie de la Gorce, *The French Army: A Military-Political History* (New York: Braziller, 1963), p. 368.

[118] Cf. William H. Draper, *Department of State Bulletin*, October 27, 1952.

[119] This criticism was made repeatedly by deGaulle, among others, and never effectively rebutted. Cf. *L'Annee Politique, 1952*, p. 342; de la Gorce, *French Army*, pp. 369ff. *The Economist*, October 25, 1952, probably intended no humor when it remarked "the surrender of national sovereignty in defense is a momentous step, even for the Germans, who have not yet regained it."

national basis." [120] American spokesmen simultaneously praised the European army scheme for just the reverse, stating as McCloy had that no national misuse of forces could occur since the treaty itself contained "the fundamental assurances against such a perversion." [121] With these basic contradictions and conflicting interpretations, it is not surprising that the ambiguities of the European army were variously perceived.

In Europe, disillusionment with the notion that Europe was ready for unity was increased by constant arguments among the Six. In midsummer there had been enormous difficulty in agreeing on a city as the seat of the newly ratified European Coal and Steel Community, with a "provisional" split solution of selecting Luxembourg for the high authority and the court, and Strasbourg for the assembly. The whole dispute had been marked by the sharpest national rivalry.[122] The same was true of other matters: the language of "Europe"—once Franco-German deadlock prevented French from being selected—was to be *four* official languages; the Saar question remained as a highly sensitive issue; the Bonn government announced that its share of the proposed EDC budget was too high; and there was almost complete disagreement among the Six on the length of military service for the soldiers of the European army.[123]

On the latter point alone, not a single member of EDC was willing to accept General Ridgway's call for a twenty-four-month conscription period, and the matter was left unresolved in spite of the treaty clause requiring a common period of service.[124] The

---

[120] Acheson, *Sketches from Life*, p. 82.

[121] Senate, *Relations with the Federal Republic*, p. 104.

[122] Stikker, *Memoir*, p. 304; *L'Annee Politique, 1952*, pp. 348ff.

[123] These matters were widely reported in the American press. See, for example, *Christian Science Monitor*, August 3, 1952; *The New York Times*, August 13 and 14, 1952.

[124] This dispute may be noteworthy not only as evidence that the EDC members were unable to agree among themselves, but also as an example of how difficult it might have been, had the treaty been ratified, to have a workable relationship between an American commander and a European army. The latter point did not come up for public discussion often, but if past U.S. attempts to guide European behavior were indicative, no easy road was in sight.

August 15, 1952, edition of the London *Times* saw these disagreements as the result of the "bland optimism" of earlier NATO meetings, but in fact they indicated that the only way agreement on the treaty was reached in the first place was because such matters were swept under the rug for later consideration. The same was true of countless matters, especially budgetary, all of which were to be parts of the "common" European army organization, and which were simply not agreed upon.

Not only were these "negative" factors of lost American leadership and intra-European quarrels characteristic of the later part of 1952, but in addition there occurred the more "positive" phenomenon of European resistance to U.S. policies amounting to a rebellion against wishes of the super-power. By the fall, a wave of anti-Americanism was reported not only in France but throughout Western Europe, and the more EDC came to be considered a U.S. rather than a European goal the more dangerous was this "revolt of Europe." This was strikingly underscored in October when the President of the National Assembly, former Premier Edouard Herriot, who was well-known for his views favoring the United States, declared the EDC treaty unconstitutional and said "our American friends are condemning France to death." This was followed shortly by an observer's dispatch that EDC had become "a test of the success or failure of American policy." [125]

Accompanying the rebellion against America in France was a new wave of anti-German feeling, as the Saar talks again collapsed. More neo-Nazi activities were reported in the Federal Republic, just as indications appeared that the United States had been financing some right-wing political groups there. The French were especially disturbed when U.S. spokesmen in Paris admitted that enough military equipment had already been set aside to supply the entire German force envisioned under EDC. These American officials, however, ingenuously denied that this was intended to pressure the National Assembly toward ratification.[126]

[125] *The New York Times,* October 18 and 26, 1952; Werth, *France,* p. xxiv; *L'Annee Politique, 1952,* p. 372.

[126] Calvocoressi, *Survey, 1952,* p. 127; *L'Annee Politique, 1952,* p. 372; *The New York Times,* December 15, 1952.

Schuman's position at the foreign ministry was by late 1952 very weak; Premier Antoine Pinay, having indicated his irritation with both Washington and Bonn, did not share Schuman's interest in quick action on EDC.[127] As time ran out for the Truman administration, *LeMonde*, on January 8, 1953, observed that "this whole business of German rearmament, which was badly started off by Mr. Acheson thirty months ago, seems to have reached a dead end."

When the conditions discussed above are taken together it was not surprising that the dominant characteristic of the period from the signing of the May agreements to the close of the year was inaction. Schuman's failure to send the treaty to Parliament seems to have been fatal, since the situation deteriorated every month. But the reason the risk was not taken was that it was considered too great; it would not have been opportune to provoke a crisis in Franco-American relations at such a critical period of U.S. transfer of presidential power. Hence Schuman's last impulse as foreign minister was virtually the same as his first response to the demand for German rearmament: to seek maximum delay.[128]

American diplomacy, it appeared, failed to induce ratification of the EDC at the only point in time when this might have been possible. In the subsequent period of the Eisenhower administration, Secretary of State John Foster Dulles made repeated, strenuous, and sometimes clumsy efforts to secure French action on the treaty. Yet Acheson's warning in the Senate following the Lisbon conference, that if not accomplished at once the projects and policies which had grown out of the German rearmament problem and emerged as the EDC might not be accomplished for a long time to come, was correct.

The North Atlantic Council met in Paris December 15 to 18, 1952, following months of American prodding and French in-

---

[127] Pinay had asked for an American guarantee, direct British participation in EDC, and other unlikely additions to the existing arrangements. Werth, *France*, p. 593.

[128] Schuman resigned on December 23, and was succeeded by George Bidault, who represented the hardline view of controlling Germany, in contrast to Schuman's orientation of reconciliation.

action. Throughout the year U.S. officials had not failed to assure each other that very shortly "countries which twice in a generation have been mortal enemies" would "join together in a common army and adopt a common defense budget" as part of their movement toward "military integration, economic unification, and political federation." [129] These countries had been reminded by U.S. military leaders that increasing the conventional strength of NATO through EDC was urgent, but in Europe "nobody at the time believed that serious efforts were necessary to raise more divisions." McCloy regretted this, but noted that "Europe, exhausted and weary, simply cannot accept the idea of war. It fears that the United States can." [130]

Secretary Acheson, whose last official act in Paris was to deliver "an eloquent and deadly serious lecture" to the NATO Council on the need for EDC, confronted a situation beyond the reach of diplomatic suasion, above all because of the conditions in Europe already described, but also because "there was no American government." [131] Nevertheless he tried to reassure the allies of EDC's importance for future U.S. policy:

It seems to me that as you create this strength and unity—this European entity—you are in effect creating a great centripetal force which will bring into an ever closer association with Europe, our British friends across the Channel and your American and Canadian friends across the Atlantic Ocean. It is as this strength is created at the center, as this vital, new, strong development occurs that you will attract strength. If this process is reversed now, in my judgment you will set up a centrifugal force.[132]

[129] From the report of William H. Draper, Jr., U.S. special representative in Europe, August 22, 1952, in Baier and Stebbins, *Documents, 1952*, p. 175. Reference is here made to American statements. It is noteworthy that there was a marked absence of European statements, and even those in Europe who favored EDC were much less optimistic in their pronouncements.

[130] Helmut Schmidt, *Defense or Retaliation: A German View* (New York: Praeger, 1962), p. 14; John J. McCloy, *The Challenge to American Foreign Policy* (Cambridge: Harvard University Press, 1953), p. 20.

[131] *The New York Times*, December 21, 1952; *L'Annee Politique, 1952*, p. 385. Three days later, there was no French government either.

[132] *Department of State Bulletin*, January 5, 1952, p. 6.

Acheson's remarks, while phrased with dignity and intended to encourage Europe to unite, did contain the implicit threat of the withdrawal of American power from the Continent. The dictum that a strong Europe would attract, and a weak one repel, Europe's Anglo-Saxon friends was a preview of the diplomacy of his successor, who changed the style rather than the substance of U.S. blandishment. But more important, it was a threat which— based on the experience of American policy since 1947 and the awareness that unified or not Europe remained vital to the United States—lacked credibility. This was so for geopolitical reasons, but it was also related to the realities of 1952. Some Europeans pointed out that even a united Europe would be indefensible (whether or not Washington reverted to isolationism), but divided, Europe "still has a chance of safety so long as the national states remain integrated in an Atlantic community, however imperfect." [133] NATO, not EDC, was the way to maintain the security which the super-power's presence provided, and whether or not German troops joined the alliance was a secondary concern of allied leaders.[134]

The NATO Council, which Acheson predicted would not reach any very great conclusions, took no action on either the Lisbon decisions or the May accords. The allied ministers, who treated the U.S. delegation "with the gentle and affectionate solicitude that one might show to the dying," agreed that it was better to reinforce existing units rather than attempt to create new ones, and reaffirmed their support for EDC.[135] Rapid ratification was stressed as a matter of paramount importance, but as expected, the council's inability to act was apparent. Noting that the Lisbon

---

[133] Raymond Aron, *The Century of Total War* (Boston: The Beacon Press, 1955), p. 312.

[134] At the time, there was a strong European apprehension that it was precisely the realization of EDC which would have the perverse consequence of strengthening domestic Anglo-Saxon arguments for continental withdrawal. Northedge, *British Foreign Policy*, p. 157. The mood of Europe was reported as apathetic about if not opposed to German participation at the end of 1952. *The New York Times*, December 21, 1952; *The Times* (London), January 20, 1953. In addition, both Paris and Bonn were already demanding revision of the EDC treaty. *The New York Times*, January 9, 1953.

[135] Acheson, *Present at the Creation*, p. 708.

goals had been "substantially achieved" (which of course was an exaggeration), and recognizing that "strong defense requires a healthy economy," [136] the alliance could do no more than mark time.

The United States, Secretary Acheson said at his last press conference, saw clouds on the horizon for EDC but affirmed America's need for partnership with Europe. "What is not so clear," he added, "is what it is that we are going to get and what it is that we shall be in partnership with. . . ." [137] The German rearmament problem had produced the EDC solution in a remarkably short period of time. All the benefits of peace, security, and prosperity already proclaimed would emerge from a united Europe, including a rearmed Federal Republic. Yet the putative panacea seemed unattractive to its very beneficiaries, above all because Europe had not solved its own problem of inner mistrust: "There is a reason for this. In the long past the military strength generated in the West has been turned upon the West. The wounds from which the West has been recovering were largely self-inflicted wounds. So there is a fear of strength itself lest the strength again be turned inwardly. That is the problem of Germany." [138]

American diplomacy during the latter half of 1952 was, as suggested, virtually suspended. There was no meeting of the NATO Council at the ministerial level until December, and by this time the allies "asked neither help nor advice nor commitment for a future we would not share with them. For this they were waiting for our successors." High Commissioner Walter Donnelly could apparently do little to hasten EDC ratification in Bonn or indeed to persuade Adenauer to comfort the French on such matters as the Saar; General Ridgway found himself unable to collect on the promises which the charm and persuasion of Eisenhower had elicited; and Secretary Acheson, long the target of McCarthyite attacks and now additionally burdened by the lame-duck condition of the Truman Administration, could hardly do much to gather

[136] *Department of State Bulletin,* January 5, 1953, pp. 3–4.
[137] *Ibid.,* January 26, 1953, p. 130.
[138] Charles Burton Marshall, *ibid.,* November 24, 1952, p. 810.

the fruits of American diplomacy's achievements at Lisbon, Bonn, and Paris.[139]

But even if the American leadership had not left Europe and even if 1952 had not been an election year, no external diplomatic suasion could have produced a continental unity, the conditions for which did not exist. Acheson's belief that "the people of Europe were disillusioned with the pettiness of their nationalisms and would unite only upon a broader and more hopeful loyalty" [140] was simply irrelevant even if correct. The lack of popular enthusiasm for EDC was due not to European distaste for German rearmament as much at it was to the persistence with which people were genuinely attached to "the pettiness of their nationalisms."

Acheson told Monnet in Paris that he sensed the troubles of EDC lay "at the very root of popular acceptance of European unity." This was an accurate impression—but the secretary still failed to appreciate that popular refusal was matched on the governmental level. "What was hard for me to understand," he said, "was how the Germans and French, who had seen us go to great lengths to respond to statesmanlike efforts on their part, could risk their own defense and future, as they were now doing, in petty political squabbling." [141]

Perhaps it was *abstractly* true, one observer remarked, that national states were anachronistic and that national passions were *supposed* to be on the way to extinction. But, he said, "The European idea is empty, it has neither the transcendence of Messianic ideologies nor the immanence of concrete patriotism. It was created by intellectuals, and that fact accounts at once for its genuine appeal to the mind and its feeble echo in the heart." [142] American leaders, who at the close of 1952 shared the President's

[139] Acheson, *Present at the Creation*, p. 708. Ridgway saw Eisenhower's job as political and his own as military: "He was the eloquent salesman who persuaded the housewife to subscribe to the pretty magazines. I was the so-and-so with the derby hat and the cigar, who came around to collect at the first of the month." Matthew B. Ridgway, *Soldier: The Memoirs of Matthew B. Ridgway* (New York: Harper, 1956), p. 239.

[140] Acheson, *Sketches from Life*, p. 82.

[141] Acheson, *Present at the Creation*, pp. 707–8.

[142] Aron, *Century of Total War*, pp. 315–16.

belief that "further delay [on EDC] was likely, though this was delay over matters of timing and emphasis, not over principles," [143] were mistaken.

On every count, the United States was impotent to change the fate of EDC as of early 1953. Paralyzed first by the election and later by the period of waiting for the new administration, unable to induce the Paris government to submit the treaty to the National Assembly, and faced with a widespread European reaction against its domination of allied policy, American diplomacy was suspended. Asked about U.S. power to achieve practical realization of the plans which were successfully formalized in the May treaties, an American official replied, "We really did not have any."

THE EISENHOWER-DULLES PERIOD

Although the advent of the Eisenhower administration again allowed Washington's voice to speak with authority, this did not remove the diplomatic impotence which had become apparent during the preceding period of suspension. The goal of rearming Germany through EDC, within the framework of the Bonn and Paris treaties of May, 1952, remained without significant redefinition until the rejection of EDC in 1954. What did change in 1953 was the style of American diplomacy, although even here it was as much a matter of the personality of the secretary of state as other factors. John Foster Dulles was very deeply committed to EDC, more so than Dean Acheson had been, especially because of his interest in the federation of Europe. It was on this political issue, more than on that of German rearmament, that EDC stumbled and fell, as France declined to ratify the treaty which had grown out of—but replaced—the Pleven Plan for a European army under supranational control.

While U.S. efforts to secure a "safely" rearmed Germany were pursued with increased verbal articulation in this period, there were very few ingredients in the EDC mixture not already present. The end of the European army story in August, 1954, might as

[143] Truman, *Memoirs*, p. 260.

well have come at almost any time during the Eisenhower-Dulles period. American diplomacy, in other words, was faced with the same fundamental situation which prevailed when Acheson left, and the frustration in Washington which began with the inaction following the signing of the Bonn and Paris treaties continued without basic change, and for basically the same reasons.

Once the Federal Republic, followed by the Benelux states, had ratified the 1952 treaties, it was up to France to take action one way or the other. Parliamentary action was subjected to lengthy delay as the National Assembly considered various amendments, interpretations, additions, guarantees, and so forth, pending the government's decision to put EDC to a vote. When a vote *was* taken, on August 30, 1954, the deputies on a procedural motion voted to end debate—and with it EDC—by 319 to 264. It is extremely difficult to summarize the manner in which the assembly finally divided, nor is it possible to say whether the votes of the deputies were representative of French public opinion.[144] To state that American diplomacy "failed" to secure ratification is somewhat misleading, since it cannot be demonstrated that the United States had this ability even potentially.

Secretary Dulles, however, behaved as if this were the case. In his first address as America's chief diplomatic spokesman, in January, 1953, he warned that if it seemed Europe was not moving toward unity, especially including France and Germany, "then certainly it would be necessary to give a little rethinking to America's own foreign policy in relation to Western Europe." [145] In terms of both style and substance, this statement was an indicative transitional one: it was, on the one hand, hardly more than a colloquial version of what Acheson had said a few weeks earlier, and on the other, it was a verbal preview of what became, by the end of 1953, the threat of an "agonizing reappraisal." [146]

[144] Furniss, *France, Troubled Ally*, pp. 99–100. The difficulty of explaining the EDC vote is apparent in Arnold Kanter, "The European Defense Community in the French National Assembly: A Roll Call Analysis," *Comparative Politics*, II (January, 1970), 203–28.

[145] *Department of State Bulletin*, February 9, 1953, p. 214.

[146] *Ibid.*, January 4, 1954; *The New York Times*, December 15, 1953. This overview of the diplomacy of Dulles does not explore the secretary's personal char-

Among the factors relevant to the continuing frustration of American diplomatic efforts for German rearmament through EDC, the following are of special importance for the 1953–54 period: (1) relationships within the NATO alliance; (2) East-West relations; (3) changes in weaponry and military strategy; and (4) differences among and within the European states, particularly developments in the French "great debate" on the EDC. American diplomacy—indeed, the diplomacy of any single state—could not influence these different elements except partially and gradually, and sometimes not at all.

The "revolt of Europe" which became apparent in the second half of 1952 continued and increased, as the NATO allies refused to respond to American prodding, not only for the European army, but in other matters. From the outset, the new U.S. secretary of state irritated his European colleagues, except for the German chancellor. Dulles's direct pressure for EDC began with his address in Paris in January, 1953, suggesting that failure to create the European army might bring an American withdrawal or independent German rearmament. This double threat was considered "shocking" and "brutal," especially since the official voice of the United States had been silent for so long.[147] Its effect was to cause even more European resentment against the super-power's behavior, which continued a trend not reversed until after the late-1954 settlements. Alliance relationships until then were poor. They extended to political-military differences about the very na-

---

acteristics. It is noteworthy that Dulles shared Acheson's attitude that "there were in fact no significant negotiable issues" between the Soviet Union and the United States, and if a settlement ever were to be possible it would only be when there was "a global imbalance of power clearly favoring the West." Seyom Brown, *The Faces of Power: Constancy and Change in United States Foreign Policy from Truman to Johnson* (New York: Columbia University Press, 1968), p. 92. See also Bell, *Negotiation from Strength,* Chap. 3 *passim.* Dulles and Acheson also shared the belief that Germany should be returned to the international family and that the mistake of the Versailles Treaty's repressive intent should not be repeated. Cf. for Dulles's views Frederick S. Dunn, *Peace-Making and the Settlement with Japan* (Princeton: Princeton University Press, 1963), pp. 98–99. For the general foreign policy views of John Foster Dulles, see his earlier work, *War or Peace* (New York: Macmillan, 1950).

[147] *The New York Times,* January 28, 1953; *New York Herald Tribune,* January 29, 1953.

ture of NATO, as the spokesmen of the Eisenhower administration gave the verbal impression of abandoning the containment policy for one of "liberation" or "roll-back," and to economic differences as American blandishments continued to stress greater European rearmament efforts while reducing military assistance funds. Even Congress managed, by 1953, to join the diplomatic forces pressing for EDC, by amending the Mutual Security Program authorization bill to provide that nonratification of the treaty would be grounds for the withholding of funds. Finally, NATO relationships were strained by the even sharper contrast between the readiness of the United States to welcome Germany back into the international family almost without restriction, and persistent European apprehension that this would generate a new danger to Western stability if not handled with extreme caution. This factor, combined with a general European impression of American militarism if not belligerence, lasted throughout 1953–54 and underscored the divergence of views in Washington from those held in other allied capitals.

East-West relations also influenced the German rearmament question's evolution in this period, especially because European disinclination to continue the rearmament effort seemed more than ever justified by the easing of earlier cold-war conditions. The death of Marshal Stalin in March, 1953, the end of hostilities in Korea in July, and an apparent decrease in Soviet pressure on Western Europe which lasted into 1954, were to many Europeans factors which should be examined before approving any device for German rearmament and hence increasing cold-war tensions. Conflicting views of the nature of the Soviet threat remained, but the impact of Stalin's demise alone was enough to take the edge off whatever momentum of apprehension might have remained from the earlier NATO period of preparation for defense.[148]

[148] Paul-Henri Spaak later said, "We were afraid, and our fear brought us together. The real father of the Atlantic Alliance was Stalin." Paul-Henri Spaak, "The Indispensable Alliance," *NATO Letter*, November, 1967.

David Bruce, who had returned to Paris as the U.S. special representative to observe the progress of the EDC project, complained a month after Stalin's death that the Soviet peace offensive was spoiling his efforts to induce EDC's ratification.

The resistance to American leadership, and the easing of the East-West confrontation's rigidity, by themselves might have been enough to discourage further interest in EDC, but another factor intervened which was even more influential. The European army solution to the problem of how to use German manpower resources to meet the ground strength deficiency of the NATO line had all along been a "conventional" military project. The Eisenhower administration, at first informally, altered the emphasis of the Western defense posture, and (perhaps unintentionally) convinced Europeans that henceforth nuclear weapons, not German troops, were the answer to the question of how to redress NATO's disadvantageous position. The so-called "new look," and the later "massive retaliation" posture, both of which envisaged the use of nuclear power virtually from the outset of hostilities, more than any other military developments, made a dozen divisions from the Federal Republic seem irrelevant.[149] In addition, the "long-haul" defense concept which looked to a stretched-out defense effort, carefully planned so as to minimize the economic dislocations of prolonged military spending, fitted well with what the European allies had long preferred. Also, the fact was noted that the alliance had actually improved its capabilities both qualitatively and quantitatively, and in the absense of new indications of Russian aggressiveness many believed NATO's strength was already enough.[150]

In any case, the factors just reviewed would have militated

He suggested that prior to this he had arranged a "deal" which would have provided sufficient votes in the National Assembly, but the easing of East-West tensions now made this look doubtful. C. L. Sulzberger, *A Long Row of Candles: Memoirs and Diaries (1934–1954)* (New York: Macmillan, 1969), p. 856.

[149] See generally Glenn H. Snyder, "The 'New Look' of 1953," in *Strategy, Politics and Defense Budgets,* by Warner R. Schilling, Paul Y. Hammond, and Glenn H. Snyder (New York: Columbia University Press, 1962), pp. 379–524. See also John Foster Dulles, "Policy for Security and Peace," *Foreign Affairs,* XXXII (April, 1954), pp. 353–64.

[150] The allies preferred the economic relief of an easier rearmament drive, not its corollary of massive retaliation. Acheson later wrote that the latter was simply "a rationalization of necessity" once Eisenhower accepted Treasury Secretary George Humphrey's retrenchment policy; it was "profoundly disturbing to our allies and to our relations with them." Acheson, *Present at the Creation,* p. 735. Cf. Hilsman, in Knorr, *NATO,* pp. 23–24.

against the Western rearmament effort as urged by Washington; they would also have made the attempt to launch EDC more doubtful than it already was. But added to the changing nature of NATO relationships, East-West relations, and military weapons and strategy, there was the question of whether developments among the Six were tending toward a "European" result, and if so, what kind. The answer to this was above all in the hands of the French, although the other parties to the EDC treaty, all of whom had manifested extensive hesitations in 1953–54, would have been less amenable to the European army scheme had not France single-handedly delayed it. There were repeated indications that dis-satisfaction in the other prospective EDC member-states was so deep that ratification could not be equated with willingness to abide by the terms of the treaty. As it was, though, Germany and the Benelux states completed ratification of the May, 1952, treaties by the first months of 1954, and it was expected that Italy would follow suit.[151]

The EDC treaty and the contractual accords with the Federal Republic had been submitted to the National Assembly at the end of January, 1953 (although the government did not request their approval), eight months after their signature. Once in the hands of the deputies, a foreign state could only indirectly hope to induce compliance, which automatically limited the amount of political leverage available, and which may have induced what some con-sidered counterproductive threats by Secretary Dulles. In any case, the French government—even under Washington's urging—did not ask the deputies to pass on the Bonn and Paris treaties, which for Paris was probably a commonsense postponement of their defeat, but which was seen by many as proof that France was afflicted with "pathological indecision." [152]

[151] By 1954, pursuant to the original treaty's provision under Article 38, the EDC had been supplemented by a draft constitution for a European Political Community. The latter was to commence with EDC and it was expected that its scope would gradually be expanded until full federation was achieved. It died with EDC. See Basil Karp, "The Draft Constitution for a European Political Community," *International Organization*, VII (May, 1954), pp. 181–203.

[152] The author was told that considerable U.S. funds were spent in attempts to bribe individual French legislators. Details were not available, but it is

For France EDC was one of the most deeply divisive questions of the postwar era, and because of its combination of political, emotional, ideological, and other ingredients should not be
superficially summarized.[153] The two main ingredients, German
rearmament and European unity, provided the substance of the
controversy; but along with these went dozens of related and collateral matters—matters whose relative weight in the mind of each
deputy as he decided his vote could not be systematically analyzed.
The main slogans of the highly confused debate in the assembly
were not even compatible *within* the anti-EDC camp. On the
German rearmament issue, the opposing sides came to justify their
arguments from opposite directions. Those in favor of EDC said
this would avoid another German army, while those opposed to
the treaty said its defeat would do the same.[154] If on no other
point, there was agreement that there should be no new German
army.

Because of the manner in which EDC had evolved away from
the Pleven Plan, particularly in the key aspects of the size of the
basic unit of the European army, the timing of the political and
military steps, and the degree of supranationality of the controlling political framework, the question of actual German rearmament assumed a peculiar character. There were, as mentioned,
divergent views in both the United States and France about
whether or not there would be "national" German rearmament

not likely that such could have determined the EDC outcome. The impact of
Dulles's threats—especially that of an "agonizing reappraisal"—is not clear. Some
analysts have concluded that the resentment provoked by such heavy-handed tactics
actually contributed to the assembly's rejection of EDC, but it is more likely that
no more than a few deputies were swayed one way or the other by the American
threats. Cf. Bell, *Negotiation from Strength*, p. 61, who said it may have affected one
or two deputies. Daniel Lerner (Lerner and Aron, *France Defeats EDC*, p. 217)
flatly rejected the charge that "American pressure" killed the EDC. See also Peter
Calvocoressi, *Survey of International Affairs, 1953* (London: Oxford University
Press, 1966), p. 50.

[153] EDC became almost equally an emotional problem for U.S. diplomacy as all
the American eggs seemed about to be spilled from the same basket. James Reston
noted that the United States was so exasperated that the French "have made
official Washington almost as irrational about France as the French are about the
Germans." *The New York Times*, December 20, 1953.

[154] Cf. Daniel Lerner, "Reflections on France in the World Arena," in Lerner
and Aron, *France Defeats EDC*, pp. 207–8.

under EDC and, if so, to what extent. But because the basic unit would be the *division* (although labeled *groupement*), because integrated control would only occur at the army corps level (common logistical services notwithstanding), and because the supranational political features would only come later, it seemed fairly clear that with or without EDC something resembling German rearmament would occur before long. Because of this, the other major issue, European unity (or, conversely, the loss of French sovereignty), transcended others, and it was upon this that EDC stumbled and fell:

Since the EDC contained two ideas, which were in principle radically distinct, it was supported and opposed in France for contradictory reasons. Certain enemies of the EDC were above all opposed to German rearmament, but others were primarily hostile to a European federation or to the abandonment of French sovereignty in the military field. . . . The camp of the supporters of EDC were hardly more homogeneous. Some saw in EDC the only hope of avoiding an autonomous German army; others saw it as a decisive step on the road to a united Europe.[155]

Political unification meant, of course, the disappearance of the component parts in the whole, a surrender of sovereignty to a non-national, and hence foreign, authority. It was this, more than a rearmed Federal Republic, that France was unprepared to accept. Even Schuman later said the one strong thread which bound together the diverse strands of those opposed to EDC was that "La France serait diminuée." If the existence of France as a nation-state was the determinative element in the defeat of EDC, then in a sense the German rearmament question was no longer the real one. But even so the story has no coherent explanation and generalizations are difficult; while understandable, the EDC rejection was *not* clearly explicable, and here as well as elsewhere "retrospection tends to clothe the past in false clarity." [156]

[155] Raymond Aron and August Heckscher, *Diversity of Worlds: France and the United States Look at Their Common Problems* (New York: Reynal, 1957), p. 37.
[156] Lerner and Aron, *France Defeats EDC*, pp. 200, 208. As one French analyst summarized the result, "France decided to broaden Germany's sovereignty in order

Once the decision in Paris had been made, the American diplomatic quest for German rearmament became submerged in the events of late 1954, with the leadership of the alliance temporarily passing to London, where Eden devised a plan to rescue U.S. diplomacy, and perhaps NATO, from the wreckage of a situation for which Dulles had not prepared an alternative.[157] The final formula, worked out after conferences in London and Paris, after German demands for full and immediate sovereignty, after American intimations of unilateral action on both the German question and NATO defense commitments, and after French realization that the Federal Republic might be rearmed with no controls at all, involved a compromise between Washington, Paris, Bonn, and London.[158]

In effect, the arrangements provided that the 1948 Brussels Treaty Organization would be revived and expanded into the Western European Union. Britain would join as a full participant, but the organization would have virtually no supranational

not to restrict her own." Guy de Carmoy, *The Foreign Policies of France 1944–1968* (Chicago: University of Chicago Press, 1970), p. 60. Cf. also Kanter, "European Defense Community," p. 210.

[157] Louis J. Halle, *The Cold War as History* (London: Chatto and Windus, 1967), p. 256. As the authors of one study pointed out, when EDC failed, "NATO was there to pick up the pieces." Fox and Fox, *NATO*, p. 44. It might be said from this that NATO was available not only—as Fox and Fox wrote—"to help manage the problem of Germany" but by its very existence to provide the missing alternative for American diplomacy, so that while *not* so perceived during the EDC period the alliance was available in case EDC failed. This was close to the early, pre-EDC shift of U.S. policymakers as a preference, but it is important not to confuse what American diplomacy wanted with the available results in terms of how the problem had to be worked out. France, which feared American withdrawal from the Continent should EDC materialize, at least knew that the entry of the Federal Republic into the American-dominated alliance would tend to counter withdrawal tendencies, since this was now the main framework for "containing" the Germans.

[158] Edinger, *West German Armament*, pp. 28ff. The 1954 settlement is summarized in Richard P. Stebbins, *The United States in World Affairs, 1954* (New York: Harper, 1956), pp. 150–83. Relevant documents are collected in Department of State, *American Foreign Policy, 1950–1955: Basic Documents* (Washington: Government Printing Office, 1957), Vol. I, pp. 483–643 (concerning restoration of sovereignty to the Federal Republic); pp. 871–73 (protocol to the North Atlantic Treaty on the accession of the Federal Republic); pp. 972–91 (the Western European Union arrangements); pp. 1470–1504 (the London and Paris conferences). See also Peter V. Curl, ed., *Documents on American Foreign Relations, 1954* (New York: Harper, 1955), pp. 107–74.

flavor. Germany would become a sovereign member of NATO, but certain restrictions would be voluntarily included in the military field. France would accept these arrangements and rely on the arms-control powers of WEU, plus the provision that forces of the organization would be under the (American) SACEUR, who would, perhaps, see to it that it would not be possible for any member of the WEU to take independent military action. The United States, settling for modest cooperation rather than political federation among her continental allies, would finally be able to anticipate the appearance of German troops, while promising (along with Britain) to leave her own on the Continent.[159] After a last, perhaps symbolic, rejection of all these arrnngements, the National Assembly at the end of 1954 accepted the London and Paris accords, having been told by Premier Mendes-France that this was "the sole means of preserving the Western alliance," and that Washington had come "within a millimeter" of deciding on German rearmament *without* the consent of France.[160]

In May, 1955, the Federal Republic became officially and effectively sovereign and a member of NATO, and the WEU came into being. German rearmament, demanded almost five years before, might now be begun, although events revealed that enthusiasm was minimal. It took Bonn until 1965 to approximate the realization of the total strength agreed on more than a decade before.[161] Germany hence rearmed on much the same basis as originally proposed by the United States in 1950, that is, on a national basis with armed forces composed of conventional-strength divisions,

[159] James B. Conant, U.S. High Commissioner and subsequently Ambassador to Bonn, observed the "incredibly tortuous process" whereby agreement was finally reached in this form which "all trained diplomatic observers and knowledgeable newsmen said could never happen. . . . There would be no automatic check on the possibility that a rearmed Germany could once again threaten the peace of Europe." James B. Conant, *My Several Lives* (New York: Harper and Row, 1970), p. 588.

[160] Janet Flanner (Genet), *Paris Journal 1944–1965* (New York: Atheneum, 1965), p. 258. The French Senate took three more months before it, too, consented to the accords.

[161] *New York Herald Tribune*, April 11, 1965. This completed the twelve divisions, the first of which had not reported to NATO until January 1, 1958. In 1969 the total strength of the Federal armed forces was about 463,000, which figure was expected to remain fairly static into the 1970's.

with little in the way of formal exterior control.[162] NATO membership for the Federal Republic was not suggested in the first American plan for German rearmament, but this would probably have followed actual defense participation rather quickly (had Bonn chosen to rearm first and bargain for equality later) if the French had been willing to go along with German rearmament in the first place.

The major distinction between the 1950 proposal and the 1955 result was the almost complete restoration of sovereignty to the Federal Republic. This, too, would eventually have been forthcoming if the cold war had gone on with two German states emerging in the respective camps of the competing super-powers, but the bargaining power afforded Bonn by Washington's call for remilitarization greatly hastened the process.

The U.S. desire for a rearmed Germany was hence frustrated during Eisenhower's term of office no less than during Truman's as long as the EDC "solution" was on the table. Once this had been disposed of, even France—albeit with the greatest reluctance—consented to German rearmament. The Federal Republic was to regain equality, but France was to retain her separate identity and her political-military independence.

---

[162] WEU was not really intended to substitute for the defunct EDC other than as an avenue of German entry into NATO. Bonn did accept its arms-control functions, and repeated the earlier willingness to abstain from making certain sophisticated military items. Since NATO forces were integrated and since all the German divisions were to be under SACEUR, the assumption was that independent action would be difficult. There was not, however, any equivalent of the automatic controls which France had demanded throughout the EDC period.

CHAPTER VI

The German Rearmament Question in Perspective

THE American attempt to rearm Germany was a part of a larger process within the Atlantic community, which in a very few years witnessed, *inter alia,* the formation of the North Atlantic Alliance; the American decision to send additional troops to Europe and to station them on the Continent indefinitely in peacetime; the transformation of the North Atlantic Treaty from a guarantee pact into an integrated military organization; and Bonn's admission to NATO and the return of the Federal Republic to the international community under conditions of dignity if not complete equality. At the same time, the states of Western Europe—especially the Six—moved closer to each other, a process which was both aided and damaged by the impact of the rearmament issue on Franco-German relations. The ultimate effects of the events examined in this study are still unclear, particularly since numerous policy courses which were followed or rejected in connection with the German rearmament question easily lend themselves to speculation on what might have happened if another path had been chosen.

Considered alone, the evolution of the original U.S. demand

for German rearmament into an ambitious scenario for the future of Europe provides a case study of the tendency of a policy chosen with a particular objective to mushroom into a much broader design the longer it is frustrated, especially if the state involved is a super-power seeking to impose its will on its allies. This assumes that other policy goals are perceived (by the super-power) as compatible with the original objective, and that the other states resist the additional goals along with the first one. In this situation, the resistance may evolve from opposition to the original goal to even greater opposition to the ones eventually demanded, just as rejection of the latter may permit the original demand to be revived successfully.[1]

In the instant case, the key to the outcome of the Franco-American struggle was probably the passing of time, as both protagonists came to realize that, eventually, Washington could rearm the Germans but could not create the EDC, just as Paris could prevent the latter but not the former. When, a decade later, the United States tried to impose upon its European allies a project which in some ways resembled an embryonic nuclear EDC, the same process of mushrooming anticipation occurred, but unlike the earlier case the Multilateral Force (MLF) was abruptly dropped. Perhaps the EDC example is not analogous to the MLF, but if not, the distinction is probably that NATO security was not perceived as dependent on the MLF, whereas it was on German rearmament, although in both projects one of the major American goals was to

[1] "The link established by the European Defense Community between German rearmament and European integration boomeranged, turning opposition to the rebuilding of German military strength into rejection of European integration." Jacques Freymond, *The Saar Conflict 1945–1955* (New York: Praeger, 1960), p. 129. The British High Commissioner, as mentioned in Chap. II, was quite convinced that even though the German rearmament issue was eventually worked out in a manner comparable to the 1950 demand, this was hardly a necessary quarrel: "The American purpose was to bring about a degree of German rearmament as quickly and effectively as possible. They would have achieved their aim more quickly if they had simply acceded to Dr. Adenauer's request [for a Federal police force]. Instead at least seven years were wasted in pressing on the Germans a proposal they disliked and the acceptance of which was made conditional on substantial concessions by the Allies." Sir Ivone Kirkpatrick, *The Inner Circle: Memoirs of Ivone Kirkpatrick* (London: Macmillan, 1959), p. 241.

lock the Federal Republic more closely into the Western camp.[2]

In some ways the 1950 demand that Germany rearm turned out to be militarily unnecessary and politically premature: these conclusions would seem apparent from the fact that there was no Soviet attack in spite of the imbalance of forces along the central front, and from the difficulty which surrounded resolution of the issue and agreement with Bonn no less than Paris. On the other hand, German rearmament finally did begin as the NATO nuclear deterrent entered the period of strategic duopoly (notwithstanding the "new look" and the presumed reliance on tactical nuclear weapons), and political rehabilitation of the Federal Republic occurred in time for less ambitious but more feasible projects for European integration than EDC. As illustrated by the rearmament issue in the early 1950's, France sought to preserve sovereignty and Germany to recover it, while the United States experienced the frustration of being caught between these conflicting forces, as both worked against a supranational EDC.[3]

Although this study emphasizes the German rearmament question during the Truman-Acheson period, neither American policy nor European reactions underwent substantial change between early 1953 and late 1954. Certain conclusions may thus emerge from the overall U.S. attempt to remilitarize the Federal Republic and unite Europe through EDC. While the success of a diplomatic

[2] In both the EDC and MLF cases, U.S. officials spoke as if the fate of the project were crucial to the fate of the Atlantic Alliance in the future, and in both cases there were American hints that if the scheme did not materialize Washington might go ahead with a bilateral arrangement with Germany. Cf. Henry A. Kissinger, *The Troubled Partnership* (New York: McGraw-Hill, 1965), pp. 133-34 and Chap. 5 *passim.*

[3] Once the German rearmament demand had been made and the three-way tangle began, "the State Department found itself a mediator, attempting to reconcile French demands for restrictions with German demands for equality." Samuel P. Huntington, *The Common Defense: Strategic Programs in National Defense* (New York: Columbia University Press, 1961), p. 321. This may in part explain the curious phenomenon of the rival conferences at Bonn and Paris in 1951, and also be relevant to why the "winner" of the Franco-American duel was the Federal Republic. Cf. Hans Speier, *German Rearmament and Atomic War: The Views of German Military and Political Leaders* (Evanston: Row, Peterson, 1957), pp. 10-13.

effort should not be confused with whether the interests of a state would have been well served thereby, the place of the German rearmament question in the history of American diplomacy is particularly ambiguous.

If only the original formulation of the German rearmament demand is considered, American diplomacy failed: additional troops were urgently sought in the wake of the Korean crisis, the Federal Republic was to have provided them, and none were forthcoming. If the ultimate formulation of the German rearmament demand, which became inextricably linked with the EDC, is considered, the result is the same: European unification was deemed a necessity, the European army was to have been the vehicle for this, and the project completely collapsed. In both cases the obstacle was France, and in both cases the immediate beneficiary of the clash between Washington and Paris was Bonn.

Yet such a limited appraisal would be incomplete. In evaluating American diplomacy, the plural nature of the goals and the mixed nature of the results should be considered. To begin with, the overriding goal of enhancing American security through augmenting the defensibility of Western Europe was not demonstrably affected, either by the nonappearance of German troops in 1950 or the nonappearance of the European army later on. Had the Federal Republic been hastily remilitarized—against the wishes of its own people in addition to those of France, Russia, and other European states—there might have been created at a stroke an element of instability far more detrimental to the American concern with a secure Europe than in fact eventuated. And had a European army been created, especially prior to the time when a political authority capable of properly using this military instrument could function, the anomalous phenomenon of EDC soldiers wearing the insignia of Europe under the command of an American general would perhaps have brought more chaos than cooperation.[4]

[4] For example, David Bruce testified that on the one hand the German forces in the European army would not be available as an instrument of the Federal Republic's policy, but on the other, each national government, including Bonn, would have a veto power over EDC activities during the opening years. See U.S. Senate, Committee on Foreign Relations, Hearings, *Mutual Security Act of 1952*,

From start to finish, the very confusion of military, political, economic, and psychological factors which the German problem automatically produced was relevant to the frustration of American diplomacy, and would have been only partially alleviated had weapons been available which only fired when pointed toward the east.

In part because there were no such weapons, there immediately arose the possibility of creating a new danger worse than the one sought to be countered—would a defeated, humiliated, divided, great power be an exception to the desire of any state in such a situation to restore and rehabilitate itself? And at the same time what should be done, asked the British in particular, to prevent a great industrial power from gaining unfair advantage due to the very absence of a large percentage of the national budget being allocated to defense? If Europe was too poor to provide more troops, if the United States was rich enough to finance the nuclear deterrent as well as a modest European conventional rearmament effort, and if America was not sufficiently concerned about ground strength to send any more than four more divisions (a negligible total if indeed a Soviet attack was imminent), then why should the European allies bother to barricade the front door of military protection with what little they had if this left the back door of social unrest and economic collapse open and unprotected?

These questions, of course, were not any more easily answerable than the overriding one of what might be the intentions of Moscow. They are among the many examples of how some of the goals of U.S. policy necessarily conflicted with each other, in the sense that the results which might have been produced were not amenable to reconciliation, especially in European eyes, which saw guns and butter as alternatives.

While Washington policymakers were not immediately concerned with further major revision of the political status of West

---

pp. 336, 339. See also the statements of General Gruenther, *ibid.*, pp. 245, 287–89, for examples of the enormously complex military mixture which EDC would have brought.

Germany prior to the Korean crisis, once it reshaped American perspectives the rehabilitation of the Federal Republic assumed a place of prominence in U.S. planning.[5] The pro-German bias of American policy from 1950 on necessarily assumed an anti-French cloak, a situation abetted by the striking domestic contrast between the Federal Republic, seemingly stable and efficient, and France, which gave the appearance of being too traumatized by the past to face and cope with the realities of the present. By making the rearmament demand, the United States necessarily raised the matter of revising the political status of the Federal Republic. Paris was more aware than Washington that there could be no such simple solution to NATO's military needs as German mercenaries, and the long struggle over the German rearmament question was accompanied from the outset by conflicting perspectives on Germany's place in international politics.

Here a distinction is appropriate between the short- and long-run aspects of American policy. The immediate U.S. goal of a German defense contribution, as soon as Chancellor Adenauer made it clear in the autumn of 1950 that the Federal Republic would not agree to rearm without substantial equality, led to the commencement of the lengthy process of working out a political settlement as part of the Petersberg negotiations. Prior to the development in 1951 of American willingness to end the occupation, the question of German rearmament was not related to political reality: only the promise of a restoration of sovereignty could have made remilitarization palatable to the Federal Republic, and even when this was made its acceptance was complete only on the official level by the Adenauer government, at least for the period under review.

The lasting importance of the German rearmament demand for the return of Germany to the international community cannot be overemphasized. Even the cold-war competition between the

[5] This is not to suggest that Germany was not seen as a crucial problem—as, indeed, the "elephantine" size of the German Bureau (which was as large as all the other European desks in the State Department combined) reflected. Political equality, however, was not immediately anticipated.

super-powers would have brought political changes in Germany only gradually (and perhaps grudgingly), since the country was already under a military occupation for which no consent was requisite. Given the enormously complicated nature of the subject matter covered by the contractual accords and the related agreements reached at Bonn, the very initiation of the process of restoring the Federal Republic's sovereignty was a highly successful result of the German rearmament demand, even if not so intended when first considered. Occupation controls could, of course, have been gradually eased over a lengthy time period, as many who were concerned with the democratization of the Federal Republic preferred. But when the historical and geographical position of Germany is considered, along with the vulnerability of Western Europe in the early 1950's, the conclusion is warranted that the political result of the military goal was in line with U.S. interests.[6] It was true, as the French pointed out, that German rearmament and a restoration of German independence did not have to coincide, but because of the dangerous international situation, and the U.S. viewpoint which gave the Bonn government the leverage to demand political equality, they did.[7]

The expanded goal of American diplomacy, once French policy had forced a tight connection between German rearmament and European unification, became the creation of the European army. Beginning with Eisenhower's sudden conversion to a belief that "the impossible" should be attempted, the United States added to its original objective a number of other goals which European unity would purportedly achieve. These included virtually every military, political, economic, and psychological benefit toward which America's European policy had looked since the beginnings of the Marshall Plan and the signing of the North Atlantic

---

[6] Even militarily this probably held; soldiers on both sides of the Atlantic were relieved that the "omelet" of the European army had not been scrambled, and that its confusions had been avoided. Lewis J. Edinger, *West German Armament*, Air University, Maxwell Air Base, Alabama, October, 1955, p. 27.

[7] Cf. Wolfram F. Hanreider, *West German Foreign Policy, 1949–1963* (Stanford: Stanford University Press, 1967), p. 82.

Treaty.[8] The general goals of political stability, economic prosperity, and military defensibility would include realization of specific objectives: Europe henceforth would need neither financial aid nor military assistance, and the German problem would be permanently solved.

Indeed, not only the problem of binding Germany to the Western community would have been solved, but also the other German problems, including the provision of a "safe" military contribution and perhaps even reunification—the latter in the sense that once the Federal Republic had been absorbed in Europe, then, strictly speaking, what was formerly Germany would no longer be divided. In either case, the traditional German problem of a Reich too powerful to take its place peacefully in the European system would never again arise.

An evaluation of the goals connected with the EDC and the results actually forthcoming presents a mixed picture. In military terms, the failure to ratify EDC meant that the defense effort continued as before. In other words, the European allies, not yet including Germany, pursued modest rearmament programs featuring small increments in troop strength and the realization of a somewhat more impressive NATO infrastructure. The economic constraints which prevented increased military spending by the individual NATO allies would not have been materially altered by a European army, so that in this respect there was no significant loss of NATO strength in this time period.[9] What was lost was the opportunity to begin raising German units, but even this must be qualified by mentioning that France would not have agreed and the Federal Republic might not have either. Pending the appearance of the common denominator of 1954, when Bonn settled for less than complete equality and Paris for less than foolproof controls, there was no way American leadership could have

[8] A good example of the list of benefits the EDC would supposedly bring is Theodore Geiger and H. van B. Cleveland, "Making Western Europe Defensible," Planning Pamphlet No. 74, National Planning Association, August, 1951, *passim*.

[9] Indeed, the situation might have been *worse* if national differences had prevented agreement on the common European army budget, without which paralysis would have developed.

solved the dilemma. Until time had passed and until France had been given an opportunity to delay German rearmament for a considerable period, the nonutilization of German military potential was a problem without a solution. It remained a problem because U.S. determination to obtain troops from the Federal Republic never wavered.[10]

One possibility not explored by the United States should be mentioned—that of German rearmament without French consent. Did France have a veto? If Bonn (and London) had not objected, could Washington have unilaterally acted? The answer depends upon several factors, and perhaps did not remain the same during the entire period of disagreement. At first, it would seem, Paris held an absolute veto. Politically, the United States as the leader of the Western alliance sought maximum cohesion in the months following the Korean attack. The possibility that this might indicate impending hostilities in Europe made an open break between the major allies out of the question. Militarily, Washington wanted to strengthen NATO, while a heavyhanded attempt to push the Germans into uniform would probably have wrecked the alliance, since no French government could have survived acquiescence in such a step, even without NATO membership for the Federal Republic. Legally, as one of the occupying powers, France had a position of full equality. The Paris government held an outright veto over national German rearmament because no change in the Occupation Statute could have been made without its consent. Nor could the United States at any time have forced the Federal Republic into NATO. Article 10 of the treaty provided that other states could accede only by unanimous agreement, and even if this had been forthcoming the Federal Republic lacked the legal capacity to join the alliance. These considerations also suggest an affirmative answer to the question whether France would (in 1950 or 1951) actually have used her veto: the combination of international factors and domestic pressures would have

[10] The distinction in this sense between EDC and MLF is clear. MLF, after it became increasingly obvious that the allies were not interested in this approach to "nuclear sharing" in NATO, was shelved in Washington with little fanfare.

made this virtually certain. Even a highly persuasive indication of Soviet intent to launch an immediate offensive on the Continent would not have altered this, since military lead time would have been too long.

The absolute nature of the French veto probably did not last in every respect. Legally, there was no change, but in other ways the power to block German rearmament might have eroded with time even if the right to do so did not. When Schuman told the National Assembly early in 1952 that he was certain the United States would proceed with national German rearmament unless the parliament approved a continued effort to reach agreement on EDC, this assumption may have been somewhat premature.[11] Acheson and other American policymakers considered this, but would certainly have hesitated to take so drastic a step, especially as Eisenhower was preparing to leave Europe and as the U.S. election campaign was getting under way. Once EDC was rejected later on, however, the pressure to act would have been enormous, with Bonn demanding sovereignty and American domestic forces demanding a compensation prize in the wake of EDC's demise and France's "misbehavior."

But even under these circumstances France could not have been ignored, particularly since international developments had fostered an all-round diminution of the belief that German rearmament was necessary. If the French veto was not so clear by 1954, neither was the need for it. Hence even following EDC's defeat France might have been unduly pessimistic in assuming the United States would ignore French legal rights and political attitudes by pressing for a bilateral arrangement between the Anglo-Saxon powers and Bonn.[12]

[11] It may also have been deliberately made by Schuman to force the issue. The personal aspect of the German rearmament story is striking in the case of the French foreign minister: while not quite a "Trojan horse" for the other occupying powers, Schuman's willingness to cooperate with the United States and Britain was certainly relevant to the EDC's lasting as long as it did. Had the ups and downs of French ministerial politics not spared Schuman the revolving-door fate of most other Cabinet members in Paris, the whole picture might have been very different had Acheson had to deal earlier with Georges Bidault, for example.

[12] Cf. Paul-Marie de la Gorce, *The French Army: A Military-Political History* (New York: Braziller, 1963), p. 368; Royal Institute of International Affairs, *Brit-*

If the failure to achieve EDC ratification was militarily no great loss, neither was it economically or politically an opportunity of unmixed character. The American goal of an economically prosperous Europe which would not need outside aid was already well on the way toward realization by the early 1950's. The allies had also by this time demonstrated that they were not in the process of internally falling prey to Communism or even neutralism, in spite of the fact that the level of economic and social stability was far from the American model. The creation of the European Economic Community (EEC) of the later 1950's, and the difficulty involved in keeping this expanded customs union operational during the years after its inauguration, suggest that even in this sector the EDC would have been premature. Economic cooperation, never divorced from political willingness to undertake common action, would under EDC have been much more difficult than it later was under EEC, since the latter was in effect an economic effort first, while EDC's requirement of a common military budget for the European army would from the outset have driven right to the heart of the political question.

Politically, the argument that EDC would create a great united ally for the United States always rested on the dubious assumption that it would be easier to deal with one large than with a number of smaller governments, and that this great ally could be relied upon to agree with American priorities. These assumptions might have been justified had the interests and outlooks of the "partners" on either side of the Atlantic been the same; but that there never has been an automatic coincidence of views, either between America and Europe, or among Europeans themselves, other than occasionally in the most basic ways, seems obvious.[13] Even at the height of the cold war, and even when NATO should have been able to present a unified appearance, political differences between Washington and the allies and between the European allies them-

---

ain in Western Europe: WEU and the Atlantic Alliance (London: Royal Institute of International Affairs, 1956), p. 26. In spite of appearances, U.S. officials were *not* determined to proceed with German rearmament without the consent of France. Interviews supported this.

[13] Cf. Kissinger, *Troubled Partnership*, pp. 241–42.

selves prevented full harmony. The notion that a united Europe, capable of defending itself, economically strong and politically cohesive, would *ipso facto* be a "partner" has simply not been proved. Even in the most basic sense, that of survival, there is no necessary reason to assume that if either the United States of America or the United States of Europe found itself at the threshold of a mortal confrontation with a third super-power, the other would perceive its interests as requiring a common stand.[14] Nonratification of EDC, even if EDC would have been capable of implementation to the degree of producing European unification, was hence not necessarily a failure for American policy, which might have lost the battle but avoided worse engagements in the long run.[15]

An assessment of the goals and results of the German rearmament policy should include a brief examination of the other major ingredient of the original American package, the sending of troops to Europe.[16] Among the reasons for doing this were the desires to increase U.S. security generally; to reassure the allies of the American commitment, and by the same token render the NATO deterrent more credible to Moscow; to achieve a limited war capability and deter a proxy attack by a satellite; to exercise the leadership of the alliance by setting an example, thereby raising the morale both of Europeans and of the American forces already there; and simultaneously to provide a screen behind which Germany could rearm while reassuring France that the new German army would be under a stronger NATO umbrella. Unlike the troops-to-Europe policy, the German rearmament goal even if realized might not have had results in line with these diplomatic objectives.

[14] Europeans themselves have tended to stress just this point, for example in relation to the consideration of separate nuclear forces for European allies or for Europe as a whole.

[15] Cf. Laurence W. Martin, "Europe and the Future of the Grand Alliance," in *Foreign Policy in the Sixties: The Issues and the Instruments,* eds. Roger Hilsman and Robert C. Good (Baltimore: The Johns Hopkins Press, 1965), pp. 29–30.

[16] Cf. Wesley B. Truitt, "The Troops to Europe Decision: The Process, Politics, and Diplomacy of a Strategic Commitment" (unpublished Ph.D. dissertation, Columbia University, 1968), Chap. 3.

For example, the original German rearmament demand and the later EDC goal shared the quality of causing the NATO allies to wonder whether the real purpose of the United States was not to increase the American commitment to military involvement in Europe, but the reverse. Nor would the reappearance of German forces so soon after the war have raised the morale of Europeans, or increased confidence in American leadership. And to the degree that a European army containing German units gave the impression of laying the foundation for conventional military self-sufficiency, this would have made the American nuclear deterrent less rather than more credible on both sides of the containment line, assuming that U.S. troops in Europe would over time have been withdrawn.

The German rearmament demand was seen in Europe not as an example of Washington's leadership but rather as evidence of its tendency to be dominant, just as the later pressure for EDC became counterproductive as this vehicle for German rearmament was increasingly perceived as a project more beneficial to the United States than to Europeans themselves.[17] Nor was the interdependent relationship between American troops in Germany and the raising of German forces sufficient to break the three-way tangle. Bonn would not have agreed to rearm without a protective screen, nor would Paris have agreed to German rearmament without Anglo-Saxon promises to remain on the Continent. But even a European army in which Germans would enjoy equality and Frenchmen security was not convincing. As long as a Soviet threat was perceived, the only ultimate source of security for Europe, with or without German rearmament, with or without EDC, was the physical presence of the United States, in NATO, perennially symbolized by an American SACEUR.

[17] "In these circumstances, even though a policy of imposing a solution was not intended, the lack of an alternative forced the United States to press so vigorously for its particular solution that it was felt to be trying to dominate." This is applicable both to the original demand and the EDC commitment. William Reitzel, Morton A. Kaplan, and Constance G. Coblenz, *United States Foreign Policy 1945–1955* (Washington: Brookings Institution, 1956), pp. 358–59. At the same time, the very existence of an "alternative" might have weakened the diplomatic attempt for the preferred objective—or so it was believed in Washington.

On the record, American goals as announced by Washington in 1950 and for a considerable time thereafter were not achieved with respect to a German defense contribution. Yet in retrospect U.S. policy *was* successful; the Soviet Union was deterred, Europe recovered from economic weakness and political infirmity, while at least beginning a military basis for security; and the unknown factor of the instability which would automatically have been introduced by the sudden reappearance of German military power did not materialize.[18] No preventive intervention was triggered; democracy in the Federal Republic was not smothered at birth; and France even though alienated was given the respite of several years' delay. It took time before the solution to the German rearmament question and its evolution into the EDC project could be worked out, and perhaps the time was really more important than the solution.[19]

Eventual French rejection of EDC was not a break in the continuity of French policy but consistent with it. The European army project as embodied in the 1952 EDC accords simply did not meet the criteria which would have made the price of ratification worth paying.[20] Nor is it certain that even the original French plan for a European army as presented by Pleven in 1950 would have generated support in Paris which would have genuinely contributed to the building of European unity. Indeed, the reverse is more likely, since if desperate enough actually to commence im-

---

[18] Scholars increasingly seem to agree, however, that even in the earlier period of the cold war "the historical record offers no evidence of Soviet intent to invade Western Europe in order to set up communist regimes, or for any other policy purpose." Bernard S. Morris, "NATO, the U.S., and the U.S.S.R.," in Edwin H. Fedder, ed., *NATO in the Seventies* (St. Louis: University of Missouri Center for International Studies, 1970), p. 26. Notwithstanding such a judgment, the success of American efforts to deter hostile acts against the NATO area remains. Since the postwar period cannot be imagined *without* what was in fact done, it must at best be a moot point whether or not measures for security were taken on false premises to counter a threat which never existed.

[19] Cf. Heinz L. Krekeler, "The German Defense Contribution," *The Annals*, CCCXII (July, 1957), p. 84. See also Edinger, *West German Armament*, p. 46, and cf. Dean Acheson, *Sketches from Life of Men I Have Known* (New York: Harper, 1961), p. 47.

[20] Cf. Nathan Leites and Christian de la Malene, "Paris from EDC to WEU," *World Politics* (January, 1957), p. 198.

plementation of the Pleven Plan, France would only have done so as an instinctive anti-German response, hardly a viable foundation stone for the rest of the European edifice.

The Federal Republic's call for equality was not so much a demand for a place alongside the other countries in Europe as it was a cry for independence. By the same token, it was in the nature of the situation that when one state sought to tap the military manpower-potential of another it could not continue to treat it as a conquered province, especially when it had recently been a great power. Hence while the United States may have been satisfied to obtain German mercenaries, such was simply not a meaningful possibility. For Germany, as for France, sovereignty was even more important than security. If security had been the highest concern then German rearmament might have preceded the fulfillment of the conditions attached to it by both Bonn and Paris. It was the failure of the United States to appreciate that the attachment to independence and sovereignty was so strong, and that national animosities were so deeply rooted, that allowed Washington's vision to be clouded.

The belief that EDC should succeed was rational and relevant; the assumption that it could do so was mistaken. This was in part due to the fact that European unity *was* so rational and so relevant, making it difficult to accept its nonmaterialization. It was also related to the American impression that supranational unification was an institutional event rather than a socio-political process, and the supposition that a result which—even if conditions were maximal—would require decades could be forthcoming in a matter of months or a few years. To subsume the explanation of the nonunification of Europe under the rubric of the persistence of sovereignty may be somewhat tautological, but as a shorthand reference for the failure of American diplomacy to induce ratification of EDC, it is not inaccurate.[21]

[21] The United States used the same diplomatic techniques toward Bonn as toward the NATO allies, even before the Federal Republic had approached an equal position, pointing up the "habit" of dealing with states as though they are sovereign even if they are not. The Petersberg talks could hardly have been held at all, had they assumed even remotely the character of leading toward a *diktat*.

From the outset of its quest for German rearmament, American diplomacy relied upon the traditional means available to a great power when dealing with weaker allies—persuasion, pressure, threats, and so forth. But because of the same cold-war conditions which gave rise to the German rearmament demand, the Federal Republic and France enjoyed positions of bargaining strength which otherwise would not have been available. Bonn and Paris could frustrate the wishes of the United States due above all to the delicate nature of the balance between the multiple American goals of (1) making German rearmament acceptable to France; (2) minimizing the risk of a future German danger; (3) allowing Adenauer to tout his willingness to remilitarize the Federal Republic as a necessary means to restore German status; and (4) generally to avoid the disruption of NATO by trampling upon the sensibilities of other allies. The most salient element in this respect was the refusal of France to consent to an American policy reversal when there was a fundamental divergence of views on the nature of the external threat, and hence on the requirements of security. Washington saw Russia as "the enemy," Paris saw Germany as at least as great a danger as the Soviet Union, and Bonn utilized this diplomatic confrontation to achieve political rehabilitation long before this would otherwise have been granted.

Perhaps, however, these results reflect the somewhat unique character of NATO. It is in the very nature of America's relationship to its European allies that the latter will not be literally forced to do the bidding of the leading power. The critical aspect of the power concept—that of its relational nature—is here readily apparent: the Atlantic Alliance for all its lopsided character was and is a grouping of states freely associating themselves to the degree which their common interests (as individually perceived) allow; and because the allies can be persuaded, cajoled, pressured, and even threatened—*but not forced*—to comply with the leader's desires, American power over the European states was necessarily circumscribed. To have changed this relationship would have

---

Adenauer's immediate reaction to the collapse of EDC was to demand not another framework for rearmament, but sovereignty.

been to wreck the very coalition the United States sought to strengthen. In this sense, Washington never had the power to insure German rearmament over either Paris or Bonn.

The mushrooming of the simple, military demand for German troops into an ambitious scenario for the future of Western Europe would probably not have occurred had the U.S. desire for a German military contribution been agreed to. The key factor in the American shift to a position in favor of EDC began with the conclusion that there was no other way to obtain German troops. All the subsequent embellishment of the European army project followed this basic evaluation. The unity of Europe had been a concern of the United States since the war, for the numerous reasons mentioned. The EDC method of unification, however, was embraced with the greatest reluctance and only by default.

Yet, once accepted, it was rapidly elevated to a position of the very highest priority. The reason for this was inseparable from its appeal as a panacea which would bring a solution not only for Europe's problems, but also for the European problem of the United States. Perceived by American policymakers as an area of recurrent wars, especially wars between France and Germany, and also as an area vital to U.S. security which was being threatened by the super-power to the east, Western Europe was on both counts considered a liability for America as long as it remained fragmented. Unification would bring internal peace to Western Europe, ending forever the cycle of wars between France and Germany and the unfortunate tendency for the United States to become involved in them, and it would bring peace in a time of cold war as a third super-power became sufficiently organized to stand alone, free of the fear of a Soviet assault, no longer dependent on American aid, and sharing the fundamental security interests of the United States. Given the benefits which U.S. policymakers believed would ensue from a Europe united through the European army vehicle, American dedication to EDC is not surprising. What remains curious is why so many believed it would work, why it was thought that if only the French would ratify the treaty then the rest would follow.

The U.S. commitment to the EDC treaty was inseparable from the assumption that its provisions could have been implemented. The weight of the evidence is against this possibility, as both the events at the time and subsequent developments among the Six have demonstrated.[22] Economic cooperation may generate the tendency to spill over into more economic cooperation, but it has yet to be shown that political interests which conflict, and which are rooted in the persistent desires of competing states to gain relative advantages for themselves rather than for the larger entity, are capable of being swept away with the magic wand of functional supranationality.[23] It is incumbent upon the proponents of such a project as EDC to demonstrate how, given the depth of national feelings and the lack of desire on both the governmental and popular levels in the European states to surrender sovereignty, the European army could have succeeded, more than it is for the critics to show why it would have failed. Eisenhower, who concluded EDC failed because it was too supranational, and Acheson, who felt that one of its main weaknesses was that it had never been properly presented to the people of France, may both have been correct. There is no simple answer to why U.S. leaders "believed in" EDC, but probably the greatest factor in their minds was that this was what they wanted.[24]

Would EDC have worked? Secretary Acheson later speculated that had the treaty been ratified promptly the political unification

[22] A survey of elite attitudes in France and Germany a decade after the defeat of EDC found that the idea still had mixed support, still tended to divide opinion in both countries, and tended to divide—not bring together—the two countries themselves. Karl W. Deutsch, Lewis J. Edinger, Roy C. Macridis, Richard L. Merritt, *France, Germany and the Western Alliance* (New York: Scribner's, 1967), p. 264.

[23] Jean Monnet, who considered EDC a political step and not a military initiative, did *not* consider the European army plan a blueprint for European unification. Rather, the idea was to start with what was possible and then continue as the new institutional framework created new conditions for other kinds of initiatives—more a trial-and-error approach than a formal or legalistic one. Monnet also felt that critics of EDC tended to make the mistake of seeing all the problems at once. There *were* problems, he agreed, but on balance EDC would have benefited rather than hindered the building of "Europe."

[24] The mystical ingredient cannot be discounted. U.S. officials who believed EDC could succeed based this to a great extent on what might be called faith. Interviews of persons involved in the American diplomatic attempt to sponsor the European army repeatedly touched on this.

of Europe might have been begun: "It is not a fantastic possibility." Even though a certain reaction against EDC would have come in either case, he added, the very establishment of the institutional framework for a European political community might have been realized "if pressure had been maintained for another year" and if Schuman had created "an organization to propagandize at the grass roots for EDC." Acheson, however, also expressed his doubts: "It is enough to suggest the might-have-been without pushing too hard." [25]

A single example might underline this, that of the likely attitude of the Federal Republic as a member of EDC. The fact that Bonn alone was not allowed in NATO would have symbolized persistent German inferiority; the device of guarantees to the EDC organization as a whole was simply a fig-leaf covering discrimination. Over time, Germany would probably not have been satisfied with its inferior place in the European army, and would have demanded revisions. This in turn would have convinced the French that the very ambitions EDC was supposed to have contained were actually being stimulated by the European army setup, and the likelihood in this case that it could have served as a solid foundation for building "Europe" is quite small. With neither Paris nor Bonn supporting the existing arrangements, their viability would surely have diminished, and it would not have been within the capability of the United States to repair the fragile shell of unity once it had been broken by the clash of national interests.

Not only would the European states have to have trusted each other before committing themselves to EDC, but they would as a group have to have trusted what the United States—because of its domination of NATO and SHAPE—would do with the European army once it came into existence.[26] Yet Europeans wanted neither the continued American domination implicit in this nor the withdrawal of U.S. troops from the Continent, which might have been

[25] Dean Acheson, *Sketches from Life of Men I Have Known* (New York: Harper, 1961), pp. 54–56.
[26] F. S. C. Northrop, *European Union and United States Foreign Policy* (New York: Macmillan, 1954), pp. 142–43.

triggered by an independently strong European army. Either way, the problems raised by this dilemma would have persisted, further clouding an already ambiguous outlook, and may have prompted a preference for a status quo characterized neither by the extended control which American command of a European army would have meant, nor by the perhaps more dangerous and illusory freedom of action which an American departure would have brought.

Eisenhower's confident assurance that the European army would work was at best misleading. The military provisions of the treaty may not have presented an insuperable bar, but such a prognosis could hardly be extended to the political aspects of the EDC once the European army is detached from the American vision of it as part of the NATO force.[27] The creation of institutional bases for cooperative efforts between states may in themselves be productive of joint action, but only when there is a willingness in the first place to implement the agreements which created the institutions. In the Western Europe of the early 1950's (and indeed since) there simply did not exist the requisite psychological or political foundation for a venture as ambitious as EDC. One study concluded that "the main reason both why the EDC was suggested in the first place and why it failed was that by 1954 the identitive power of the European ideal was not strong enough to overcome national loyalties, suspicions, and fears of other nations, especially the fear of Germany." [28] By implication, EDC could not have been implemented even if the policymaking elites had been more willing, due to underlying socio-political factors which necessarily meant that unifying efforts could succeed only gradually, if at all.

Looking back, U.S. interests did not seem to have suffered demonstrable ill-effects as the result of the failure to gain either German rearmament in 1950 or a European army thereafter. On the contrary, the continued imbalance of conventional strength

[27] Eisenhower quite confused the two aspects. Dwight D. Eisenhower, *The White House Years: Mandate for Change, 1953–1956* (Garden City: Doubleday, 1963), pp. 398–99.

[28] Amitai Etzioni, *Political Unification* (New York: Holt, Rinehart, and Winston, 1965), p. 267, and see Chap. 7 *passim*.

between NATO and Soviet forces—perhaps for entirely separate reasons—did not tempt an aggressive adventure either before or after the addition of the present dozen divisions of Federal troops.[29]

More important, the political outcome of the German rearmament effort was consistent with American interests. The premature demand for German troops and the premature attempt to unite Europe through EDC were both advantageous in terms of the adjustment of attitudes relevant to the Federal Republic's return to the international community. By raising the military issue, the United States hastened the political rehabilitation of Germany and forced the French to accustom themselves to the fact that the perpetuation of second-rate status for the Germans could not be had.[30] Franco-American relations and Franco-German relations both suffered in the short run from the inevitably emotional struggle surrounding the German rearmament question. But compared with the post-1919 mistakes in the wake of "the first German war," these events which partially contributed to the liquidation of the second should not be faulted, at least not as aspects of an informal settlement which will perhaps never be memorialized in an all-round treaty of peace.[31]

Whether by pressing for German rearmament long after the original stimulus of the Korean attack had passed the United States lost one or more opportunities to ease the cold-war confrontation, to reintroduce Germany into the Western family in less emotionally and politically disturbing circumstances, to build a relationship with France uncluttered by the debris of past

[29] NATO officials, however, continued to be apprehensive. Following the Russian invasion of Czechoslovakia in mid-1968, senior allied officers warned that a Soviet offensive would reach the Rhine River in forty-eight hours if not met with nuclear weapons. *The New York Times*, November 29, 1968.

[30] "It is surprising to the historian that anti-German feeling in France, far from being revived by the rejection of the EDC, had on the contrary been weakened." Guy de Carmoy, *The Foreign Policies of France 1944–1968* (Chicago: University of Chicago Press, 1970), p. 92.

[31] The temporary allied occupation and administration of Germany after the war gave time for stable political and economic conditions to develop before responsibility was handed over to a German government. Kirkpatrick, *Inner Circle*, p. 238.

traumas, or to accelerate European cooperation and integration in nonmilitary sectors, is beyond the scope of this study. These questions provide ample room for speculation, but each would involve an investigation in which the German rearmament question would be only a part, a variable whose weight would be difficult to assign.

Whether or not bringing the Federal Republic into the Western fold by the military avenue was a mistake will become less demonstrable with time. America's interests in terminating the wasting asset of the occupation, and in holding the alliance together, probably were well-served by the participation of Bonn in NATO, although the justification for this, that Russia was about to swallow Western Europe, gave the United States "the equivalent of a vested interest in the Soviet menace." [32] The cold war may have been prolonged unnecessarily, yet in the period studied American policymakers could not be certain that the Soviet Union was "satisfied." [33] The lasting importance of the American diplomatic attempt to rearm Germany was thus not in its belated success as a dozen more divisions were produced, but in its political by-products: the restoration of the sovereignty of the Federal Republic in a manner acceptable to all the major Western states concerned; the inauguration of more modest and hence more successful European integration projects; [34] and an easing of the cold-war confrontation itself once the German rearmament question was finally answered, and answered in a manner which did not leave

[32] Louis J. Halle, *The Cold War as History* (London: Chatto and Windus, 1967), p. 261, and see Chap. 15 *passim*. See also Hanreider, *West German Foreign Policy*, p. 89.

[33] John J. McCloy, "Challenge to Europe," *Interplay*, February, 1968, p. 33. The former High Commissioner said "Those who lived through the period and faced the problems . . . can never be persuaded that the threat was unreal."

[34] Cf. Etzioni, *Political Unification*, Chap. 7 *passim;* Karl W. Deutsch and Lewis J. Edinger, *Germany Rejoins the Powers: Mass Opinion, Interest Groups and Elites in Contemporary German Foreign Policy* (Stanford: Stanford University Press, 1959), pp. 246–47.

It was *after* the German rearmament question's settlement in 1954–55 that the Soviet Union offered disarmament proposals, concluded the Austrian treaty, agreed to a summit meeting, and recognized the Bonn government. Coral Bell, *Negotiation from Strength: A Study in the Politics of Power* (London: Chatto and Windus, 1962), p. 113.

the Federal Republic adrift and without at least indirect supervision.[35]

One great question which remains, whether the division of
Germany (which the remilitarization question seemed to affirm)
will become a cause for a future war, has probably been exaggerated. In the age of super-powers, a state in the position of the
Federal Republic would not have among its options the reunification of the nation by force, especially as long as NATO remained.[36] The other side of the coin is that the splitting of the
former Reich into a number of areas and entities may prove a
stabilizing influence. In this respect, it has been observed, "the
German problem is solved: there is no Germany." [37]

The Federal Republic today remains at the very center of the
East-West arena of confrontation, and judged by criteria which
incorporate the complexities, and perhaps the chaos, of the postwar era, the record of American diplomacy emerges as mixed but
without irreparable flaw. If German rearmament was something
of a mistake, this has been compensated for by NATO, just as
Western Europe has become a "zone of peace" *without* the political unification of its ancient antagonists.[38]

The conflicting perspectives of Americans and Europeans, in

[35] George Kennan, for example, would completely disagree. He found the whole
thrust of American foreign policy mistaken after 1950, including German rearmament and the entry into NATO of Bonn. By these steps, he said, flexibility for
negotiation with Moscow was lost; it later became necessary to conjure up such
projects as MLF; France was denied the leadership of Europe which she deserved;
and a European settlement was put off indefinitely. George F. Kennan, *Memoirs
1925–1950* (Boston: Little, Brown, 1967), pp. 448–50, and Chap. 18 *passim*. Kennan,
however, does not mention the success of U.S. diplomacy in achieving what Acheson
considered the enormous task of "pushing, persuading, inspiring the Germans to
rejoin Western civilization and the community of Europe." Acheson, *Sketches from
Life*, p. 174. See also Dean Acheson, *Present at the Creation: My Years in the State
Department* (New York: Norton, 1969), pp. 731–32.

[36] Cf. Helmut Schmidt, *Defense or Retaliation: A German View* (New York:
Praeger, 1962), pp. 174–75. See also Julian Lider, *West Germany in NATO* (Warsaw:
Western Press Agency, 1965), p. 77, for an Eastern European view.

[37] Arthur Lower, "The West and Western Germany," *International Journal*
(Autumn, 1951), pp. 300–1.

[38] By the mid-1950's the real reason for German rearmament in NATO was political, not military; the Federal Republic's membership in NATO was less important as a source of troops than as a device to tie Bonn firmly to the West.
Edinger, *West German Armament*, p. 114.

retrospect, seem to have become less divergent. Europeans never quite agreed with the United States on the degree of likelihood of a Soviet attack, and at no time shared the enthusiasm of the Americans for German rearmament. The United States, on the other hand, simply did not fear a resurgent Germany to a degree comparable to the more proximate victims of the aggressions of the recent war. One of the ironies of the postwar period might be that both were correct. American pressure for German rearmament led to the political rehabilitation of the Federal Republic, just as rigid French resistance to German resurgence would in the long run have been counterproductive. The history of international relations in the twentieth century suggests that there justifiably has been abiding concern with the German problem. As an element in this problem's resolution, the outcome of the rearmament question has probably served American interests, and those of the Atlantic community, rather well in light of not only what has developed but also what has not.

Bibliography

PUBLIC DOCUMENTS

Public Papers of the Presidents of the United States. Harry S Truman. 1950. Washington: Government Printing Office, 1965.

Public Papers of the Presidents of the United States. Harry S Truman. 1951. Washington: Government Printing Office, 1965.

Public Papers of the Presidents of the United States. Harry S Truman. 1952–53. Washington: Government Printing Office, 1966.

U.S. Department of State. *American Foreign Policy, 1950–55: Basic Documents.* Vols. I and II. Washington: Government Printing Office, 1957.

———. *Department of State Bulletin.* Vols. XXII–XXVII.

———. *Germany, 1947–1949, The Story in Documents.* European and British Commonwealth Series, No. 9. Washington: Government Printing Office, 1950.

———. *The United States and Germany 1945–1955.* Washington: Government Printing Office, 1955.

U.S. High Commissioner for Germany. "Information Bulletin." Frankfort (monthly).

U.S. House of Representatives. Committee on Foreign Affairs. Hearings. *Mutual Security Act of 1951.* 82nd Cong., 2nd Sess., 1952.

———. Hearings. *The Mutual Defense Assistance Program, 1950.* 81st Cong., 2nd Sess., 1950.

U.S. Senate. Committee on Appropriations. Hearings. *Supplemental Appropriations for 1952.* 82nd Cong., 1st Sess., 1951.

———. Committee on Foreign Relations. Hearings. *North Atlantic Treaty.* 81st Cong., 1st Sess., 1949.

———. Committee on Foreign Relations. Hearings. *Relations with the Federal Republic of Germany.* 82nd Cong., 2nd Sess., 1952.

———. Committees on Armed Services and Foreign Relations. Hearings. *Military Situation in the Far East.* 82nd Cong., 1st Sess., 1951.

————. Hearings. *Assignment of Ground Forces of the United States to Duty in the European Area.* 82nd Cong., 1st Sess., 1951.

————. Hearings. *The Mutual Defense Assistance Program, 1950.* 81st Cong., 2nd Sess., 1950.

————. Hearings. *Mutual Security Act of 1951.* 82nd Cong., 1st Sess., 1951.

————. Hearings. *Mutual Security Act of 1951 Extension.* 82nd Cong., 2nd Sess., 1952.

————. Hearings. *Mutual Security Act of 1952.* 82nd Cong., 2nd Sess., 1952.

White Paper 1970 on the Security of the Federal Republic of Germany and on the State of the German Federal Armed Forces. Bonn: Press and Information Office of the German Federal Government, 1970.

BOOKS

Abosch, Heinz. *The Menace of the Miracle: Germany from Hitler to Adenauer.* New York: Monthly Review Press, 1963.

Acheson, Dean. *Power and Diplomacy.* Cambridge: Harvard University Press, 1958.

————. *Present at the Creation: My Years in the State Department.* New York: Norton, 1969.

————. *Sketches from Life of Men I Have Known.* New York: Harper, 1961.

Adenauer, Konrad. *Memoirs, 1945–1953.* Trans. Beate Ruhm von Oppen. Chicago: Regnery, 1966.

Aron, Raymond. *France Steadfast and Changing.* Cambridge: Harvard University Press, 1960.

————. *The Century of Total War.* Boston: The Beacon Press, 1955.

————, and Heckscher, August. *Diversity of Worlds: France and the United States Look at Their Common Problems.* New York: Reynal, 1957.

Attlee, C. R. *As It Happened.* London: Heinemann, 1954.

Augstein, Rudolf. *Konrad Adenauer.* London: Secker and Warburg, 1964.

Baier, Clarence W., and Stebbins, Richard P., eds. *Documents on American Foreign Relations, 1952.* Vol. XIV. New York: Harper, 1953.

Bailey, Thomas A. *A Diplomatic History of the American People.* 5th ed. New York: Appleton-Century-Crofts, 1955.

Ball, M. Margaret. *NATO and the European Union Movement.* New York: Praeger, 1959.

Barber, Hollis W. *The United States in World Affairs, 1955.* New York: Harper, 1957.

Bathurst, M. E., and Simpson, J. L. *Germany and the North Atlantic Community: A Legal Survey.* New York: Praeger, 1956.

Bell, Coral. *Negotiation from Strength: A Study in the Politics of Power.* London: Chatto and Windus, 1962.

Beloff, Max. *The United States and the Unity of Europe.* Washington: The Brookings Institution, 1963.

Beugel, Ernst van der. *From Marshall Aid to Atlantic Partnership: European Integration as a Concern of American Foreign Policy.* Amsterdam: Elsevier, 1966.

Bowie, Robert R. *Shaping the Future: Foreign Policy in an Age of Transition.* New York: Columbia University Press, 1964.

Brookings Institution. *Major Problems of United States Foreign Policy, 1952–1953.* Washington, D.C.: Brookings Institution, 1952.

Brown, Seyom. *The Faces of Power: Constancy and Change in United States Foreign Policy from Truman to Johnson.* New York: Columbia University Press, 1968.

Buchan, Alastair. *NATO in the 1960's: The Implications of Interdependence.* Rev. ed. New York: Praeger, 1963.

Bundy, McGeorge, ed. *The Pattern of Responsibility.* Boston: Houghton Mifflin, 1952.

Calvocoressi, Peter. *Survey of International Affairs, 1949–1950.* London: Oxford University Press, 1953.

———. *Survey of International Affairs, 1951.* London: Oxford University Press, 1954.

———. *Survey of International Affairs, 1952.* London: Oxford University Press, 1955.

———. *Survey of International Affairs, 1953.* London: Oxford University Press, 1956.

Campbell, John C. *The United States in World Affairs, 1945–1947.* New York: Harper, 1947.

———. *The United States in World Affairs, 1948–1949.* New York: Harper, 1949.

Clay, Lucius D. *Decision in Germany.* Garden City: Doubleday, 1950.

———. *Germany and the Fight for Freedom.* Cambridge: Harvard University Press, 1950.

Conant, James B. *Germany and Freedom.* Cambridge: Harvard University Press, 1959.

———. *My Several Lives.* New York: Harper and Row, 1970.

Craig, Gordon A. *From Bismarck to Adenauer: Aspects of German Statecraft.* Baltimore: The Johns Hopkins Press, 1958.

Curl, Peter V., ed. *Documents on American Foreign Relations, 1953.* Vol. XV. New York: Harper, 1954.

————. *Documents on American Foreign Relations, 1954.* Vol. XVI. New York: Harper, 1955.

de Carmony, Guy. *The Foreign Policies of France 1944–1968.* Chicago: University of Chicago Press, 1970.

Dehio, Ludwig. *Germany and World Politics in the Twentieth Century.* New York: Knopf, 1959.

Dennett, Raymond, and Turner, Robert K., eds. *Documents on American Foreign Relations, 1950.* Vol. XII. Princeton: Princeton University Press, 1951.

————, and Durant, Katherine D., eds. *Documents on American Foreign Relations, 1951.* Vol. XIII. Princeton: Princeton University Press, 1953.

Deutsch, Karl W., and Edinger, Lewis J. *Germany Rejoins the Powers: Mass Opinion, Interest Groups and Elites in Contemporary German Foreign Policy.* Stanford: Stanford University Press, 1959.

————, Edinger, Lewis J., Macridis, Roy C., and Merritt, Richard L. *France, Germany and the Western Alliance.* New York: Scribner's, 1967.

Dulles, John Foster. *War or Peace.* New York: Macmillan, 1950.

Dunn, Frederick S. *Peace-Making and the Settlement with Japan.* Princeton: Princeton University Press, 1963.

Eden, Sir Anthony (Lord Avon). *Full Circle.* Boston: Houghton Mifflin, 1960.

Edinger, Lewis J. *West German Armament.* Research Studies Institute, Documentary Research Division, Air University, Maxwell Air Force Base, Alabama. October, 1955.

Eisenhower, Dwight D. *The White House Years: Mandate for Change, 1953–1956.* Garden City: Doubleday, 1963.

Epstein, Leon D. *Britain—Uneasy Ally.* Chicago: University of Chicago Press, 1954.

Etzioni, Amitai. *Political Unification.* New York: Holt, Rinehart, and Winston, 1965.

Fedder, Edwin H., ed. *NATO in the Seventies.* St. Louis: University of Missouri Center for International Studies, 1970.

Flanner, Janet (Genet). *Paris Journal 1944–1965.* New York: Atheneum, 1965.

Fox, William T. R. *The Super-Powers.* New York: Harcourt, Brace, 1944.

————, and Fox, Annette B. *NATO and the Range of American Choice.* New York: Columbia University Press, 1967.

Freund, Gerald. *Germany Between Two Worlds.* New York: Harcourt, Brace, 1961.

Freymond, Jacques. *The Saar Conflict 1945–1955.* New York: Praeger, 1960.

Furniss, Edgar S., Jr. *American Military Policy: Strategic Aspects of World Political Geography.* New York: Rinehart, 1957.

————. *France, Troubled Ally: DeGaulle's Heritage and Prospects.* New York: Praeger, 1960.

Geiger, Theodore, and Cleveland, H. van B., *Making Western Europe Defensible.* Planning Pamphlet No. 74. Washington, D.C.; National Planning Association, August, 1951.

Gorce, Paul-Marie de la. *The French Army: A Military-Political History.* New York: Braziller, 1963.

Graebner, Norman A., ed. *An Uncertain Tradition: American Secretaries of State in the Twentieth Century.* New York: McGraw-Hill, 1961.

————. *The New Isolationism.* New York: The Ronald Press, 1956.

Grosser, Alfred. *The Colossus Again: West Germany from Defeat to Rearmament.* New York: Praeger, 1955.

Halle, Louis J. *The Cold War as History.* London: Chatto and Windus, 1967.

Hanreider, Wolfram F. *West German Foreign Policy, 1949–1963: International Pressure and Domestic Response.* Stanford: Stanford University Press, 1967.

Hilsman, Roger. *To Move A Nation: The Politics of Foreign Policy in the Administration of John F. Kennedy.* Garden City: Doubleday, 1967.

————, and Good, Robert C., eds. *Foreign Policy in the Sixties: The Issues and the Instruments.* Baltimore: The Johns Hopkins Press, 1965.

Hoffmann, Stanley, and others. *In Search of France.* Cambridge: Harvard University Press, 1963.

Horne, Alistair. *Return to Power: A Report on the New Germany.* New York: Praeger, 1956.

Huntington, Samuel P. *The Common Defense: Strategic Programs in National Politics.* New York: Columbia University Press, 1961.

————. *The Soldier and the State: The Theory and Politics of Civil-Military Relations.* Cambridge: Harvard University Press, 1957.

Ismay, Lord (Hastings L.). *The Memoirs of General Lord Ismay.* New York: The Viking Press, 1960.

————. *NATO: The First Five Years, 1949–1954.* Paris: NATO, 1955.

Kahn, Herman. *On Thermonuclear War.* Princeton: Princeton University Press, 1961.

Kaufman, William W., ed. *Military Policy and National Security.* Princeton: Princeton University Press, 1956.

Kennan, George F. *Memoirs 1925–1950.* Boston: Little, Brown, 1967.

Kirkendall, Richard S., ed. *The Truman Period as a Research Field.* Columbia: University of Missouri Press, 1968.

Kirkpatrick, (Sir) Ivone. *The Inner Circle: Memoirs of Ivone Kirkpatrick.* London: Macmillan, 1959.

Kissinger, Henry A. *The Troubled Partnership.* New York: McGraw-Hill, 1965.

Knorr, Klaus, ed. *NATO and American Security.* Princeton: Princeton University Press, 1959.

L'Annee Politique, 1950. Paris: Presses Universitaires de France, 1951.

L'Annee Politique, 1951. Paris: Presses Universitaires de France, 1952.

L'Annee Politique, 1952. Paris: Presses Universitaires de France, 1953.

Lerner, Daniel, and Aron, Raymond. *France Defeats EDC.* New York: Praeger, 1957.

Lider, Julian. *West Germany in NATO.* Warsaw: Western Press Agency, 1965.

Litchfield, Edward H., and others. *Governing Postwar Germany.* Ithaca: Cornell University Press, 1953.

Lowenstein, Prince Hubertus zu, and Zuhlsdorff, Volkmar von. *NATO and the Defense of the West.* New York: Praeger, 1962.

Macridis, Roy C., ed. *Foreign Policy in World Politics.* 2nd ed. New York: Prentice Hall, 1962.

McCloy, John J. *The Challenge to American Foreign Policy.* Cambridge: Harvard University Press, 1953.

McInnis, Edgar, Hiscocks, Richard, and Spencer, Robert. *The Shaping of Postwar Germany.* New York: Praeger, 1960.

McKay, Donald C. *The United States and France.* Cambridge: Harvard University Press, 1951.

Millis, Walter, Mansfield, Harvey C., and Stein, Harold. *Arms and the State.* New York: Twentieth Century Fund, 1958.

Moch, Jules. *Alerte! Le probleme crucial de la Communaute Europeenne de Defense.* Paris: Laffont, 1954.

———. *Histoire du rearmement allemand depuis 1950.* Paris: Laffont, 1965.

Montgomery, Bernard L. *The Memoirs of Field-Marshal The Viscount Montgomery of Alamein.* New York: New American Library, 1958.

Moore, Ben T. *NATO and the Future of Europe.* New York: Harper, 1958.

Murphy, Robert. *Diplomat Among Warriors.* Garden City: Doubleday, 1964.

Northedge, F. S. *British Foreign Policy: The Process of Readjustment, 1945–1961.* London: Allen and Unwin, 1962.

Northrop, F. S. C. *European Union and United States Foreign Policy.* New York: Macmillan, 1954.

Osgood, Robert E. *NATO: The Entangling Alliance*. Chicago: University of Chicago Press, 1962.

Patterson, Gardner, and Furniss, Edgar S., Jr. *NATO: A Critical Appraisal*. Princeton: Princeton University Press, 1957.

Reitzel, William, Kaplan, Morton A., and Coblenz, Constance G. *United States Foreign Policy, 1945–1955*. Washington: Brookings Institution, 1956.

Richardson, James L. *Germany and the Atlantic Alliance: The Interaction of Strategy and Politics*. Cambridge: Harvard University Press, 1966.

Ridgway, Matthew B. *Soldier: The Memoirs of Matthew B. Ridgway*. New York: Harper, 1956.

Rostow, Walt W. *The United States in the World Arena*. New York: Harper, 1960.

Royal Institute of International Affairs. *Atlantic Alliance: NATO's Role in the Free World*. A Report by a Chatham House Study Group. London: Royal Institute of International Affairs, 1952.

———. *Britain in Western Europe: WEU and the Atlantic Alliance*. A Report by a Chatham House Study Group. London: Royal Institute of International Affairs, 1956.

Schilling, Warner R., Hammond, Paul Y., and Snyder, Glenn H. *Strategy, Politics, and Defense Budgets*. New York: Columbia University Press, 1962

Schmidt, Helmut. *Defense or Retaliation: A German View*. New York: Praeger, 1962.

Snyder, Richard C., and Furniss, Edgar S., Jr. *American Foreign Policy*. New York: Rinehart, 1954.

Spanier, John W. *American Foreign Policy Since World War II*. 2nd rev. ed. New York: Praeger, 1965.

Speier, Hans. *German Rearmament and Atomic War: The Views of German Military and Political Leaders*. Evanston: Row, Peterson, 1957.

Stebbins, Richard P. *The United States in World Affairs, 1950*. New York: Harper, 1951.

———. *The United States in World Affairs, 1951*. New York: Harper, 1952.

———. *The United States in World Affairs, 1952*. New York: Harper, 1953.

———. *The United States in World Affairs, 1953*. New York: Harper, 1955.

———. *The United States in World Affairs, 1954*. New York: Harper, 1956.

Steel, Ronald. *The End of Alliance: America and the Future of Europe*. New York: Viking, 1964.

Stein, Harold, ed. *American Civil-Military Decisions: A Book of Case Studies*. A Twentieth Century Fund Study. Birmingham: University of Alabama Press, 1963.

Stikker, Dirk U. *Men of Responsibility: A Memoir*. New York: Harper and Row, 1966.

Strauss, Franz-Josef. *The Grand Design: A European Solution to German Reunification*. New York: Praeger, 1966.

Sulzberger, C. L. *A Long Row of Candles: Memoirs and Diaries (1934–1954)*. New York: Macmillan, 1969.

Truman, Harry S. *Memoirs: Years of Trial and Hope*. Vol. II. Garden City: Doubleday, 1956.

Turner, Gordon B., and Challener, Richard D., eds. *National Security in the Nuclear Age*. New York: Praeger, 1960.

Vagts, Alfred. *Defense and Diplomacy: The Soldier and the Conduct of Foreign Relations*. New York: King's Crown Press, 1956.

Vali, Feranc A. *The Quest for a United Germany*. Baltimore: The Johns Hopkins Press, 1967.

Werth, Alexander. *France: 1940–1955*. London: Hale, 1956.

Wettig, Gerhard. *Entmilitarisierung und Wiederbewaffnung in Deutschland, 1943–1955*. Munich: Oldenbourg, 1967.

White, Theodore H. *Fire in the Ashes: Europe in Mid-Century*. New York: Sloane, 1953.

Wighton, Charles. *Adenauer—Democratic Dictator: A Critical Biography*. London: Muller, 1963.

Wilcox, Francis O., and Kalijarvi, Thorsten V. *Recent American Foreign Policy: Basic Documents 1941–1951*. New York: Appleton-Century-Crofts, 1952.

Willenz, Eric. *Early Discussions Regarding a Defense Contribution in Germany*. RAND Research Memo. No. 968, October 15, 1952.

Willis, F. Roy. *France, Germany and the New Europe, 1945–1963*. Stanford: Stanford University Press, 1965.

Wolfers, Arnold, ed. *Alliance Policy in the Cold War*. Baltimore: The Johns Hopkins Press, 1959.

———. *Britain and France Between Two Wars: Conflicting Strategies of Peace Since Versailles*. New York: Harcourt, Brace, 1940.

Wylie, Laurence. *Village in the Vaucluse*. Cambridge: Harvard University Press, 1961.

Zink, Harold. *The United States in Germany, 1944–1955*. New York: Van Nostrand, 1957.

ARTICLES

Acheson, Dean. "Ethics in International Relations Today." *The Puritan Ethic in United States Foreign Policy.* Ed. David L. Larson. Princeton: Van Nostrand, 1966.

———— ["Anonymous"]. "The Balance of Military Power," *The Atlantic Monthly,* CLXXXVII (June, 1951), 21–27.

Adenauer, Konrad. "German Reunion and the Future of Europe," *International Journal,* IX (Summer, 1954), 173–76.

Bracher, Karl Dietrich. "Foreign Policy of the Federal Republic of Germany." *Foreign Policies in a World of Change.* Eds. Joseph E. Black and Kenneth W. Thompson. New York: Harper and Row, 1963.

Brandt, Willy. "German Policy Toward the East," *Foreign Affairs,* XLVI (April, 1968), 476–86.

Cole, Taylor. "Neo-Fascism in Western Germany and Italy," *American Political Science Review,* XLIX (March, 1955), 131–43.

Craig, Gordon A. "Germany and NATO: The Rearmament Debate, 1950–1958." *NATO and American Security.* Ed. Klaus Knorr. Princeton: Princeton University Press, 1959.

————. "NATO and the New German Army." *Military Policy and National Security.* Ed. William W. Kaufmann. Princeton: Princeton University Press, 1956.

Dallin, David J. "France and German Rearmament," *The New Leader* (October 15, 1951).

Deutsch, Karl W., and Edinger, Lewis J. "Foreign Policy of the German Federal Republic." *Foreign Policy in World Politics.* Ed. Roy C. Macridis. 2nd ed. New York: Prentice-Hall, 1962.

Dulles, John Foster. "A Policy of Boldness." *Life* (May 19, 1952).

————. "Policy for Security and Peace," *Foreign Affairs,* XXXII (April, 1954), 353–64.

Duroselle, J.-B. "French Diplomacy in the Postwar World." *Diplomacy in a Changing World.* Eds. Stephen D. Kertesz and M. A. Fitzimons. Notre Dame: University of Notre Dame Press, 1959.

Etzioni, Amitai. "European Unification: A Strategy of Change." *World Politics,* XVI (October, 1963), 32–51.

Fox, William T. R. "Korea and the Struggle for Europe." *Journal of International Affairs,* VI (Spring, 1952), 129–34.

Friedrich, Carl J. "Why the Germans Hesitate." *The Atlantic Monthly,*
CLXXXVII (April, 1951), 40–41.
Furniss, Edgar S. Jr. "French Attitudes Toward Western European Unity."
International Organization, VII (May, 1953), 199–212.

Garthoff, Raymond L. "On Soviet Military Strategy and Capabilities." *World
Politics,* III (October, 1950).
Goodpaster, Col. Andrew J. "The Development of SHAPE, 1950–1953."
American Military Policy. Edgar S. Furness, Jr. New York: Rhinehart, 1957.
Goormaghtigh, John. "France and the European Defense Community." *In-
ternational Journal,* IX (Spring, 1954) 96–106.

Hammond, Paul Y. "NSC-68: Prologue to Rearmament." *Strategy, Politics,
and Defense Budgets.* By Warner R. Schilling, Paul Y. Hammond, and
Glenn H. Snyder. New York: Columbia University Press, 1962.
Head, Brigadier A. H. "European Defense." *International Affairs,* XXVII
(January, 1951), 1–9.
Healey, Denis. "Britain and NATO." *NATO and American Security.* Ed.
Klaus Knorr. Princeton: Princeton University Press, 1959.
Hilsman, Roger. "NATO: The Developing Strategic Context." *NATO and
American Security.* Ed. Klaus Knorr. Princeton: Princeton University Press,
1959.
———. "On NATO Strategy." *Alliance Policy in the Cold War.* Ed. Arnold
Wolfers. Baltimore: Johns Hopkins Press, 1959.
Hoffmann, Stanley. "Paradoxes of the French Political Community." *In
Search of France.* By Stanley Hoffmann and others. Cambridge: Harvard
University Press, 1963.
Holborn, Hajo. "American Foreign Policy and European Integration." *World
Politics,* VI (October, 1953), 1–30.

Ismay, Lord. "Atlantic Alliance." *International Journal,* IX (Spring, 1954),
79–86.

Kanter, Arnold. "The European Defense Community in the French National
Assembly: A Roll Call Analysis." *Comparative Politics,* II (January, 1970),
203–28.
Karp, Basil. "The Draft Constitution for a European Political Community."
International Organization, VII (May, 1954), 181–203.
Kelleher, Catherine M. "The Issue of German Nuclear Armament." *Proceed-
ings of the Academy of Political Science,* Vol. XXIX, No. 2 (1968), 95–107.
King, James E. Jr. "NATO: Genesis, Progress, Problems." *National Security*

in the Nuclear Age. Eds. Gordon B. Turner and Richard D. Challener. New York: Praeger, 1960.

Kirchheimer, Otto. "Notes on the Political Scene in Western Germany." *World Politics*, VI (April, 1954), 306–21.

Krekeler, Heinz L. "The German Defense Contribution." *The Annals*, CCCXII (July, 1957), 84–88.

Laukhuff, Perry. "German Reaction to Soviet Policy, 1945–1953." *Journal of International Affairs*, VIII (Winter, 1954), 62–72.

Leites, Nathan, and de la Malene, Christian. "Paris from EDC to WEU," *World Politics*, IX (January, 1957), 193–219.

Lower, Arthur. "The West and Western Germany," *International Journal* (Autumn, 1951), pp. 300–1.

Macridis, Roy C. "French Foreign Policy." *Foreign Policy in World Politics*. Ed. Roy C. Macridis. 2nd ed. New York: Prentice-Hall, 1962.

Martin, Laurence W. "The American Decision to Rearm Germany." *American Civil-Military Decisions: A Book of Case Studies*. Ed. Harold Stein. Birmingham: University of Alabama Press, 1963.

McCloy, John J. "Challenge to Europe," *Interplay* (February, 1968), p. 33.

McLellan, David S. "The Role of Political Style: A Study of Dean Acheson." *Foreign Policy in the Sixties: The Issues and the Instruments*. Eds. Roger Hilsman and Robert C. Good. Baltimore: The Johns Hopkins Press, 1965.

———, and Reuss, John W. "Foreign and Military Policies." *The Truman Period as a Research Field*. Ed. Richard S. Kirkendall. Columbia: University of Missouri Press, 1968.

Morgenthau, Hans J. "Sources of Tension Between Western Europe and the United States." *The Annals*, CCCXII (July, 1957).

Mosely, Philip E. "Soviet Policy and the War." *Journal of International Affairs*, VI (Spring, 1952).

Onslow, C. G. D. "West German Rearmament." *World Politics*, III (July, 1951), 450–85.

Schilling, Warner R. "The Politics of National Defense: Fiscal 1950." *Strategy, Politics and Defense Budgets*. By Warner R. Schilling, Paul Y. Hammond, and Glenn H. Snyder. New York: Columbia University Press, 1962.

Schmid, Carlo. "Germany and Europe." *International Affairs*, XXVII (July, 1951), 306–11.

Schuman, Frederick L. "The Soviet Union and German Rearmament." *The Annals*, CCCXII (July, 1957), 77–83.

Servan-Schreiber, Jean-Jacques. "Europe and America: Views on Foreign Policy." *Journal of International Affairs,* V (Winter, 1951).
Snyder, Glenn H. "The 'New Look' of 1953." *Strategy, Politics and Defense Budgets.* By Warner R. Schilling, Paul Y. Hammond, and Glenn H. Snyder. New York: Columbia University Press, 1962.
Speier, Hans. "German Rearmament and the Old Military Elite." *World Politics,* VI (January, 1954), 147–68.
Spofford, Charles M. "Toward Atlantic Security." *International Affairs,* XXVII (October, 1951), 434–39.

Vigers, T. W. "The German People and Rearmament." *International Affairs,* XXVII (April, 1951), 151–55.

Walton, Clarence C. "Background for the European Defense Community." *Political Science Quarterly,* XLVIII (March, 1953), 42–69.
Walton, Clarence C. "Background for the European Defense Community." VI (May, 1952), 175–91.

UNPUBLISHED SOURCES

Kelleher, Catherine McArdle. "German Nuclear Dilemmas, 1956–1966." Unpublished Ph.D. dissertation, Massachusetts Institute of Technology, 1967.

Truitt, Wesley B. "The Troops to Europe Decision: The Process, Politics, and Diplomacy of a Strategic Commitment." Unpublished Ph.D. dissertation, Columbia University, 1968.

Index